The Best from Helen Corbitt's Kitchens

edited by
Patty Vineyard MacDonald

Number 1 in the
Evelyn Oppenheimer Series

University of North Texas Press
Denton, Texas

Permissions
University of North Texas Press
PO Box 311336
Denton TX 76203-1336
940-565-2142

Library of Congress Cataloging-in-Publication Data
Corbitt, Helen.
The best from Helen Corbitt's kitchens / edited by Patty Vineyard MacDonald. –1st ed.
p.   cm.
(Evelyn Oppenheimer series; no. 1)

ISBN 1-57441-076-8 (alk. paper)
1. Cookery. 2. Corbitt, Helen. I. MacDonald, Patty Vineyard. II. Title. III. Series.

TX714.C679 2000
641.5—dc21   99-053514
                                         CIP

Design by Angela Schmitt
Cover art by Charles Shaw

Dedicated to Edith Cagle Pool
whose friendship has transcended generations and miles.

Contents

Foreword

❧

During my father's lifetime he insisted that the cuisine in his home, and later in the Store, must be distinguished. My mother bore the brunt of the home assignment, while to me went the responsibility to establish and maintain a successful food operation that would make Neiman Marcus food as famous as its fashions.

He was willing to suffer a restaurant that did not make a profit, but only if the restaurant was packed and jammed.

This goal was hard to achieve and most managers turned out to be poor restaurateurs, who were serving half-filled dining rooms. All of this is a true description of the Neiman Marcus Restaurant Division until we were able to persuade Helen Corbitt to come to Dallas to take over the food service of the Store. I had known about her for years, shortly after she migrated to Texas from upstate New York and created a reputation for sensational food at the Houston Country Club.

She told me she was not ready to leave Houston, but she very soon found that the country club was a huge responsibility that she did not want. She was approached by Joske's downtown Houston store to run the store's restaurants and accepted the position when assured that she would have complete control. The department store management in that particular store did not agree with her insistence on top quality of food.

I recall having one of many delicious luncheons with her in my attempt to win her to Dallas. She was reluctant to leave Houston, but I made her promise to call me night or day if she ever changed her mind.

Five months later she called to tell me that she had broken her promise, but only partially. She said that an old friend of hers, Herman Brown, an eminent Houston business leader, had insisted she move to Austin to supervise the food operations at the Driskill Hotel, which he had recently purchased. She ended by saying, "I had to do this for him, but I will end up with you." So I accepted her decision with good humor and urged her to do a fine job at the Driskill.

Almost four years later, in March 1955, I received a midnight call from her! "Stanley, Herman didn't tell me he wanted me to manage the whole hotel as well as the food. I can't take it any more. Do you still want me?"

"Of course," I replied. "When can you get here? By noon tomorrow?" She said she could not, so we compromised her arrival to the evening of the next day.

This was a remarkable woman and a superb designer of food and food sensations, as I have pointed out in a miniature book titled, *Helen Corbitt—The Balenciaga of Food* (Somesuch Press, 1992).

Overnight our food business boomed and we had people standing— at every meal, every day. We continued to lose money but we had a packed house that benefited from her ingenious food ideas. Her extravagance was legendary, but the dishes that came out of her kitchen left nothing to be desired.

A few years after Helen's death, a woman whom I did not know, Patty Vineyard MacDonald of Hot Springs Village, Arkansas, called for an appointment. She said, "It is about Helen Corbitt. I want to bring her cooking back to life."

We met and she told me it was her opinion that the Helen Corbitt cookbooks were the best in the world, but they needed some modifications to meet changes in food preparation. As she went through her revival of "La Grandeur de Helen Corbitt," I told her "Just writing a food book is an achievement in itself, but writing one that has recipes that can be produced by ordinary mortals is an artistic triumph; it will become a commercial success."

So here it is: *bon appétit*!

—Stanley Marcus

Preface

❧

L ike many of you, I sharpened my culinary skills on Helen Corbitt's five cookbooks and have been a devoted fan ever since. Corbitt's special way with food and words has delighted us for the past half century. My purpose in republishing this collection of Corbitt's best recipes is not merely to preserve them, but to make them accessible and useful to a wider audience. My challenge has been to reconcile recipes from Corbitt's five cookbooks, published over a span of twenty years. The University of Dallas houses Corbitt's personal papers, consisting of boxes and files crammed with recipes, newspaper articles about her that contain still more food ideas, plus cooking school booklets she used. This motherlode of material made recipe selection my most daunting task in putting this book together. Cookbook author Edie Acsell and I read and discussed hundreds of recipes, selecting the ones we thought most appealing for today's cooks. I hope I have included your personal favorites.

Recipes marked "Previously Unpublished" are taken from cards or booklets Corbitt provided for her students at cooking schools. Members of her men's cooking school kept their recipes on no-nonsense golden-rod colored cards held together by two metal rings. Smaller booklets, attractively designed and decorated, were handed out at Corbitt's various cooking schools around the country. The schools served as a testing ground for recipes, many of which later found their way into her cookbooks.

Corbitt's published recipes have idiosyncrasies not seen in contemporary recipes: she mixed narrative into the list of ingredients and her directions for combining ingredients were often cryptic. She neglected to include visual descriptions to help us judge when recipes are done: for example, oysters are cooked when their edges begin to ruffle; a cake is done when it pulls away from the edges of the pan and springs back when touched lightly in the center. In addition, her recipes had certain problems common to all historic recipe collections. Who remembers how many cups a #2½ can holds? As new foods are introduced, some of the old standbys are no longer on supermarket shelves. Today's food packages sometimes contain less product than they did when Corbitt was writing her books. In her last cookbook, Corbitt anticipated our switching over to metric measurements, but to date only the beverage industry has done so in this country. Information I have added to Corbitt's original published texts is enclosed in square brackets throughout this book. I trust my occasional editorial interventions will make these recipes easier for today's cooks.

Most of Helen Corbitt's recipe titles were descriptive, meeting modern criteria. For reasons of privacy and the difficulty in locating individuals to obtain permission to publish, I did not include names of persons in recipe titles. A few other titles were changed to prevent duplicates and to more accurately describe the dish being prepared. My apologies for any disappointment or inconveniences these changes cause.

On page 195 of *Helen Corbitt's Cookbook*, we are instructed to save the leaves from cauliflower heads and cook them like broccoli and do them *au gratin*. In the fields, cauliflower leaves are tied up over the heads to blanch them. Today most of the leaves are removed before packaging and shipping.

In her cookbooks Helen Corbitt repeatedly used the words "chop parsley," to be used for garnishing when "mince parsley" may have been closer to her true meaning. According to one of the men from her cooking class, "You could never mince parsley fine enough to suit Helen."*

Kitchen equipment has changed in the past fifty years, too. Corbitt often specified a blender for mincing ingredients; she also used a food grinder. Food processors and Pam were introduced toward the end of her writing career and Corbitt referred to their use in passing. She showed less enthusiasm for microwaves. I assume that if these are among your favorite kitchen tools, you will know when and how to substitute them for her suggested methods.

How to reconcile these various editorial problems has been the subject of much discussion and concern. Corbitt's recipes are intelligible to my generation because we learned to cook at our mothers' elbows. As

*Attributed to Tom Courtin by Tom Hunt in an interview, Dallas, March 15, 1995.

our daughters deserted their kitchens for the workplace, however, these basic skills too often were not passed along to their offspring. To meet the needs of less experienced cooks, contemporary food writers have standardized recipe formatting in an effort to make them more comprehensible and efficient. The result according to Judith Jones, Julia Child's editor for the past fifty years, is that recipes have become so sanitized, they're boring. I have tried to steer a middle road between these opposing editorial philosophies. Readers can be assured, however, that the foods they prepare from these recipes will be the same as Corbitt intended. I hope you'll also find her ebullient personality in them, for she wrote just as she talked.

Cooking temperatures throughout this book are in Fahrenheit. To convert Fahrenheit to centigrade, subtract 32 from Fahrenheit degrees, multiply by 5, then divide by 9. Most European cooks will find the following scale sufficiently accurate for their cooking needs:

Oven Temperatures, British and U.S.

°Fahrenheit	200	225	250	275	300	325	350	375	400	425	450	475
°Centigrade	95	110	120	135	150	165	175	190	200	220	230	245

Compared to English cooks, we Americans have fewer choices available in types of cream. Perhaps knowing our standards will help you select an appropriate substitute: light whipping cream, the kind most readily available here, contains 30 to 36 percent butterfat. Light cream or coffee cream contains about 20 percent butterfat and will not whip. Half-and-half refers to a combination of milk and light cream with 10 to 12 percent butterfat. Ultrapasteurized cream has been heated to 300° to give it a long shelf life; it's a bit more difficult to whip.

Unsalted butter was not widely available to home cooks in the 1950s, so unless specified, use salted butter in these recipes. Because many of us favor less salt today, you may want to scant that seasoning. This works in recipes other than those for pickles, where it is a preservative, and yeast breads, where salt is needed to strengthen cell walls and control the leavening process as bread rises and expands. Corbitt employed sugar substitutes extensively in *Helen Corbitt's Greenhouse Cookbook* and *Helen Corbitt Cooks for Looks* recipes. Still inconclusive research casts doubt on the advisability of some people's use of these sweeteners. It's your call.

In this day of heightened awareness of the hazards of food-borne illnesses, there is a question about the wisdom of using uncooked eggs in any form. Foods containing uncooked eggs, such as chiffon custards or eggnog, must be handled with extreme care because of the danger of salmonella poisoning. This is why I omitted some otherwise delectable recipes. However, recipes like mayonnaise are too basic to ignore. Refrigerate such foods immediately after preparing and consume them as quickly as possible. When you cook whole eggs or yolks, hold them at 140° for 3½ minutes. Pasteurized whole eggs and whites, liquid or dried, are a safe alternative. (I shudder to think what Corbitt would make of that statement, for her associates say she never allowed a powdered egg in her kitchens; however, that product has improved significantly since her day.)

Large eggs are the right size for these recipes. Eggs are considered a liquid ingredient in recipes, so their size will affect the "wetness" of a mixture. Extra large eggs may necessitate adding a little more flour; very small eggs make it necessary to decrease the amount of flour in the recipe. The shells of commercial eggs are washed and sanitized, so do not wash again. Discard any eggs that are not clean or have broken shells. Refrigerate raw shell eggs in their cartons on a middle or lower inside shelf, not on the door.

All meats, not just poultry, pose a hazard for salmonella poisoning. Immediately sterilize work surfaces, cutting boards and knives that are used to prepare raw meats. A kettle of boiling water is an easy, effective way to clean your sink and equipment. It is important to boil marinade used on meat for at least 10 minutes before serving it at the table.

Corbitt sometimes instructs us to flame brandy or other liqueur to lend a moment of high drama to our entertaining. Here are a few tips for your safety and success: Be sure the food to be flambéed is bubbling hot. Set the dish over its heat source on a large tray to protect your table from scarring. Never open a bottle of liqueur near any open flame nor pour it from the bottle directly into the dish. Flames can climb up the stream of alcohol into the bottle, exploding it. Pour the liqueur into a long-handled pan or ladle, warm it separately, and light it with a long kitchen or fireplace match before pouring it, flaming, into the dish. Allow flames to burn out before serving.

Today's pork is raised to be leaner and more disease-free than was true in Corbitt's day. Then pork was always cooked to an internal temperature of 170° because it was safer and the extra fat kept it moist. If you cook today's pork that long, you will turn it into leather—160° is sufficient.

Know which flour to use in different recipes: cake flour is made with soft wheat, which makes it suitable for delicacies. Sift it before measuring. Pre-sifted all-purpose flour is the choice for quick breads, including pancakes and pie crust; use a fork to aerate it before lightly spooning it into a measuring cup. You can also use it to thicken gravies and sauces, but it's easier to use one of the special blending flours. Bread flour, milled from hard winter wheat, should be your choice for all yeast-raised breads; its higher gluten content provides more elasticity to ensure lighter loaves. Most of the specialty flours such as whole wheat, oat and rye flour do not contain sufficient gluten to make a light loaf of bread. This is why you add them to white bread flour, in proportions of less than 50%. You can add 1 to 1½ tablespoons of gluten to bread recipes. For potato bread, you can substitute dried potato flakes and water, mixed according to package directions.

Helen Corbitt's Story

ૐ

With little more than soufflés and sass, Helen Corbitt became a food legend. This brash transplanted Yankee firebrand waged her own revolution on the naive palates of hungry Texans. She once claimed to have brought elegance to the Lone Star State, an imagined slur that caused the Texas food writers to rise up in wrath. "I couldn't believe the food they were eating," she said about her early days in Texas. "Chicken fried steak, I couldn't eat one yet. Everything overcooked, salads over-dressed."[1] Inevitably, her innovations came to define our culinary standards and this outlander, hatched in the northern woods, was eventually named one of the ten most influential women in Texas.

Stanley Marcus, scion of the famous Dallas mercantile family and a renowned taste-maker himself, declared Helen "the Balenciaga of Food,"[2] referring to the great post-war Spanish fashion designer known for classic lines and elegance. Earl Wilson described her simply as "the best cook in Texas."[3] She was the 1968 recipient of the solid gold Escoffier plaque from the Confrérie de la Chaîne des Rôtisseurs, the world's oldest gourmet society, founded in 1248. It is unclear how she managed to keep their requisite ancient vow "never to desecrate a roast by cooking it in any other way than on a turning spit."[4] She was also an honorary member of the exclusive gourmet society Confrérie des Chevaliers du Tastevin,[5] which resulted in her assessment "the Chaîne has more fun."[6]

The professional honor Helen Corbitt most treasured was the Golden Plate Award given her by the Institutional Food Service Manufacturers' Association in 1961.[7] She was the first woman thus honored by her peers. Skidmore College awarded a Doctor of Letters degree to its distinguished alumna and trustee.[8] The University of Dallas presented her its coveted Athena Award, not for her cooking, but for her indomitable spirit and impeccable character.[9] These two attributes served her well, for the road to international fame led from hospital dietetics to conquer-

Helen Corbitt, c. 1906–07

ing Texas, to international travels, authorship and cooking schools and
on to directing the restaurants of Neiman Marcus during its most glamorous days.

High Buttoned Shoes and Morals

Helen Lucy Corbitt was born in Benson Mines, New York, in 1906.[10]
During her childhood, her father was a prosperous attorney-
businessman and her mother had her own dressmaking business, "but
we always had good cooks, and mother baked her own bread."[11] Her
mother's artistic bent was reincarnated in Helen's unique food presenta-
tions, for which she relied on esthetic combinations and contrasts of

color, texture and sometimes even serving temperatures. She remembered her proper Edwardian upbringing as a time when quality was a password in food, clothes, discipline and lifestyle.

Looking back, Helen recalled the first dishes she learned to cook were those universal childhood favorites: macaroni and cheese combined with enough egg and milk to bake into an almost-custard and, when she was seven years old, "June Cake," a kissin' cousin to a pound cake. She liked macaroni and cheese with creamed potatoes so much that she prepared that identical dinner every time the cook had a day off. She later reported that her father wouldn't have given even odds that she could make it in the food service business because he was sure that menu was the extent of her talent.[12] "Food was important at our house," she said. "At home in upstate New York we cooked with coal. You know, I don't think pot roast ever tasted as good as when it was cooked in a coal stove."[13] Helen always claimed that she never could best her mother when it came to making chocolate pie.[14]

The Skidmore Coed

Helen earned a BS degree in Home Economics in 1928 from Skidmore College, located in the lovely Victorian spa and thoroughbred racing town of Saratoga Springs, New York. The school, now a prestigious independent liberal arts college with 2,100 men and women studying on its modern campus, was the inspiration of Lucy Skidmore Scribner, who started a school in 1903 to teach young women to sew and cook and to instruct them in the art of gracious living. In her acceptance speech for her Doctor of Letters Degree, Helen said that she had chosen Skidmore a half-century earlier because "it quietly let a few people know it had extremely high standards. . . . True we were housed in rickety old buildings, mine had a rope coiled under the bed in case of fire. I have no doubt it was used at other times." She credited the school with having shown her how important it is throughout life to learn to distinguish the excellent from the second-rate and to care about the difference.[15]

She had wanted to become a doctor, but after college the Depression detoured her into the dietary kitchen. Her father had lost everything he owned, even the family home. Her first job was as therapeutic dietitian at Presbyterian Hospital in Newark, New Jersey, and a short time later she became administrative dietitian at Cornell Medical Center in New

York City.[16] In those days interns received only about ten dollars a month, but they and their families had the privilege of eating in the doctors' cafeteria once a week. The young doctors claimed that Helen's food did more to build that medical center than did the illustrious faculty.

"Deep in the Heart of ... Texas"?

Helen needed a more creative outlet than hospital dietetics and soon she was tramping the streets of New York seeking another job. Nobody but Helen could see beyond her hospital work. The only job offer she snared was to teach large quantity cooking and tea room management at the University of Texas in Austin. She didn't want to accept the job. "I said, 'Who the hell wants to go to Texas?' Only I didn't say hell in those days. I learned to swear in Texas,"[17] and "to tell a cockroach from a scorpion."[18] She had a long way to go, but still, a job was a job in those lean years. She soon discovered that her Texas students had learned nothing more than how to make fancy sandwiches. "I had to teach those people how to cook!"[19]

Adjusting to her new home was not easy for this strong-willed young Irish redhead. She hated Texas! After two weeks in Austin, she was asked to do a convention dinner using only Texas products. "What I thought of Texas products wasn't fit to print," she later confessed. Almost in defiance, she concocted for that dinner a mélange of garlic, onion, vinegar and oil mixed in with black-eyed peas. She called it "Texas Caviar," and Neiman Marcus later put it up in cans that Texans ordered by the case [see recipe on page 39].[20]

She was entertaining thoughts of going back home to "God's country," when the Houston Country Club offered her a job that came with an apartment and a decent salary. She turned it down. They came back again and she agreed to try it for a year, but only because she was broke. "I thought I would stay just until I got on my feet and then go back to New York. The first six months I didn't unpack my suitcases. Then I unpacked the suitcases but not my trunk. After a year I unpacked the trunk and decided to stay." Helen finally had made her peace with Texas and through later years described herself as a "Texan by adoption."[21]

This was just at the beginning of World War II and the country club was losing money. The board told her to do whatever she wanted. Soon

Helen's dining room was a bigger draw than the nineteenth hole. "They told me I took the 'class' out of the club," she chuckled. "I also paid off their debt."[22] She was there for more than six years.

The Al Dente War

Part of Helen's hands-on management style was to perch on a kitchen stool to inspect every plate before it was served. One of her innovations was to steam all vegetables briefly so that they remained slightly crisp and brightly colored. A former employee tells the story about one particular day when Corbitt spied limp broccoli about to be covered with turkey breast before being slathered with Mornay Sauce and dolloped with Hollandaise Sauce [see recipes on pages 226 and 224]. In high Irish dudgeon, she ordered all of the broccoli thrown out. The diners waited meekly while their entrées were re-created to Corbitt's exacting standards.[23]

This was only the opening skirmish in the Al Dente War that Helen waged all her life. She insisted on the freshest fruits and vegetables, steamed in small batches. Her credo was the less time the pot boils, so to speak, the better the flavor, better for health. Why destroy the vitamins? They are sensitive. Less stirring, less handling gives food a chance to show its au naturel look.[24]

As might be anticipated, green bean cookery became the principal battleground in all her kitchens. Once when a hapless waitress returned a plate to the kitchen because her customer had complained that the vegetables were raw, Corbitt thundered, "What do you mean the green beans weren't done? God put me on this earth to teach you Southerners how to cook green beans!"[25]

Smoke-Filled Rooms

Helen had moved on to operating the tearoom at Joske's department store in Houston and had started her own catering business, when the Driskill Hotel called her back to Austin. The good news spread quickly among well-connected Texas politicos. Paul Wakefield wrote to a friend in Lampasas, "I am pleased to report that Travis County tavern cooking has improved a great deal with the appearance here of the distinguished and gifted Miss Helen Corbitt, who is doing some lyrical things in the way of food . . . at the old Driskill. . . . I was told by one of the economy-minded members that the old [Houston Country] club just couldn't afford her fine gifts."[26] The truth was that Helen was far more concerned with taste than she was with the bottom line in all her food operations.

While she was at the Driskill, Helen made the acquaintance of many of the state's "movers and shakers," who lunched and dealt in the old paneled hotel dining room. Under her watchful eye, the staff became known for both service and discretion. Here a lifelong friendship with the Lyndon B. Johnsons was formed, which culminated in the President applying his legendary powers of persuasion to try to get Helen to manage his White House kitchen. Although she was their guest many times, she was adamantly opposed to working at the White House. In a 1969 letter written to her on White House stationery, LBJ complained, ". . . my waistline isn't getting me down, my diet is."[27] After the president's retirement, Lady Bird Johnson wrote to Helen, "Lyndon once said, 'What we need is a Helen Corbitt to take care of the entertaining we do at the [LBJ] Library and at the ranch, and help keep our guests comfortable.' I am sure he was thinking of himself, too, and the surprises he would find at the dinner table."[28]

LBJ Library Collection. Photo by Yoichi R. Okamoto.

Big City Lure

Stanley Marcus courted Helen Corbitt for eight years before she finally agreed to give up her job at the Driskill and come to Dallas. Each turndown would end with his saying, "Just let me know when you're ready to come to work for me, Helen." Late one night the phone rang and a woman's voice said, "I'm ready. When do you want me to start?" Helen asked to bring along her major-domo, Clarence White—called Captain White—who quickly became a mainstay of the Zodiac Room.[29]

In the Texas of those days it was hard to escape the glamour and allure of Neiman Marcus—even for those like Helen, who were already well up the prestige ladder themselves. Marcus, a gourmet and perfectionist, had hoped to provide the best restaurant in the region to attract more people to the downtown area and keep them in the store longer. However, his first few restaurant directors had not been successful in establishing such a reputation. Helen was characteristically blunt when she finally accepted. "They say Jesus Christ couldn't please you," she told him. "I'd like to see whether I can."[30] Years later she said, "A lot of people think Stanley Marcus made me. I'm very fond of Stanley, and my years at Neiman Marcus were the most rewarding of my life, but I had my reputation before I came to him."[31]

The Zodiac Room was the upper-floor restaurant in the flagship Dallas store. Furred and sparkling ladies, usually accompanied by their illustrious men, found it an oasis for daytime glamour. Dallas citizens and out-of-town visitors could enjoy a noonday feast along with a display of the latest fashions worn by sleek, slim Neiman Marcus models. Raquel Welch won her break in the movies as a store model.[32]

Food served in the Zodiac attracted as much attention as the models. It was imaginative, delicious and presented with flair. The Zodiac Room projected the Neiman Marcus image as much as the store's advertisements, sumptuous displays or even its famous Fortnights. Demand soon created a Thursday evening buffet, as well, since there were few good downtown restaurants convenient for customers during extended store hours. Before long, affluent Texans began driving miles into town to wait in long lines for a Corbitt meal.

Not only Texans, but every visiting celebrity that came through Dallas vied for a seat in the Zodiac Room—names like Bob Hope, Zsa Zsa Gabor, Carol Burnett, Charlton Heston, Kaye Kayser, the Duke and Duchess of Windsor, Princess Margaret, Lily Pons and Greer Garson. Van

Cliburn lunched while his mother was having her hair done in the adjacent beauty salon. They were guests and they were welcome, but Helen's standards and sense of fairness prevailed. One morning operatic diva Maria Callas made a luncheon reservation for her party of thirty. Renowned for keeping everyone waiting, she was over a half-hour late, so Corbitt instructed the staff to break down the long table and serve people who had been waiting patiently in line. Callas's retinue swept in still later and were consigned to the end of that long line.[33]

A Feisty Cook

In *Minding the Store,* Stanley Marcus writes, "I had been forewarned that I might have difficulty holding on to her, for she had a record of getting bored with her jobs. Very quickly, I discerned that beneath her facade of self-assurance and belligerence, she had a basic need for appreciation."[34] He made a point of complimenting her several times a week on some particular menu offering. "Helen, that was the best Lamb Curry I've ever eaten," or "Our Canadian visitor said that your Steak and Kidney Pie was better than any he's had in London." A bit sheepishly, Marcus confessed that he even invented a few compliments. Corbitt invariably harrumphed, "I've been makin' it that way for a long time."[35]

How she must have tried his patience! Accustomed to poking into every corner of his store, one morning Marcus strolled into Helen's institutional kitchen. "Stanley, did I invite you into my kitchen?" boomed Helen. "No? Then walk right out and don't come back until I do!"[36] Times like that may have originated his other pet name for her, his "Wild Irish genius."[37] In a speech at Skidmore in which she recalled the particular joys of her life, she mentioned "sixteen wonderful years trying to get the best of Stanley Marcus."[38]

Part of Helen's success was her bed-rock knowledge of food—part was her feisty attitude. "I'm kind of an individualist and he [Marcus] let me go ahead and create my own climate without interference."[39] Soon the Zodiac Room began to reflect Helen's ideas and especially her favorite color, blue. The hue was carried out in linens, dishes, menus and even in the oft-noted blue sugar on the tables.[40] It was Marcus's genius that he gave her elbow room to create not only the most famous restaurant in the Southwest, but one of the premier dining establishments in this country.

Of course Helen and Stanley both knew who really owned the store. A story holds that when Helen had cooked in Houston, Mrs. Bernard Sakowitz, wife of the owner of Houston's most exclusive fashion store, indulged in the Baked Shrimp so often that the recipe came to be known as "Shrimp Saki" [see recipe on page 212]. Stanley Marcus told Helen to rename the dish for the Zodiac menu, explaining "I'm not going to advertise the competition!"[41]

Potluck? Well Really!

The Zodiac menu was soon enlarged to nine hot and nine cold dishes every day. "Potluck," a trademark of her restaurant, was anything she wished to concoct that day. There were always four different Potluck entrées so that each person at a table could be served something different. With the waiters sworn to secrecy, guests were invariably delighted with their surprise entrées. The cream of these improvised recipes was gathered into her popular cookbook, *Helen Corbitt's Potluck*.

Operating under the dictum that the most expensive food is that which is not eaten, Helen never cut corners on quality. She insisted on the freshest produce, sometimes shopping for it herself. One morning a new employee of Dallas' gourmet grocery store spotted a well-dressed, determined woman selecting mushrooms from the crates in the back of the store. "I'm sorry, but the manager doesn't allow customers back here," he said. The woman continued to fill her bag. "Go tell the manager Helen Corbitt is here," she said. "I've got pickin' privileges."[42]

Wider Horizons

Once the late Broadway playwright Moss Hart was eating lunch with Edward Marcus. The Zodiac Room served only custom-made soups—all but the cream of tomato. "I used Campbell's, with coffee cream and butter added to make it like velvet," Corbitt recalled. "Mr. Hart first had a cup, then a bowl, then he wanted the recipe. I refused to give it to him." Edward was hurt and surprised until Helen later explained to him that "we couldn't tell Moss Hart he ate Campbell's soup at Neiman Marcus."[43]

Helen junketed around the globe to bring back new ideas and authentic foreign recipes, which she then adapted to Texans' palates. On a trip to Paris she discovered candied violet petals, which she crushed to dust over choice desserts. They were as expensive as gold dust. It's been told that when Stanley Marcus complained about cost over-runs in her operation, Helen defended herself, "You said you wanted the best. And I've given you the best. You didn't say anything about cost!"[44]

Beneath the Crust

Neiman's kitchen staff started off integrated, but wound up almost all African-American. Helen preferred to hire people who had not previously worked in food service, because she found it easier to train them to her own standards. Admittedly a demanding taskmaster, she also took their personal problems to heart. Those were the days when the government's welfare net was frayed to nonexistent. Helen often used her own money to pay medical and food bills for her troubled employees. Sensitive to their pride, she might preface her offer with "I know how it feels to be without funds but now that I have some money, I hope you will let me help you."[45] After her retirement from Neiman's, she helped two of her former employees start their own catering business.[46]

"She could see our potential when we couldn't see it ourselves," commented one of the cooks she trained. "She brought in a young woman who had an artistic flair for arranging salads. When bill collectors began to hound her, Miss Corbitt realized that the woman couldn't handle her own money. So she established a bank account for the woman and taught her money management."[47]

In 1955 the University of Dallas was taking root on the rolling hills between Dallas and Fort Worth. Flying in the face of liberalism that was beginning to challenge other colleges, UD based its curriculum on the supposition that truth and virtue exist. Youngest of the nation's Phi Beta Kappa schools, it decided to focus its core curriculum on the great deeds, ideas and works of Western civilization. These were concepts that had guided Helen through her entire lifetime, so it was natural that she would be among the school's idealistic supporters. Her papers, cooking awards and personal effects are in the "Helen Lucy Corbitt Suite" on campus, which is used by visiting professors and researchers. An endowment set up by her estate supports UD's Helen Corbitt Awards for Excellence given at graduation each year, and it supports special activities on the university's Rome campus, a handsome permanent facility in the Alban hills outside Rome, where virtually all 1100 undergraduate students spend a semester of full-time study.

A deeply religious woman who attended mass every morning before work, Helen's concern sometimes appeared to be prompted as much by guilt over her high temper as by spirituality. The story goes that she fired one of her employees in a rage. Soon she began to ponder how this young single mother would scrape by without a job. So she called an associate and gave the woman such a glowing recommendation that her friend replied, "But Helen, if she was this good, why did you fire her?"[48]

Sometimes her concern may have sprung from more practical concerns, too. Part of Helen's legend is that in a fit of pique, she once fired the entire kitchen staff on the spot. As they disappeared down the elevator, the reality of having a dining room full of hungry customers set in. She immediately phoned store security and told them to lock the employees' doors so that they couldn't leave, and then send them all back upstairs. "I was very tough, but I was fair and I fought for them," she said about her employees. "I got them recognition and gave them tradition. I demanded a lot and I got a lot." Then she smiled, "Every place I worked since I was twenty-one, except Neiman Marcus, my kitchen people called me Mama."[49] To a person, though, her employees took pains to tread lightly on the days she came to work in a red dress.[50]

Back in those days Texas was still officially dry, but Helen was not always orthodox in regard to wines and wine cookery. "I remember a time when, if I wanted wine in the kitchen, I had to disguise it," she said "The produce dealer also carried wines. In our secret code, a half case of lemons meant a gallon of sherry and a half case of oranges a gallon of burgundy." Did the kitchen help nip into the vino? She laughed, "In all my years I fired only one cook for drinking, and I used a lot of wine, even in the hospital. All you have to do is add some salt to the wine and they won't bother it."[51]

Helen Corbitt's Cookbook, her first, made its debut in 1957 to immediate critical and popular success, ultimately selling over 350,000 copies. It was followed in 1962 by a slender volume, *Helen Corbitt's Potluck*. Then in 1974 came *Helen Corbitt Cooks for Company*. Warned by her doctor that she had to lose weight, Helen relied on her dietetic training. She went from a self-admitted dress size of twenty to a size fourteen. Never one to waste a worthwhile experience, she gathered her favorite lower calorie recipes in *Helen Corbitt Cooks for Looks*. Anticipating today's leaner cuisine, these recipes furthered her reputation as a trendsetter. Shortly before her death, she completed the manuscript for her last book, *Helen Corbitt's Greenhouse Cookbook,* which was published post-humously.

Sharing

Partially to get ideas for future books, Helen began teaching cooking classes for non-profit groups. Her schools were great "draws" and she raised substantial amounts of money for charities all over the country. When she rolled up the sleeves of her navy silk shirtwaist, her big diamond ring flashing under the spotlights and her heavy horn-rimmed glasses slipping down her nose, she worked the crowd like a ball of dough. She became the first honorary member of the local Junior Symphony Orchestra League in recognition of her sixteen annual benefit cooking schools that netted the Dallas orchestra well over $100,000.

In 1968 several men requested equal cooking school time. By invitation only, this spirited group consisted of wealthy and influential Dallas men. Originally calling themselves the "No Name Gourmet School for Men," Helen came to refer to them as her "perpetual cooking school." The group eventually settled on a membership of fourteen who met in Corbitt's kitchen every third Wednesday night for years. She joked, "I can't get rid of them. Wouldn't you call that perpetual? I told them, 'I've taught you everything I know,' and they said, 'Then start over again.'"[52] Membership in the select group came to be such a coveted social cachet that the waiting list expanded to thirty-seven. There were no drop-outs.

At the organizational meeting of her innovative cooking school, one of the men asked about her attitude toward bringing their wives to class. "Well, I have no objections to the wives coming to the dinners as long as they stay out of the kitchen . . . the reason is very simple. If I told somebody to do something, say peel the onions, his wife would say, 'You don't like to peel onions,' . . . and I can't take it. I'm sorry . . . the wives can come and play cards or get drunk or anything they want to—but out of the kitchen."[53] The issue was compromised by having two formal couples' dinners a year prepared by the men and served by Helen's trained employees under the watchful eyes of Captain White.

Corbitt established control of her high-spirited group during the first session. "Now, I am not a chef. I am not an exponent of French cooking. I am just an ordinary, American girl who has liked to cook and has had a fair success in teaching other people to do it. Now, you may have done some French cooking . . . or you watched Julia Child . . . or somebody and that is fine—but I am going to teach you my way and I don't particularly care if you think your way is better. . . . In other words, I don't want any argument. . . . Now, you all came to me—I didn't go to you. Take it or leave it boys. Fair enough?"[54]

There were some strict rules laid down at that first meeting. Although menu suggestions were to come from both pupils and teacher, she warned them, "I don't want to hear anybody saying that they don't like something . . . because you really don't know whether you like it or not. Most of you have preconceived ideas of what you like and don't like because your mother didn't like them. When I entertain at my home, I am noted for calling up the people that I invite and saying, 'What does your husband not like?' and then I serve that; and you know, they eat two or three servings and then turn to their wives and say, 'Why don't you have that at home?'"[55]

The men also were not supposed to drink or smoke while they were cooking. One of her former students summed the group this way, "We were a smart alecky bunch, so sometimes we intercepted Captain White on the way to the bathroom. He would fix us a small libation for the journey."[56]

"To help us develop our palates, appropriate wines were always served with our dinners. One evening we found several partial bottles of leftover wine in Helen's refrigerator, which we secretly mixed and served for her approval. After she had remarked on the fine bouquet and quality, we confronted her with its mongrel appellation." Helen prided herself on always being able to spot a phony, but this deception so amused her that she later recounted it before a cooking school audience of Houston doctors' wives.[57]

Helen Corbitt always liked men. Intimates had heard that she once had been engaged to a young man back East. Perhaps he died before they could be married. In later years she confided, "I'm not married, not because I have never had the chance—but the last time I was dating someone serious and we went out to eat, I was so tired, I literally went to sleep over the steak."[58]

Although she had close women friends, Helen's Yankee directness seemed easier for Southern men to accept than it was for conventionally reared Southern belles. She had a long running cooking school for women in her home, but it didn't receive the publicity of her classes for men. Apparently operating on the "man bites dog" theory, the tabloids considered it less newsworthy for women to study the culinary arts.

Her women's class, too, had a regular membership of around fourteen, dictated by Helen's chair count. It was made up of both those who really cooked and those who enjoyed good cooking. Reminiscing about the classes, a former member recalls that when Helen had enough of a lady's questions about possible substitutions for the dish she was demonstrating, she snapped, "You can substitute anything you like, but if you want to achieve this result, you will follow my directions!" On another day, a talkative member caught the rough side of Helen's tongue, "Be quiet! You don't even know where your kitchen is!"[59]

Helen once confided to a long-time colleague that one of her great gripes was that she didn't get invited out to dinner often enough. The inference was that everyone, professional or amateur, was so intimidated by the presence of "La Corbitt" that they were reluctant to set their own dishes before her. Her cohort replied, "Well, who wants to play 'Chopsticks' for Van Cliburn?"[60]

Out of her various cooking schools and a lecture series on entertaining that she gave at Southern Methodist University in 1971, came the book that Helen's admirers had asked for, *Helen Corbitt Cooks for Company*. This book contained not only delectable Sunday-best recipes, but menus for every type of entertaining from easy informal brunches to wedding receptions. With her usual pragmatism, she graded the menus according to cost, using from one to three cornucopias to signify the price of the ingredients.

On Her Own Again

In June 1969, Helen gave up day-to-day management of Neiman's restaurants to become a food services consultant, to lecture, and to write. After the fuss and feathers of her retirement party, one of the kitchen employees reminded her how, when irritated, she had always threatened to "go back to Ireland and never come back." On behalf of her staff, he handed her an envelope which contained an airline ticket to Ireland. Blinking, Helen said, "So you want to get rid of me completely?" "No ma'am," the man answered gently. "If you'll notice, that ticket is round trip."[61]

Her new interest was creating enticing recipes for the 850-calorie a day regimen served at The Greenhouse, the posh new health and beauty spa developed just outside Dallas. Corbitt brooked no more foolishness from the wealthy clientele that returned year after year to be pampered back into health and svelte at the Greenhouse than she had from a self-important opera star.

"We have a Dallas woman who comes to the Greenhouse twice a year for two weeks. Every time she comes, she brings two loaves of San Francisco sourdough rye and she doesn't think we know about it," confided Corbitt. "A Houston woman recently complained that she didn't lose any weight during her stay. I suggested next time she gather up the chocolate bar wrappers and put them in her purse instead of throwing them in the wastebasket in her room."[62]

Her dieting secrets found their way into print in Helen Corbitt's *Greenhouse Cookbook*. Helen once said that all good cooks would arrive at the pearly gates "with an onion in one hand and a pound of butter in the other."[63] She often predicted that her own hostess gift was more likely to be a jar of "Poppy Seed Dressing" [see recipe on page 122]. "Personally, I can't stand it!"[64]

Balenciaga and Bouillabaisse

Dick Hill, writing a farewell in the *Dallas Times Herald* after Helen's death in 1978, seemed to have gotten it about right: "she was 'a no-nonsense woman.' She was capable of humor, often of the rapier variety, but she used it as she would a pungent spice: for hinting at the substance of a point. She was a curious combination of elegance and gusto, impatience and painstaking perfectionism, femininity and jaunty zest. She was subtle and imperious, ebullient and unerringly correct. Lots of things that you wouldn't think would go together in a person, went together in Helen Corbitt. She was a bouillabaisse of a person, part administrator, part hostess, part duchess and part Mother Superior."[65]

[1] Frances Raffetto, "The Texas Star," *The Dallas Morning News*, 26 March 1972, 13 Supplement.

[2] Stanley Marcus, *Minding the Store* (Denton: University of North Texas Press, 1997), 181.

[3] Claire White, Editor, "Tempo," *Roanoke* (Virginia)*Times*, 17 April 1974; and Earl Wilson, quoted in "Woman's World," *The Houston Post*, 5 October 1971.

[4] Presentation plaque, Confrérie de la Chaînes des Rôtisseurs–Vows of the Ancient Spit-Roasters, 1968, Helen Corbitt's personal papers: University of Dallas, Irving, Texas.

[5] *The Dallas Morning News*, 17 January 1978.

[6] Transcript of tape recording made during the organizational meeting of Helen Corbitt's Men's Gourmet Cooking Class, 31 January 1968, Helen Corbitt's personal papers: University of Dallas, Irving, Texas.

[7] Connie Lunnen, "She's Cookin' on All Burners," *The Houston Chronicle*, 20 June 1976.

[8] Dr. Louise Cowan, presentation remarks as reported in a newspaper clipping, Helen Corbitt's personal papers: University of Dallas, Irving, Texas.

[9] Text of presentation remarks given at ceremony in Dallas on 12 July 1977, Helen Corbitt's personal papers: University of Dallas, Irving, Texas.

[10] Memo to Helen Corbitt, written on Skidmore College letterhead, dated 10 February 1978, Helen Corbitt's personal papers: University of Dallas, Irving, Texas.

[11] Raffetto.

[12] Judith Collins, *Times Record*, 20 April 1974.

[13] Raffetto.

[14] *Rochester Times-Union*, New York, 23 March 1972.

[15] Text of presentation remarks given at ceremony in Dallas on 12 July 1977, Helen Corbitt's personal papers: University of Dallas, Irving, Texas.

[16] Ernest Kay, Hon., General Editor, *Two Thousand Women of Achievement*, Vol. III, (London: Melrose Press, Ltd., 1971).

[17] White.

[18] Lunnen.

[19] White.

[20] Mary Bell, "Black-eyed Peas Make New Pickle," from Dallas INS, as reprinted in *Mid-Ocean News*, Hamilton, Bermuda.

[21] Photocopy of fragment of Corbitt interview in Dallas newspaper. Helen Corbitt's personal papers: University of Dallas, Irving, Texas.

[22] White.

[23] Robert Jones, telephone interview with editor, 25 February 1995.

[24] Jean Moore, interview with editor, Universitiy of Dallas, March 1995.

[25] Ibid.

[26] Letter from Paul Wakefield to Stanley Walker of Lampasas, Texas, dated March 11, 1952. Helen Corbitt's personal papers: University of Dallas, Irving, Texas.

[27] Letter from Lyndon B. Johnson, to Helen Corbitt, dated 5 May 1969.Helen Corbitt's personal papers: University of Dallas, Irving, Texas.

[28] Letter from Lady Bird Johnson to Helen Corbitt, dated 5 March 1973. Helen Corbitt's personal papers: University of Dallas, Irving, Texas.

[29] Stanley Marcus: interview with editor at his Dallas office, March 1995.

[30] Photocopy of fragment of printed newspaper article (no headline, date or page number). Helen Corbitt's personal papers: University of Dallas, Irving, Texas.

[31] Ibid.

[32] Moore interview.

[33] Beverly Bennett: interview with editor in the Zodiac Room, downtown Neiman Marcus store, Dallas, March 1995.

[34] Marcus, 182.

[35] Marcus interview.

[36] Jean Moore and Clarence White: interviews with editor at University of Dallas, Irving, Texas, March 1995; confirmed by Beverly Bennett: interviewed in the Zodiac Room, downtown Dallas Neiman Marcus store in March 1995.

[37] Marcus, 181.

[38] Corbitt's remarks on receiving Skidmore College's Doctor of Letters degree. Typewritten fragment signed by Helen Corbitt, no date. Helen Corbitt's personal papers: University of Dallas, Irving, Texas.

[39] Newspaper interview that omitted source and date. Helen Corbitt's personal papers: University of Dallas, Irving, Texas.

[40] Bennett interview.

[41] Jones interview.

[42] Julia Sweeney, *Dallas Times Herald,* 16 January 1978 (no page number).

[43] Raffetto. (Although widely circulated, this story may be apocryphal, according to Miss Corbitt's contemporaries.—Editor)

[44] Marcus interview.

[45] Bennett interview.

[46] Moore and White interviews. Confirmed by Beverly Bennett, interview.

[47] Maxine Johnson: interview with editor at the Zodiac Room, downtown Dallas Neiman Marcus store, March 1995.

[48] Jones interview.

[49] Raffeto.

[50] White interview.

[51] Raffeto.

[52] Newspaper interview that omitted source and date. Helen Corbitt's personal papers: University of Dallas, Irving, Texas.

[53] Transcript of tape recording made during organizational meeting of Helen Corbitt's Men's Gourmet Cooking Class, Dallas, 31 January 1968. Helen Corbitt's personal papers: University of Dallas, Irving, Texas.

[54] Ibid.

[55] Ibid.

[56] Robert Gaylord, interview with editor at his Dallas office, March 1995.

[57] Jerry Jerico: Telephone interview, Dallas, March 1995.

[58] Beverly King, *Times* Women's Editor, *Shreveport Times* (Louisiana), (date missing).

[59] Harriet "Dolly" Kelton, telephone interview with editor, 15 October 1995.

[60] Dick Hitt, "Helen Corbitt: The grande dame of gourmets," *Dallas Times Herald*, 18 January 1978 (page numbers missing).

[61] Raffeto.

[62] Gay McFarland, "Greenhouse," *The Houston Post*, 28 March 1971 (no page number).

[63] Letter to Neiman Marcus InCircle director from Mrs. C.N. Wilkinson, Jr., Midland, Texas, 1995.

[64] Dorothy Sinz, *Dallas Times Herald*, 16 January 1978 (no title or page number).

[65] Hitt.

Kitchen staff for the Zodiac Room (from left to right) Grace Baker, John Elliott, T. Bowman (kneeling), Helen Corbitt, Lula B. Paul, Carol Grinsted, Wallace Taylor, and Dorothy Mitchell. From the Neiman Marcus collection, Texas/Dallas History and Archives Division, Dallas Public Library.

Photo by Michael Olsen. © The Conde Nast Publications, Inc.

Neiman Marcus during Corbitt's reign. From the Neiman Marcus collection, Texas/
Dallas History and Archives Division, Dallas Public Library.

Appetizers

The cocktail party has become the American way of turning everyone into a "Blithe Spirit." How we do it depends entirely on the host—or hostess. Informality is its purpose, as munching on such oddments before or in place of a meal should keep conversation on the lighter and brighter things of the day.

Where to serve? Anywhere—the living room, the back porch, the kitchen; anywhere your guests or family choose to light.

If you are interested in its family tree, go to the Russian Zakouska. Being a hearty race, before dinner the Russians gather around a sideboard in a room adjoining the dining room and partake of all kinds of special pastries, smoked fish and such, with much conversation and strong drink. The French Hors d'oeuvre, the Scandinavian Smörgåsbord, the Italian Antipasto, all are offshoots of the Zakouska. . . . I like to keep [the cocktail tidbit] as uncomplicated in flavor as possible, freshly made, cold and crisp—or hot—as the case may be. . . . These few ideas, I think, will answer for all kinds of tastes, for the hostess who has time, or not much time; an unlimited budget, or just a few spare dimes. I think you should let guests pile as high and wide as they like, so very few of these ideas are to be spread on silly little squares of this and that by the hostess beforehand.

CRABMEAT GRUYÈRE

1 cup canned crabmeat
¼ cup shredded Swiss Gruyère cheese
1 tablespoon Sauterne
½ teaspoon salt
Mayonnaise to moisten

Mix and pile high on sautéed rounds of white bread and run into a
450° oven until hot.

DEVILED CRABMEAT MARYLAND

1 pound fresh white crabmeat
Juice of 1 lemon
⅛ teaspoon Worcestershire sauce
Few drops of Tabasco
1 teaspoon Dijon mustard
4 tablespoons butter [divided use]
2 tablespoons chopped onion
1 tablespoon flour
1 cup half-and-half
Salt and white pepper to taste
[½ cup white bread crumbs]
[2 tablespoons mayonnaise]

Mix crab, lemon juice and seasonings. Melt [2 tablespoons] butter, add
onion and cook 1 minute. Stir in flour, cook until bubbly. Pour in
cream [gradually], cook until thick. Add to crabmeat mixture. Correct
seasonings. Pile into clam shells, onto toast rounds or artichoke
bottoms. Mix bread crumbs with 2 tablespoons melted butter and
mayonnaise. Crumble on top of crab mixture. Bake at 375° until hot.
Run under broiler to brown. [Do] ahead and refrigerate but do not
freeze.

CHEESE-CRAB DIP

½ cup Roquefort or blue cheese
⅓ cup cream cheese [about 3 ounces]
2 tablespoons mayonnaise
½ teaspoon Worcestershire sauce
1 small clove garlic, finely chopped [you may leave it out]
1 teaspoon lemon juice
½ cup crabmeat, fresh or canned, but fresh is better, as always

Mix the two cheeses together until soft and add the rest of the ingredients in the order given. Place in a bowl on a large tray or plate and surround with potato chips that have been sprinkled with garlic salt and heated.

To make a simple heavily laden cocktail table takes only time, and not much money. For instance:

Chipped crisp bacon mixed with grated orange peel and cream cheese on rounds of whole wheat bread for a sweet tidbit.

Thin slices of ham rolled up with cream cheese, chives and capers, and then sliced as thin as you like.

Small oysters, drained and rolled in white bread crumbs, broiled in butter and served on rounds of crisp garlic buttered toast.

Buy prepared deviled ham and mix with chopped salted pecans— two parts of ham to one part nuts—and serve with thin slices of whole wheat or rye bread.

Small apple balls, made by cutting fresh apples with a French ball cutter, dipping in lemon juice and coating with cream cheese, mixed with finely chopped candied ginger and slivered blanched almonds. Dip one end in minced parsley.

You don't have to give up dips just because you are counting calories. Here is a case in point:

BUTTERMILK DIP

⅔ cup fresh buttermilk
½ cup shredded or minced cucumbers
¼ cup [reduced fat] mayonnaise
2 tablespoons lemon juice
1 teaspoon dried dill weed
Salt and cracked pepper to taste

Mix the ingredients and use as a dip for crisp fresh vegetables.

Or how about this one?

Whip cottage cheese with skim milk until consistency of whipped cream. Add herbs or chopped clams or curry or horseradish. Or carefully stir in caviar, with or without the horseradish. Or chop up very fine whatever raw vegetables you have and add. Add melted gelatin to any of this mixture and mold. You can balance your slice on a slice of cucumber while the rest indulge in crackers or melba toast.

To make your own Melba toast, buy a loaf of the best unsliced bread you can find and refrigerate until you can slice easily. Slice paper-thin, put on a cookie tray in a cold oven and turn to 200°. Leave until dry and light brown. The melba toast at The Greenhouse is so thin a guest suggested serving it with solid-gold tweezers to pick it up with. Your toast, too, should be that thin.

My most successful dip is made by mixing 1 cup sour cream with ½ to ¾ cup of chopped French-fried onions to make a crunchy paste. You may buy the onions already fried, in cans—or fry them yourself.

STEAK TIDBITS

When I really want to impress my male guests at a cocktail party, I serve what I call Steak Tidbits. They could be a successful backyard supper dish, or for an informal buffet supper anywhere. If you are extravagant minded, use a sirloin strip. If you are not, have your butcher cut a 2-inch-thick round steak. Marinate in red wine, bourbon whiskey, or beer, garlic, and olive oil, for at least 1 hour (1 cup of wine or liquor to ¼ cup of oil). [Discard marinade.] Broil medium rare, remove and cut into ½-inch squares. Be sure to save the drippings and add to:

½ cup butter
1 tablespoon dry mustard
½ teaspoon garlic salt
1 teaspoon Worcestershire sauce
Dash Angostura bitters
2 tablespoons red wine
A twist or two from the pepper grinder

Heat and pour over the beef cubes and keep hot in a chafing dish. *Please!* Not well done! I might add, I have to feel really extravagant when I do this. They are much too popular.

A popular cocktail item, or dessert, is the apple and cheese combination. Almost any kind of cheese will do, but Camembert, Liederkranz or Roquefort served with a cold crisp Jonathan apple has a certain something that satisfies.

In these days of waist watching, honeydew or cantaloupe balls, encircled with a thin slice of ham, held together with a toothpick or plastic spear, make an interesting taste experience. The better the ham, the better the morsel.

I never saw a place where everyone likes hot hors d'oeuvres as well as they do in Texas. They should be hot, and I mean hot! *And you should not try to serve them unless you can arrange for them to be passed many times, either by yourself or your jewel from your kitchen, or else kept hot in a chafing dish.*

PRAIRIE FIRE

1 quart red beans, cooked and put through a sieve
    [or use the steel blade on your food processor to purée]
½ pound butter
½ pound grated Provolone cheese
4 jalapeño peppers, chopped very fine
1 teaspoon jalapeño juice
2 tablespoons minced onion
1 clove garlic, chopped very fine

Mix and heat over hot water until cheese is melted. Serve hot from chafing dish with fried tortillas or potato chips.

ᴈ❧ *Reader's Request*

HAM-STUFFED MUSHROOMS

½ pound ground cooked ham
1 clove finely minced garlic
1 cup finely minced parsley
1 cup finely minced mushroom stems
½ cup fine white bread crumbs
½ cup grated Parmesan cheese
Salt and pepper [optional]
24 medium-sized mushrooms
Pine nuts
½ cup melted butter

Mix ham, garlic, parsley, mushroom stems, crumbs and cheese. Taste for more salt and pepper if needed. Stuff the mushrooms (you have removed the stems for mincing). Decorate with the pine nuts. Place in a buttered casserole, pour butter over and bake at 375° for 25 minutes.

๛ *Previously Unpublished*

CRAB-STUFFED MUSHROOMS

12 large mushrooms
¼ cup butter
½ cup Medium Cream Sauce
½ teaspoon white wine Worcestershire sauce
½ cup mayonnaise
¼ cup fine white bread crumbs
2 pounds fresh crabmeat, diced
Gruyère cheese, shredded
Parmesan cheese, shredded

Rinse mushrooms and remove stems. Sauté whole mushroom caps in butter over low heat until they change color. Follow directions for Medium Cream Sauce on page 223. (This recipe will require only half a recipe of Cream Sauce.) Season with Worcestershire and fold in mayonnaise, crumbs and crabmeat. Place mushroom caps on a flat oiled pan and pile the mixture onto the mushrooms. Mix equal amounts of the two cheeses and sprinkle them over the tops. Bake at 350° for 15 minutes to heat through, run the pan under the broiler to brown.

LEMON BROILED CHICKEN DRUMSTICKS

½ cup vinegar
2 tablespoons cracked pepper
1 teaspoon salt
¼ cup brown sugar
¼ cup lemon juice
2 cups salad oil (I like peanut oil.)
18 chicken drumsticks [or 3 dozen wing drumettes]

Bring the vinegar, pepper, salt and sugar to a boil. Remove from stove; add lemon juice and oil. Marinate drumsticks several hours. Place on a rack over broiler pan and broil, basting with the marinade about 10 minutes on each side. Serve them with a container of soy sauce nearby for those who like to use it.

I like to serve these as a cocktail tidbit. They are low in calories and light enough not to interfere with the main course.

MARINATED FRESH ARTICHOKES

8 fresh artichokes
½ lemon, sliced
Few slices onion
2 tablespoons olive oil

Wash artichokes in cold salted water, drain and snip off the sharp tips of the leaves with scissors. Stand in a kettle and cover with fresh cold salted water, lemon, onion slices and olive oil. Cover and boil until leaves pull away easily. Remove, turn upside down and drain. Cool. Turn right side up and pour marinade over. Refrigerate for several hours or overnight.

MARINADE
½ cup salad oil
½ cup olive oil
Juice of 2 lemons
2 tablespoons chopped chives or green onions
¼ cup chopped parsley
¾ teaspoon dry mustard
1½ teaspoons each salt and freshly cracked pepper

Mix thoroughly all ingredients and pour over artichokes. Lift the artichokes onto plates and pour a little of the marinade over.

Anchovies have an affinity for cheese. Sometime try these Anchovy Sticks. First, you fry pieces of bread in butter until crisp, then cut them in fingers wide enough to lay an anchovy fillet on each. Mix Parmesan cheese and a little chopped parsley and moisten with dry sherry to make a paste. Spread the paste rather thickly over the anchovy fingers; sprinkle with melted butter and grill under the broiler. Serve very hot!

This is strictly a cocktail item as it has lots of flavor. It freezes well and makes a wonderful canapé, if you are canapé-minded.

HAM MOUSSE

½ pound boiled ham
¼ pound butter
1 cup whipping cream
1 tablespoon salt
1 teaspoon white pepper
1 tablespoon Dijon mustard
1½ tablespoons unflavored gelatin
½ cup Madeira
1 cup chicken broth
¼ cup cognac

Put ham through the meat grinder [or use the steel blade on the food processor to mince]. Combine the ham and butter in a bowl, mixing well. Blend in the cream; stir vigorously. Add salt, pepper, and mustard. Soften the gelatin in the Madeira. Bring broth to a boil, remove from flame, and add gelatin, stirring to dissolve. Cool, add to the ham. Check seasoning. Mix well with cognac and pack in 1½-quart soufflé dish or mold. Refrigerate. Unmold and serve with lightly salted toasted crackers or dark bread.

❧ *Reader's Request*

CHEESE AND RED CAVIAR

1 cup cream cheese [8 ounces]
2 tablespoons cream
1 teaspoon onion juice
1 teaspoon lemon juice
2 tablespoons red caviar

Soften the cream cheese with cream and onion juice (obtained by grating onion and straining—you will weep bitterly but it is good for you). Add lemon juice and using a fork, mix the caviar in carefully to avoid breaking the eggs. Dark rye bread squares are mighty good with it.

CHEESE STRAWS

1 cup butter or margarine
1 cup grated sharp cheese
2 cups flour
1 teaspoon salt
⅛ teaspoon cayenne pepper
Parmesan cheese

[Preheat oven to 350°.] Have butter and cheese at room temperature. Mix all ingredients and either put through a cookie press or roll out very thin and cut into narrow strips. Sprinkle lightly with Parmesan cheese. Bake for 15 minutes.

Sometimes I use grated Swiss Gruyère in place of the sharp cheese and add 1 teaspoon fines herbes [or dried dill weed]. Especially nice with salads. Whatever kind of cheese you use, be sure you grate it finely.

An elegant party start:

GRAPEFRUIT AND SHRIMP COCKTAIL

3 large grapefruit
1 pound cooked, cleaned shrimp
1 ripe avocado
Lemon juice
Russian Dressing

Cut the grapefruit in two and with scissors or a very sharp knife cut out the center portion. Loosen the sections without cutting the membrane from the skin and remove every other section. Fill the empty sections with the shrimp and a thin slice of avocado placed in the split cleaned back of each shrimp. Fill centers of each grapefruit with Russian Dressing [page 116] and garnish the edge of each with chopped watercress or parsley. If you are extravagant minded, put ¼ teaspoon of caviar in the center of each.

⅜ *Reader's Request*

No one will deny that pickled shrimp are delicious:

PICKLED SHRIMP

1 pound cooked and cleaned shrimp
2 tablespoons olive oil
1 cup vinegar
2 tablespoons water
¼ cup paper-thin slices of onion
8 whole cloves
1 bay leaf
2 teaspoons salt
1 teaspoon sugar
Dash of cayenne pepper

Dribble the oil over the shrimp. Bring to a boil the rest of the ingredients and while hot pour over shrimp and olive oil. Cool and then refrigerate for at least 24 hours.

Angels on Horseback (oysters broiled, wrapped in bacon) are the usual. Be unusual with the Irish version.

ANGELS ON HORSEBACK

4 dozen medium-sized oysters
1 cup chili sauce
2 tablespoons chopped green pepper
2 tablespoons Worcestershire sauce
12 slices uncooked bacon
¾ cup grated Parmesan cheese

[Preheat oven to 350°.] Place oysters, well drained, in a skillet or saucepan; cover with chili sauce mixed with green pepper and Worcestershire sauce. Place in oven until oysters begin to puff. Remove and sprinkle with the bacon cut in fine dice and the cheese. Return to oven and bake 10 minutes. Keep hot while serving; and give your guests a square of dark rye bread to rest them on.

Snails I like, but not in their shells. (Somehow I feel the snails might resent them.)

SNAILS IN PASTA SHELLS

I like to serve snails in the pasta shells you find in the grocery stores—the sea shell macaroni is best. Drain and wash the snails and for 2 dozen, which is the small can size, sauté in 2 tablespoons butter and 2 cloves of finely chopped garlic for about 5 minutes. Cool and stuff each snail into a cooked macaroni shell.

Cover with the following butter mixture:

> ½ cup softened butter
> 1 teaspoon chopped shallots
> 2 tablespoons minced parsley
> 1 additional clove garlic, finely minced
> Juice of ½ lemon
> Few drops Worcestershire sauce

Refrigerate several hours, then bake in 350° oven until sizzling. You eat the snail with the pasta and all the butter. I find they disappear like magic. You can prepare these several days ahead and freeze.

HONEY AND MUSTARD SPARERIBS

> 1 tablespoon dry mustard
> 1 teaspoon chili powder
> 1 teaspoon sage
> 1 tablespoon salt
> 10 pounds spareribs, cut in 3-inch pieces (the butcher will do it
>   for you.)
> 1 [12 ounce] bottle beer
> 1 cup honey
> 1 tablespoon lemon juice

Mix the spices and rub on the ribs. Mix the beer, honey and lemon juice. Pour over the ribs and marinate overnight. Roast uncovered at 350° for 2 hours. Baste with the leftover marinade.

You may put bits and pieces of many foods on bamboo skewers. How much you like to spend determines the kind of food. The morsels should be small, though, as they are eaten off the stick.

CHICKEN SATÉS

1 broiler-sized chicken [or 5 boned skinless chicken breast halves]
6-inch bamboo skewers
1 cup soy sauce
2 slices fresh ginger
2 cloves garlic, mashed
Fresh ground pepper, a twist or two
½ cup dry white wine or sake

Remove skin from chicken and cut off all the meat from the carcass. Cut into ½- to 1-inch size pieces and thread 5 or 6 onto each skewer. Be sure you leave enough space at the end of the skewer to hang onto. Place in a shallow pan and cover with marinade consisting of remaining ingredients. Refrigerate for several hours. Remove from marinade. Place on a shallow pan or rack and broil, about 5 minutes, on each side. Baste with marinade. Serve hot or warm. Beef, lamb, shrimp, scallops, pork—try any of them.

Sometimes I have a Peanut Sauce handy to dip the satés into before eating.

PEANUT SAUCE

⅔ cup peanut butter
2 tablespoons butter
6 tablespoons soy sauce
2 tablespoons lemon juice
2 teaspoons fresh garlic juice
⅔ cup whipping cream

Cook all except cream over hot water until hot. Add whipping cream. Keep warm. Use for egg rolls and tempura, too.

Terrines and pâtés are a part of the French gastronomical scene. Basically, this pâté is a mixture of pork, veal, fowl, game and liver baked in a terrine or casserole lined with pork fat. If it is baked in a crust, it is called pâté en croûte. If it is made of all fowl or birds of any kind, and boiled or steamed, it is a galantine.

TERRINE PÂTÉ

1 pound chicken livers
¼ teaspoon salt
⅛ teaspoon poultry seasoning
1 tablespoon cognac
½ pound fresh pork
½ pound veal
¼ cup sherry
Dash of salt and pepper
1 egg
¼ pound salt pork, sliced paper-thin
1 bay leaf

Dice half of the livers. Add the salt, poultry seasoning and cognac. Refrigerate for a few hours. Put the rest of the livers, the pork and veal through your meat grinder. Add the sherry, salt, pepper, egg and mix well. Line the bottom and sides of the terrine or casserole with pork. Put a layer of the ground mixture, then a few pieces of the diced liver. Repeat until the terrine is filled, ending with mixture layer. Top with the salt pork. Place the bay leaf on top. Cover the terrine and seal the edges with foil. Place in a shallow pan with about an inch of hot water and bake at 375° for 2½ hours. Remove cover and bay leaf, and refrigerate for 24 hours. You may add truffles if you feel extravagant. Slice and serve on soft lettuce or watercress with or without Melba toast.

This pâté substitutes very well for the imported pâté de foie gras.

PÂTÉ

1 pound chicken livers
Chicken broth

Bring chicken livers to a boil in chicken broth barely to cover and simmer them for 15 to 20 minutes in a covered saucepan. Drain and put the hot livers through the finest blade of the food chopper [or use food processor with the steel blade to purée them].

Mix the livers with:

2 teaspoons salt
Pinch cayenne pepper
½ cup softened butter
½ teaspoon dry mustard
2 tablespoons finely minced onion
1 tablespoon dry sherry

Blend well; pack the mixture in a crock and chill in the refrigerator. You may freeze.

Ripe olives lend extra-special appeal to any relish or canapé tray. To provide a rich gloss, drain olives well and pat dry with paper towels, then roll in a bowl with a few drops of salad oil. Serve some of the olives with coatings of parsley, toasted sesame seeds or instant minced onion. To toast sesame seeds, place on a shallow pan or baking sheet in 200° to 250° oven; watch closely and stir frequently. They should be just golden brown to bring out the flavor, but will become bitter if toasted until they are dark.

Christmas is a "nutty" time of year, and nuts prepared by loving hands are far more exciting than out of a can. They make nice neighborhood Christmas gifts, too.

ORANGE PECANS

1¼ cups sugar
Grated rind and juice of 1 orange
⅛ teaspoon cream of tartar
Pecans

Cook sugar, orange juice, rind and cream of tartar to soft ball stage [234° to 238° on candy thermometer]; remove from heat and beat until creamy. Dip pecans into the mixture, forming small clusters, or coating singly if they are large. Keep mixture in pan of warm water while dipping.

SALTED NUTS

To roast any nuts, put 1 pound of nuts in a shallow pan with 4 tea-spoons butter or oil and roast in a hot oven until they are golden-brown, stirring frequently to obtain an even color. Sprinkle with salt while the nuts are still hot.

Cooking nuts over direct heat produces a more uniform effect than can be obtained by roasting. Use 1 cup oil or butter for 2 cups nutmeats and cook over a low flame for 3 to 5 minutes, or until the desired shade of brown is obtained. Some nuts take longer to color than others, so only one variety should be fried at a time.

GLAZED NUTS

Cook together 2 cups sugar, ⅛ teaspoon cream of tartar, ⅔ cup water, and a dash of salt. Stir only until the sugar is dissolved and cook the syrup to 310° or until a little of the syrup dropped into very cold water separates into brittle threads. Remove immediately from the fire and dip the base of the saucepan for a second in cold water to stop the cooking and then put the pan over hot water to keep the syrup from hardening. Drop perfect whole or half blanched nutmeats into the syrup, one at a time, and lift them out with a dipping fork or spoon. Let any excess syrup drain off and turn the coated nuts upside down on an oiled slab or platter to cool. They will harden almost immediately. The syrup may be gently reheated over hot water.

❧ *Previously Unpublished*

SPICED NUTS

2 cups sugar
2 teaspoons salt
1 teaspoon ground nutmeg
3 tablespoons ground cinnamon
2 teaspoons ground ginger
1 tablespoon ground cloves
2 egg whites
2 tablespoons cold water
1¾ cups nutmeats

Sift the sugar, salt and spices together 3 times. Beat the egg whites until they are foamy, gradually adding the cold water. Dip the nuts into the slightly beaten egg whites, coating each nut completely. Putting them in a wire strainer will make this easier. Drain the nuts well and roll them in a small amount of the spiced sugar. Make a ¼-inch deep layer in a shallow pan with the remaining dry sugar mixture and place the nuts on this, separating each one. Cover the nuts with the rest of the dry sugar and bake in a very slow oven, 250°, for about 3 hours. Remove the nuts from the oven and shake off excess sugar. You can keep the spiced sugar in a closed jar in a cool dry place and use it for another batch of nuts. It would also be good sprinkled on top of whipped cream for holiday desserts.

It goes without saying that thin slices of smoked salmon do things for a cocktail party. Have a pepper mill handy. The pepper brings out the taste. Smoked sturgeon, too. I like small Matzo crackers with it, flavored subtly with garlic and poppy seeds.

PICKLED OKRA

Choose small tender okra; wash and leave stem ends on. Fill each jar tightly, but do not bruise okra. For each *pint*:

2 teaspoons dill seed
2 strips jalapeño peppers
½ teaspoon red chili pepper flakes
2 cloves garlic, cut in half

Cover with the following which have been boiled together:

1 quart white vinegar
1 cup water
½ cup non-iodized or kosher salt

This syrup is enough for 4 to 6 pints. One pound okra fills 2 pints. Seal jars as soon as filled. Pour paraffin on top to seal properly.

A hot Roquefort Cheese Puff smells to high heaven, but is so good you can hardly wait for "seconds." Merely mix Roquefort cheese with a little Worcestershire sauce and butter. Pile high on toast rounds, or better yet, pastry bases you make yourself from pie crust. Bake these in a 450° oven until hot. Too, mix with toasted chopped almonds for a more delightful experience.

Mash together equal quantities of sweet butter and Roquefort or Danish blue cheese. Sandwich a little of the mixture between two walnut or pecan halves. Chill before serving.

❧ Reader's Request

In the South, the black-eyed pea is the traditional good-luck food for New Year's Day and a good Texan eats them some time during the day to insure prosperity for the coming year—whether he likes them or not. I came to Texas wide-eyed and innocent about such shenanigans—I didn't like the peas either. So-o-o, I pickled them. Since then I serve few parties at any time of the year without them. And the men, how they love them!

PICKLED BLACK-EYED PEAS

2 15-ounce cans cooked dried black-eyed peas
1 cup salad oil
¼ cup wine vinegar
1 whole clove garlic—or garlic seasoning
¼ cup thinly sliced onion
½ teaspoon salt
Cracked or freshly ground black pepper

Drain liquid from the peas. Place peas in a bowl, add remaining ingredients and mix thoroughly. Store in a jar in refrigerator and remove garlic bud after one day. Store at least two days and up to two weeks before eating. You'll need a plate and fork for these. Red kidney beans and garbanzos, do the same.

Let's appreciate the green chile more. It adds spice to meat, sandwiches—just about everything. This concoction will keep for several days:

PICKLED CHILES

3 7-ounce cans whole green chiles or 5 4-ounce cans
1 cup white vinegar
1 cup sugar
1 teaspoon dill seeds
1 teaspoon salt

Cut chiles into bite-sized pieces. Leave all seeds in. Mix sugar, vinegar, dill and salt, until sugar is dissolved. Pour over chiles. Refrigerate at least 24 hours before serving. I add strips of red sweet pepper when it's in season.

Beverages

The cup that cheers, be it made with spirits or not, has its place in every home. For graduation parties, large get-togethers, lounging on the back porch or terrace, after football games, any time more than two people get together.

MINT PUNCH
For 12

1 cup sugar
½ cup water
Juice of 6 oranges
½ cup grapefruit juice
Juice of 6 lemons
½ cup crème de menthe
Rind of ½ cucumber
Rind of ½ orange
1 quart ginger ale
¼ cup grated fresh pineapple

Boil the sugar and water, cool and add the juice of oranges, grape-fruit, lemons and crème de menthe, cucumber rind and the rind of ½ an orange. Chill several hours, remove cucumber and orange rinds, add the ginger ale and fresh pineapple and pour over the ice cubes.

CRANBERRY ORANGE PUNCH
For 12

6 cups cranberry juice cocktail
1 cup orange juice
3 tablespoons lemon juice
1¼ cups pineapple juice
3 cups ice water
Fruit sherbet (optional)

Mix together in the order given [except for the sherbet] and pour over an ice block in a punch bowl. Serve plain or with fruit sherbet float-ing on top. Place your punch bowl in the center of a polished table and surround it with greens from your yard or sprigs of holly at holiday time. Or serve as a first-course cocktail.

❧ *Reader's Request*

Punch comes from a Hindu word meaning "5," so a fruit punch should have at least five ingredients.

FRUIT PUNCH
For 30

4 cups pineapple juice
4 cups fresh lime juice
1 quart orange juice
2 cups sugar
1 quart orange ice
2 quarts ginger ale

Mix fruit juices and sugar and refrigerate. Pour over a quart of orange ice and add ginger ale. Garnish with fresh mint and thin slices of orange.

RASPBERRY CUP
For 12

1 cup frozen raspberries
¾ cup grated fresh pineapple
Juice of 3 lemons
1 cup sugar syrup (see next page)
3 cups cold tea
1 quart ginger ale

Crush the fruit with the lemon juice, syrup and tea. Allow to stand several hours, strain, forcing as much fruit pulp through your sieve as possible. Just before serving, add the ginger ale and pour over ice. It is a pretty punch.

If you dilute your frozen orange juice concentrate with apricot nectar, you will enjoy it more.

SIMPLE SUGAR SYRUP

2 cups boiling water
2 cups granulated sugar

Cook for 15 minutes. Cool and pour into jars to use when needed.
Add 2 tablespoons lemon or lime juice to each cup of syrup to use
over fruit.

*I recommend this coffee punch for all occasions: cocktail parties,
weddings, teas, receptions . . . you will find men sometimes like it better
than whiskey.*

COFFEE PUNCH
For 50

2 gallons strong coffee (I add 2 tablespoons instant Espresso to
    the coffee), cooled
2 gallons vanilla ice cream
1 pint half-and-half
Sugar to taste
2 bottles cognac or brandy, $^4/_5$ quarts each
    [6 cups plus 6½ tablespoons total.]

Freeze 1 quart of the coffee in a ring mold. Pour the rest into a punch
bowl. Add ice cream, cream, sugar and [unmolded] frozen coffee. Stir
well and add cognac.

IRISH COFFEE
For 1 cup

2 sugar cubes
2 jiggers [3 ounces] hot coffee
2 jiggers [3 ounces] Irish whiskey
Dab of whipped cream

Put sugar in bottom of cup, add the hot coffee, then the whiskey. Add
the whipped cream. Do not stir. You may do it in a punch bowl, but
for goodness sakes know your Irish—friends and whiskey.

SPICED TEA
For 50

6 quarts boiling water
1½ pounds sugar [3 cups]
2 lemons, juice and rind
4 oranges, juice and rind
4 teaspoons whole cloves
8 sticks cinnamon
3 tablespoons tea

Let first 6 ingredients [all ingredients except tea] stand 20 minutes, keeping hot but not boiling. Add tea. Let stand 5 minutes. Strain. Serve from a tea urn in punch or demitasse cups.

TEA PUNCH
For 75 to 80

Make a syrup of:

8 quarts water
8 pounds sugar

When cool, add:

2 quarts lemon juice (3 dozen lemons)
1 pint orange juice (½ dozen oranges)
¼ pound black tea steeped in 1 pint water (strained)
Rind of cucumber, chopped
¼ scant teaspoon cayenne pepper (optional)
1 bunch fresh mint, minced
2 quarts strawberries
1 cup grape juice
1 can of chunk pineapple, sour cherries or raspberries

Serve over ice and ladle into punch cups.

HOT CHOCOLATE
For 20

⅔ cup cocoa
¾ cup sugar
½ teaspoon salt
1 cup water
3 quarts scalded milk
1 teaspoon vanilla
1 cup cream, whipped
[Ground cinnamon (optional)]

Mix cocoa, sugar, salt and water. Add to the scalded milk and beat
with a rotary or wire whip. Return to heat and bring to a boil.
Remove; add vanilla and pour into warm cups. Put a teaspoon of
whipped cream on top. A touch of cinnamon in the cream for
grownups who indulge.

*Eggnog is as personal as you make it. This one is mine. I remember the
first time I made it, for the Houston Country Club Woman's Golf
Association Christmas party. They were sure a Yankee couldn't, but
afterwards this recipe was always used.*

EGGNOG
For 30

24 eggs, separated
2 cups sugar
1 quart bourbon
1 pint brandy
1 quart heavy cream
2 quarts milk
1 quart vanilla ice cream
Nutmeg

Beat the egg yolks and sugar until thick. Add the bourbon and brandy
and stir thoroughly. . . . Add the cream and milk and continue whipping. Break up the ice cream and add. Beat the egg whites until stiff
and fold in. Refrigerate if possible for 30 minutes before serving.
Sprinkle lightly with nutmeg. This is a drinkable eggnog, not too
thick, but speaks with authority.

DAIQUIRI PUNCH
For 75

2 quarts lemon juice
4 quarts lime juice
4 quarts orange juice
1 pound confectioners' sugar
4 quarts club soda
2½ fifths light rum [2 quarts]

Mix fruit juices and sugar and refrigerate several hours. Add soda and rum and serve with cracked ice and fresh mint in cold glasses.

WHISKEY SOUR PUNCH
For 50

1 quart lemon juice
1 quart orange juice
1 quart whiskey
3 quarts sparkling water
Sugar to taste
Fresh pineapple slivers

Pour over ice, and sprinkle with slivers of fresh pineapple. Serve in cold glasses.

GOLDEN SPIKE
For 1 quart

For a change and good for large occasions. Half fill a blender with crushed ice and pour in 3 jiggers [4½ ounces] of vodka and 3 jiggers of orange juice. Blend for 30 seconds and pour into stemmed glasses. Nice for a morning wedding or any time.

BORDER BUTTERMILK
For 1 quart

1 6-ounce can frozen lemonade concentrate
Tequila to fill 1 lemonade can

Put in blender. Fill with crushed ice. Blend at high speed until smooth and frothy and milky looking.

This drink, invented by Père Kir of Dijon, France, in the late twenties or early thirties, has become a most popular aperitif.

KIR
For 1 serving

$^1/_5$ ounce crème de cassis
3 or 4 ounces Chablis or dry white wine

Mix and serve very cold in a stemmed glass.

I use this drink frequently for all-women gatherings, especially in the early part of the day. It doesn't tickle your nose as much as plain champagne, and it is better for you to start the day with a little Vitamin C.

MIMOSA
For 10 or 12

1 quart cold freshly squeezed orange juice
1 bottle chilled Brut champagne [750 ml.]

Mix and pour into stemmed glasses, and please, no maraschino cherry.

WEDDING OR RECEPTION PUNCH
For 50

¾ cup sugar
Juice of 3 lemons
2 quarts of fresh strawberries or 3 10-ounce packages of frozen
    sliced strawberries
1½ cups orange juice
1½ cups Cointreau
3 bottles champagne [750 ml. each]
1½ quarts sparkling water

Dissolve the sugar in the lemon juice. Slice berries. Add with orange juice and Cointreau to the sugar mix. Chill for 1 or 2 hours. [At serving time] pour into a punch bowl, add champagne and sparkling water.

There are several ways to make Sangría and only a few ways are good. This classic recipe is the best.

SANGRÍA BASE
For 50

2 large oranges, sliced
3 lemons, sliced
3 limes, sliced
3 quarts water
2 pounds sugar

Slowly boil mixture for 3½ hours or more until it is reduced by one-half. Cook until syrupy and a bitter taste begins to appear. Cool to room temperature.

To make Sangría for 8: Pour ⅓ cup of Base into a pitcher, add 1 bottle of an inexpensive red wine. Add 1 dozen ice cubes and about half of a 10-ounce bottle of soda water. Stir well and add diced peaches, strawberries, cherries or whatever fresh fruit you wish, and thin slices of lemon, oranges and limes. There is a great difference between the taste of this Sangría and the simple kind. For a white Sangría use a dry white Burgundy wine in place of the red. You may also add brandy or vodka, 1 cup for each bottle of wine.

CHAMPAGNE PUNCH
For 30

1 quart Sauterne
2 cups brandy
2 quarts champagne
1 quart sparkling water

[It may be easier to buy the ingredients using the following units:

1 litre Sauterne
2¼ cups brandy
2 litres champagne
1 litre sparkling water]

Mix Sauterne and brandy. Pour over ice, then add the champagne and sparkling water. Serve it right now.

SPRITZERS
For 1

Usually served in a tall glass; they will last longer than champagne. Pour about 6 ounces of California white or Rhine wine over ice, add a twist of lemon peel and fill up with club soda. Or you may serve it in a stemmed glass, using lesser amounts of the ingredients. They are cool and especially good for a summer wedding or reception.

In the middle of the afternoon, if you need an added push and crave some flavor to it, fresh fruit of any kind, put into a blender with cracked ice, makes a delightful pick-me-up. Use it for the before-dinner cocktail, too. I like to take a few pieces of fresh pineapple, perhaps a few strawberries, a small piece of melon, any fruit as long as it is fresh (about 1 cup altogether), add a couple of ice cubes, a sprig of mint if I have it, and put them all in the blender until they form a mush. Not many calories, but so refreshing.

Soups and Stews

A good soup does fine things for the soul at times, so give them a try. These have always been popular.

Cream of Corn Soup is my favorite of all soups.

CREAM OF CORN SOUP
For 6

2 strips of finely chopped bacon
2 tablespoons finely chopped onion
2 cups frozen or fresh corn
2 tablespoons butter
2 tablespoons flour
2 cups milk
1 teaspoon salt
½ teaspoon pepper
2 cups light cream [or half-and-half]

Fry finely diced bacon until crisp; add onion and sauté until soft. Put corn through a food chopper [or food processor, using the steel blade], add to onion and bacon, and cook until it begins to brown. Add butter and then the flour. Cook slowly for 3 minutes. Add milk, salt, and pepper and cook until thickened, then add cream and heat until smooth. Serve with hot crackers.

❧ *Reader's Request*

Chicken Velvet Soup. . . . tastes the way it sounds.

CHICKEN VELVET SOUP
For 8

⅓ cup butter
¾ cup flour
6 cups chicken stock [divided use]
1 cup warm milk
1 cup warm cream [or half-and-half]
1½ cups finely diced chicken
½ teaspoon salt
Pepper to your taste

Melt butter, add flour and cook over low heat until well blended. Add 2 cups hot chicken stock and the warm milk and cream. Cook slowly, stirring frequently, until thick. Add remaining 4 cups of the chicken stock and chicken, and heat to boiling. Season with salt and pepper.

CHICKEN BROTH À LA ZODIAC

A demitasse cup of this flavorful steaming broth was served to every diner in the Zodiac Room. It put the customers in the right frame of mind and quickly became our trademark. The broth was prepared when we simmered hens as a first step to other preparations.

["Another Corbitt item was her absolute insistence that every lunch or dinner begin with a cup of steaming hot chicken broth, and woe to the person who did not relish and consume his chicken soup. Such a person absolutely did not belong in the Zodiac level of society." —Evelyn Oppenheimer, an old friend of Corbitt's and, as a great supporter of letters, one for whom the University of North Texas Press' book series is named. She was delighted to learn that Corbitt's book would be the first book in the Evelyn Oppenheimer Series.]

[For complete directions, see page 128; proceed to the point where you remove the chicken, strain the broth and serve.—Editor]

For a clearer broth, break two eggs into the pot of broth. Bring to a fast boil. Set aside until eggs float to the top. Strain through a fine sieve or through cheese cloth.

Add gelatin for a jellied soup, 1 teaspoon for each cup of broth. Dip out a little of the measured cold broth and stir the gelatin into it to soften. Heat the rest of the broth to boiling; mix in softened gelatin. Remove from heat and chill until set.

COLD TOMATO AND SHRIMP SOUP
For 6

1 10-ounce can beef bouillon
¼ cup diced cucumber
½ cup peeled diced fresh tomato, seeded
2 tablespoons wine vinegar
1 cup diced cooked shrimp
1 teaspoon finely chopped onion

Mix, chill, and serve. It is a pretty soup and could be served in scooped-out tomatoes.

🎋 Reader's Request

By far the most asked-for soup everywhere I have been is Canadian Cheese Soup. My men customers are mad about it. Where it comes from I do not know; it has been a part of my life so long it could have come with the stork.

CANADIAN CHEESE SOUP
For 8

¼ cup butter
½ cup finely diced onion
½ cup finely diced carrots
½ cup finely diced celery
¼ cup flour
1½ tablespoons cornstarch
1 quart chicken stock
1 quart milk
⅛ teaspoon soda
1 cup [grated] processed Cheddar-type cheese
Salt and pepper
2 tablespoons parsley, chopped fine

Melt butter in the pot you are going to make the soup in; add onion, carrots, and celery and sauté over low heat until soft. Add flour and cornstarch and cook until bubbly. Add stock and milk and make a smooth sauce. Add soda and the cheese. Season with salt and pepper. Add parsley a few minutes before you serve.

Another light soup the Zodiac customers always enjoyed was chicken broth with thin slices of avocado, mushrooms and water chestnuts added. We never found a name for it.

꒰ *Reader's Request*

Soups made with seafoods intrigue me—my customers, too.

LOBSTER BISQUE
For 4

3 tablespoons butter
3 tablespoons finely minced onion
2 cups chopped lobster meat, fresh or frozen
3 tablespoons flour
5 cups half-and-half or milk
1 teaspoon salt
⅓ cup sherry

Melt the butter, add the onion and sauté until soft, but not brown. Add the lobster and cook at low heat until thoroughly heated. Remove the lobster; add the flour, cook until bubbly. [Gradually] add half-and-half and cook until thickened. Return the lobster, correct the seasonings and let stand over hot water until ready to serve. Heat the sherry and float on top. It will mix as the Bisque is ladled out into cups.

꒰ *Previously Unpublished*

BRIE SOUP WITH MADEIRA
For 4 to 6

2 tablespoons butter
½ teaspoon salt
4 large onions, thinly sliced
4 cups beef broth or consommé
⅓ cup dry Madeira
½ pound Brie cheese

Melt butter in a heavy saucepan with a tight lid. Salt onions and stir them into the butter. Cover the pan and cook over very low heat, "sweating" them until they are tender—about 15 minutes. Shake the pan occasionally. Add the broth and simmer for 20 minutes. Correct the seasoning. Strain or not and add the Madeira, which should not have a hint of sweetness. Dice Brie into the bottoms of warmed soup cups before you ladle the broth into them. Serve immediately, if not sooner.

❧ Reader's Request

Senegalese, for the information of my Southern gals, is a popular cold soup served for the most part in exclusive restaurants and private clubs in the East. You can do it, too, and you will find it to be a talked-about addition to your menu. Serve this soup very cold in bowls surrounded by crushed ice, a nasturtium blossom and leaf peeping from under, if you go for such. I do.

[The following recipe is a combination of two versions of Senegalese Helen Corbitt published.—Editor]

SENEGALESE
For 6

2 tablespoons minced onion (optional)
3 tablespoons butter
3 teaspoons curry powder
3 tablespoons flour
4½ cups chicken stock
1½ cups heavy cream
1 cup finely diced white meat of chicken (or cooked shrimp)
Salt and pepper
1 tablespoon minced chives

Sauté onion in the butter until soft, but do not brown. Add curry powder and flour and cook slowly for 5 minutes. Slowly add stock and bring to a boil, stirring until smooth. Put through a fine sieve and chill. Add the chilled cream and chicken or cooked shrimp. Season when cold; sprinkle each serving with chives.

Condensed Cream of Chicken soup becomes a specialty when finely shredded cucumber is added with cream or milk to dilute it. Heat long enough to blend the flavors, then chill; or prepare in a blender and sprinkle with chopped chives or watercress. This could make a quick delightful supper dish when served with whole cold shrimp and halves of hard-cooked eggs, mayonnaise whipped up with lime juice in which to dunk the eggs and with salty rye crisp wafers.

▪ *Reader's Request*

If you want to be exotic, make this India-born creation, full of subtle flavors, which became a favorite American dish a century ago. Mulligatawny, a fascinating name, a fascinating dish; and definitely a soup any guest in your house will rave about.

MULLIGATAWNY
For 6

2 tablespoons butter
½ cup onion, chopped fine
1 small clove garlic, crushed
2 tablespoons flour
1 tablespoon curry powder
1 pint half milk and cream [1 cup milk and 1 cup cream]
1 quart chicken stock
1 raw apple, peeled and chopped
1 tablespoon salt
Dash of pepper

Melt the butter in the pot you are going to make the soup in. Add onion and crushed garlic and cook over low heat until the onion is soft. Add the flour and curry powder and cook 2 minutes. [Gradually] add milk and chicken stock; cook over hot water until smooth. Add apple, peeled and chopped, 10 minutes before serving. Season with salt and freshly ground pepper—just a dash. It is the apple that throws them; no one can figure it out, unless they are Mulligatawny addicts.

Canned condensed Cream of Celery soup diluted with cream, generously combined with finely chopped cooked broccoli or raw spinach, served icy cold with chopped fresh tomato floating in the center and a faint dusting of curry powder, goes well with a make-your-own sandwich tray of assorted breads and cheeses. [Read about Moss Hart's encounter with Corbitt's tomato soup on page 9.]

One of the most popular cream soups that I have served is Cream of Fresh Pea. In the summer, I add finely chopped fresh mint just before serving, or chopped fresh chives. Every time I serve it, I always have notes sent back for the recipe or for a jar to take home. You know, cream soups of any kind are much better if just before serving you add a bit of the freshly chopped vegetable you are using; for example, freshly chopped celery to cream of celery, chopped tomatoes to cream of tomato, etc. It just does something to them. Try it sometime.

CREAM OF FRESH PEA SOUP
For 6

3 cups fresh or frozen green peas
½ cup chopped onion
Dash of sugar—what you can get on the tip of a teaspoon
2 cups water
3 cups Thin Cream Sauce [triple recipe for Cream Sauce, page 223.]
Fresh mint or chives, minced
Nutmeg

Cook peas [and onion], adding sugar, in water until they are soft but still green. Force onions, peas, and liquid through a food mill or sieve, or put in an electric blender if you have one [or use your food processor with the steel blade]. Combine the pea mixture with cream sauce and heat in a double boiler. The mint or chives are added 10 minutes before serving. A dash of nutmeg added last makes people sit up and take notice. It is good served icy cold in the hot days of summer—and the color is lovely.

Cream of Green Pea soup combined with fresh mint, served cold with well-chilled fresh fruit and Lime Honey Dressing [page 123], would make a summer luncheon party a joy for both hostess and guests. Serve with crisp cheese wafers—packaged and bought, of course.

𝕒 *Reader's Request*

She-Crab Stew is something you should try. Now to me a crab is a crab, whether hard shell or genus homo, *but those who know their crabs say that She-Crabs are the best. . . . She-Crabs are more tender and tasty, according to those who know.*

SHE-CRAB STEW
For 6

¼ cup chopped or sliced onions
2 tablespoons butter
2 cups She-Crab meat
2 tablespoons flour
4 cups milk
1 cup cream
1 cup cooked corn kernels (fresh is the best)
1 teaspoon Worcestershire sauce
Salt and pepper to taste
4 tablespoons sherry

Simmer onions in butter until tender. Add crabmeat with their eggs, and heat thoroughly. Add flour; [gradually add] milk and cream and cook until thick. Add corn and Worcestershire sauce and season to your taste. Add the sherry just before serving. [This is a taste that pleases that premier taste-maker, Stanley Marcus.]

Cold Avocado Soup is beautiful to look at and to taste. I serve it in a ceramic tulip cup. . . . I use this for a luncheon soup, with a good big spoonful of chicken salad nested in fresh fruit.

AVOCADO SOUP
For 8 or 10

4 tablespoons butter
4 tablespoons flour
2 cups milk
2 cups cream [or half-and-half]
3 avocados
¼ teaspoon powdered ginger (you may omit)
Grated rind of 1 orange
Salt to taste

Melt butter, add flour. Cook until bubbly. [Gradually] add milk and cream. Cook until thickened and smooth. Cool. Peel and mash [about 2½] avocados. Add to the cream sauce with the ginger and orange rind. Put in electric blender until smooth as velvet. Chill. Serve very cold with reserved avocado diced on top, and whipped cream if you like and grated orange peel.

This soup is especially nice in spring and summer because you need only two courses. I slice cinnamon bread paper-thin and oven brown to serve. You can buy Cinnamon Bread or make your own [page 73].

BLACK BEAN SOUP
For 12

4 cups dried black beans
4 quarts cold water
1 cup sliced onion
2 cloves garlic, minced
4 stalks celery, chopped
8 peppercorns
1 bay leaf
2 carrots
Few sprigs parsley
Ham bone or ½ pound salt pork or leftover ham scraps
Salt and pepper

Cover beans with the water, bring to the boiling point and simmer for 10 minutes. Cool. Add remaining ingredients and cook about 4 hours below the boiling point until beans are soft. Add more water if necessary. Remove ham bone or salt pork, and put beans and vegetables through a Foley mill or purée in your blender. [Or purée in a food processor, using the steel blade.] Correct seasonings. If you like, add sherry or Burgundy to taste. Sometimes I add rice, bits of avocado, sour cream, lemon or eggs poached in the soup. You may add the ham scraps too if you wish.

No time? Use canned Black Bean Soup as label directs and sherry or Burgundy will help it.

Once you meet the deep South in your travels, you find all kinds of interpretations of gumbo. Some serve it as a soup, some as an entrée. This recipe is a compromise; add more shrimp and crabmeat or oysters and pour it over a mound of hot cooked rice and you have an entrée; serve it as written for a soup.

SEAFOOD GUMBO
For 6

¼ pound bacon, diced
¼ cup diced onion
¼ cup diced green pepper
1 cup diced celery
¼ cup chopped parsley
1 clove garlic, minced
2 cups peeled diced tomatoes, fresh or canned
4 cups fish or chicken stock
2 cups okra
2 cups raw cleaned shrimp
2 cups crabmeat or fish, fresh or frozen
1 cup oysters
[Salt and pepper]
Gumbo filé

In the pot in which you plan to prepare the soup, sauté the bacon until limp. Add the onion, green pepper and celery and sauté until onion is yellow, but not brown. Add parsley, garlic, tomatoes and stock. Cook at low heat until vegetables are soft. Add the okra, cover and cook 5 minutes. Add the seafood, cook 5 minutes more. When ready to serve, add gumbo filé to your taste, and salt and pepper. Do not boil after this step. Never put the filé in before you are ready to serve as it becomes stringy. You might have extra filé available for those who like more. Serve from a tureen or the soup pot over rice. You may vary this by adding ham or chicken or both in place of the crabmeat or use all three.

Being a Yankee, Friday to me always means Fish Chowder Day, and I find others are becoming addicted, too—the Yankee infiltration into many ports, no doubt. As they say up there, when the frost is on the pumpkin, there isn't anything better than a bowl of chowder, especially with hot Johnnycake (cornbread to you) dripping with butter. Chowder made with red snapper is wonderful, but any fish will do. During cold weather, I like to use smoked haddock or finnan haddie. And when I am really homesick, I use clams, fresh, frozen or canned.

NEW ENGLAND FISH CHOWDER
For 6

1 cup chopped onion
½ cup diced salt pork or bacon
1 cup butter
1 cup finely diced raw potatoes
½ cup water
2 tablespoons flour
2 cups milk
1 cup cream
2 cups flaked cooked fish

Sauté onion and salt pork in the butter and cook until soft, but not brown. Add potatoes and water and cook until the potatoes are soft. Add flour, cook 2 minutes and add the milk. Cook 5 minutes, stirring constantly; add the cream and fish, then cook until hot.

Having a few canned cold soups in the pantry is a good time saver in planning a menu. Anyone who spends the time and money to make jellied consommé today has more time and money than I. Dressing up the canned variety is fun. For instance:

Jellied Chicken Consommé is made pleasing by adding fresh mint or rosemary with cooked fresh vegetables spooned in just before serving; or try slivers of chicken or ham and white grapes.

Jellied Green Turtle soup with lump crabmeat—why go on? Use your imagination and dress up cold soup with anything.

❧ Reader's Request

Gazpacho is a good bad-temper medicine. I keep a gallon of it around at all times.

GAZPACHO
For 4 or 6

4 large ripe tomatoes, peeled
½ cucumber, peeled
¼ cup chopped green pepper
A dash of Tabasco
4 tablespoons olive oil
4 teaspoons wine vinegar
1 cup tomato juice
½ teaspoon salt
1 teaspoon grated onion
Fresh-ground pepper

Chop the tomatoes and cucumber fine, and add the rest of the ingredients. Strain through a sieve and chill, or put everything in an electric blender. Serve with an ice cube floating in the center of the chilled cup. Pass a tray containing a bowl of chopped cucumbers, a bowl of chopped tomatoes, tiny croutons, and one of chopped chives or parsley for each to add their own, and a bowl of sour cream would not be amiss.

❧ Previously Unpublished

COLD CARROT SOUP WITH GUACAMOLE
For 6 to 8

¼ cup butter
1 cup chopped onions
1 quart chopped fresh carrots
3 cups chicken broth, canned or fresh
1 cup half-and-half cream
Pinch chervil (optional)
Few drops Tabasco
1 teaspoon salt
White pepper
Avocado or purchased spicy guacamole

Melt butter, add onions and sauté for 1 minute. Use carrots sold in bunches with their tops for this recipe, rather than packaged carrots from cold storage. Discard the tops and scrape the carrots. Add them along with the chicken broth. Cover and simmer together for 10 minutes. Put this in a blender or food processor, using the steel blade, to purée it. Chill and add the cream and the rest of the ingredients. Serve this very cold in icy soup dishes. Float a generous amount of mashed avocado or guacamole in the center. If you use purchased frozen guacamole, taste for spiciness before adding Tabasco to the soup.

Mention Vichyssoise and immediately the housewife goes into a dither. In reality it is the easiest soup there is to make. No fuss about getting it to the table hot, no worrying guests or family to hurry. . . . Cold soup does not stimulate the appetite, so in using it make it a part of the meal instead of the "come on" to bigger and better things. Amazing, too, is the fact that almost all cream soups are good cold—but they have to be really cold.

CHILLED CREAM VICHYSSOISE
For 8

4 leeks, white part, finely sliced
¼ cup finely chopped onion
¼ cup butter
5 medium-sized potatoes (Idaho variety)
1 carrot
1 quart chicken stock
1 teaspoon salt
2 cups milk
3 cups cream [or half-and-half]
Chives, finely chopped

Sauté leeks and onion in butter until yellow. Add potatoes, carrot, chicken stock and salt. Bring to a rapid boil, cover and reduce heat to simmer until potatoes and carrot are soft. Mash and rub through a fine strainer [or purée it in your food processor or blender]. Return to heat and add milk. Season to taste and cool. Add cream and chill thoroughly. Serve in very cold cups with a sprinkling of finely chopped chives.

SPINACH VICHYSSOISE: [Use only 2 potatoes and replace the milk and cream above with only 2 cups. Purée 1 pound of slightly cooked spinach with the potatoes.]

JELLIED CONSOMMÉ HELENNAISE

4 cups canned jellied beef consommé
1 cup seeded cucumber, finely diced
2 cups peeled, seeded and finely diced fresh tomatoes
½ cup thinly sliced green onion
1 cup finely diced celery
½ cup diced avocado
1 tablespoon olive oil
2 tablespoons red wine vinegar
Sour cream (optional)
Caviar (optional)

Mix together lightly all ingredients [except sour cream and caviar] and refrigerate. Serve from a punch bowl or in individual soup cups. You may serve with or without sour cream. Caviar is a nice addition, but expensive. I sometimes add diced cooked shrimp, chicken or roast beef.

The flavor of this soup is best if it is made the day before. With thin cucumber sandwiches and fresh pineapple fingers sprinkled with brown sugar for dessert, you have a delightful luncheon. Change in the weather? Reheat it—and change the cucumbers to very thin ham.

COLD CURRIED CRABMEAT SOUP INDIENNE
10 or 12 small cups

1 tablespoon chopped chives or green onion tops
2 tablespoons butter
2 teaspoons curry powder
2 tablespoons flour
3 cups milk
2 cups crabmeat, fresh, frozen or canned, cut into small pieces
¼ cup sherry
2 cups light cream [or half-and-half]

Sauté the chives in the butter for 1 minute. Add the curry powder and flour and cook until well blended. Add the milk and [gradually] cook until thick. Heat the crabmeat in the sherry, add the cream and bring to a boil. Add to the curry mixture and cool. Serve very cold, surrounded by ice, for informal entertaining.

Why fight it? There is nothing greater than a good stew. I know! There are never any leftovers. By the same rule, there is nothing worse than a poor one.

BEEF STEW IN BURGUNDY WITH PARMESAN CRUST
For 8 to 10

¼ cup salad oil
4 pounds beef round or tenderloin, cut in l-inch cubes
2 tablespoons flour
3 cloves garlic, minced
3 cups dry red burgundy
2 cups beef broth or water
1 stalk celery
Few sprigs parsley
1 carrot
½ pound diced salt pork
20 small white onions, cooked
20 fresh mushrooms, quartered
Salt and pepper to taste

Pie crust
Melted butter
Parmesan cheese

Heat the oil in the pot you will cook the stew in. Add the beef and brown on all sides. Drain the oil. Add flour and cook until foamy. Stir in garlic; [gradually add] wine, broth or water and bring to a boil. Add the celery, parsley and carrot. Cover and simmer about 2 hours or put in a [preheated] 350° oven to cook until meat is tender. Remove the celery, parsley and carrot. Add the salt pork, onions and mushrooms and simmer until thoroughly hot. Skim off any excess fat from the top. Season with salt and pepper. Transfer to a shallow 2½- or 3-quart casserole. Cover with pie crust, brush with melted butter and sprinkle with Parmesan cheese, freshly grated if possible. Return to oven to bake at 350° until crust is brown. I like to serve this also as a stew over crisp hashed brown potatoes or thin cornbread—but then I like stew.

❧ Reader's Request

I always make this stew the day before serving, as the flavor is better the second day. I freeze it, too.

GERMAN BEEF STEW
For 6 or 8

Mix, put in a bowl [or large, self-sealing plastic bag], cover and marinate overnight:

> 3 pounds beef stew meat
> ⅔ cup water
> ⅔ cup vinegar
> 1 clove garlic, slivered
> 1 bay leaf
> 4 whole cloves

Then prepare the following:

> [¼ cup vegetable oil]
> 1 cup sliced onion
> ½ cup chopped parsley
> 1 cup sliced carrots
> ½ cup slivered celery
> 1 cup peeled diced tomatoes
> 4 cups beef broth
> ½ cup gingersnap cookie crumbs
> 1 tablespoon vinegar
> Salt and pepper

Remove meat from the marinade, put into a heavy saucepan and brown [in hot oil] with the onion. Add the parsley, carrots, celery, tomatoes and beef broth. Cook uncovered at medium heat until meat is tender (approximately 1½ hours). Skim off any fat; add the gingersnaps and vinegar. Cook until sauce is thickened. If during the cooking the meat becomes dry, add more broth or water. Season with salt and pepper.

Serve on rice or noodles [or Späetzle, page 290]. . . . Crisp coleslaw will never argue with a stew . . . nor will an ice cream pie for dessert [page 360].

Jessie was one of my cooks at the Driskill Hotel in Austin, and he made the chili. I still use his method and keep the chili frozen. Using this recipe I have substituted lower-in-calorie chicken and turkey for the beef.

JESSIE'S CHILI
4 quarts

¼ pound chili pepper pods
1 quart water
1 pound coarsely ground beef suet
5 pounds coarsely ground beef
3 to 4 cloves garlic, finely chopped or 1 tablespoon garlic powder
2 teaspoons ground cumin
¾ cup chili powder
2 cups chopped onion
2 cups canned tomatoes
4 tablespoons cornmeal
2 tablespoons flour
Salt

Boil the chili pods in a covered pot with 1 quart of water for 15 minutes. Remove the pods, and save the water they have boiled in. Remove pods' stems, seeds and slip off the skins. Chop the pods. Sauté the suet, beef and garlic until the meat is thoroughly cooked, about 40 minutes, along with the cumin and chili powder. Add the onions and cook 10 minutes, add tomatoes mixed with the cornmeal, flour and chopped pods. Cook another 5 minutes. Add the chili water plus enough water to make 2 quarts. Simmer for about 45 minutes or until all the flavors are well blended. Correct seasonings.

When I substitute coarsely ground turkey or chicken for the beef I add ½ cup of butter or salad oil in place of the suet.

When I make Enchiladas, I dip each tortilla in the fat from making the chili, or in broth or salad oil, fill with chili, grated cheddar cheese or half cheddar, half Provolone cheese and grated onion. Roll up and arrange side by side, seam side down, in a shallow oiled casserole. Pour chili over and sprinkle grated cheese. Bake at 350° for 15 minutes. Run under broiler until piping hot. Serve right away, but you may assemble them ahead of time and freeze before baking.

≥ Previously Unpublished

A delicately flavored fish stew, this will conjure images of Marseilles.

BOUILLABAISSE DE HELEN
Serves 8 to 10

6 tablespoons olive oil
4 white onions, sliced thinly
4 leeks, white parts only, sliced thinly
6 fresh tomatoes, peeled, seeded and diced
3 quarts water (or fish stock)
Bouquet garni (see below)
1 piece slivered orange peel (zest)
4 cloves garlic, crushed
½ teaspoon crushed saffron
1 cup clam juice
1 cup white wine
1 pound red snapper, cut in 1-inch pieces
1 pound cod or haddock, cut in 1-inch pieces
2 lobster tails, sliced (or monk fish)
2 pounds shrimp, cleaned and washed (or any fish you prefer)
2 dozen clams (or mussels)
Minced parsley
Salt and freshly ground pepper
¼ teaspoon cayenne pepper

Heat the oil in a 12-quart heavy stockpot and sauté the onions and leeks (which must be carefully washed through several waters) until they are transparent, but not browned. Add the tomatoes, water or stock, a bouquet garni (wrap and tie a rib of celery, a carrot and one bay leaf together with parsley), orange zest, garlic and saffron. Simmer over medium heat for 30 minutes, stirring occasionally. You can prepare the broth to this point early in the day and cool. Reheat before adding the rest of the ingredients.

Add the clam juice, wine, snapper and cod. Cook for 10 minutes, then include the cleaned and peeled lobster and shrimp. Scrub the clam or mussel shells vigorously with a brush before adding them. Continue to cook until the clams or mussels open. If any shells fail to open, discard those immediately. Remove from the heat; you can keep the stew over hot water for up to 45 minutes without toughening the shrimp. Add the parsley and black and cayenne pepper. Taste before adding salt, which may not be needed if you used well-seasoned fish stock. Correct seasonings, remove bouquet garni, and ladle generous portions into heated soup plates.

Spread one side of sliced French bread with cheese mixed with finely chopped garlic (1 clove garlic to ½ cup cheese) and toast; turn, spread the other side with cheese mixed with garlic, and toast. Serve with Bouillabaisse.

This is a pretty buffet dish—and the leftovers are delicious.

VEAL STEW WITH ZUCCHINI
For 16

4 pounds lean veal, cut in 1-inch cubes
½ cup thinly sliced onion
[¼ cup fat, half butter and half vegetable oil]
4 cups chicken broth
Salt to taste
1 teaspoon grated lemon peel
8 medium zucchini
1 tablespoon slivered lemon peel [zest]
Fresh chopped parsley

Lightly brown veal and onion in butter and oil in a shallow pot. Add broth. Simmer until veal is tender, about 1 hour. Add seasoning and grated lemon peel. Let stand 1 hour. Quarter zucchini lengthwise. Reheat veal; add zucchini and slivered lemon peel. Cover and simmer 3 minutes. Sprinkle with parsley.

Yeast Breads and Quick Breads

Did you know that white bread was made only for royalty in Roman times? (Now royalty is looking for some good whole-wheat or rye bread.)

Your bread recipe reads: "knead until smooth and satiny." How long is that? You've never made bread before! Most doughs require from 8 to 10 minutes of kneading before you recognize a smooth and satiny surface. After 10 minutes, grasp the dough in one hand, squeezing it slightly with your fingers. If fully developed, the opposite side of the dough ball should feel smoothly taut; you will see bubbly blisters under the surface.

Yeast bread likes a warm draft-free and moist place for rising. If you don't have a cozy, private nook for "proofing" (rising) dough, make a "mini sauna" in your oven. Turn your oven to 400° for one minute only and then turn it off. It should have reached a temperature between 80° and 100°—just what the dough likes. Situate your dough in the warm oven so it has plenty of room to rise. Place a pan of hot water on the oven floor before closing the door. Or place dough in bowl beside your stove, turn one burner on to low. Be sure to cover the bread with a towel or napkin if proofing outside the oven. [Before putting yeast bread dough aside to rise, roll the ball of dough inside a heavily greased bowl to coat all sides and prevent it from drying out while it rises.—Editor]

Almost any yeast dough or batter may be refrigerated if the amount of yeast in the recipe is doubled. A sweet dough, that is, one that is high in sugar, refrigerates best. You can refrigerate the dough immediately after mixing, kneading or after it has risen once and been punched down. Proofing before refrigeration, however, helps the dough retain its rising power.

[To test bread dough to see if it has doubled in bulk, press the tips of two fingers lightly and quickly about ½-inch into the top of the dough. If the dent stays, the dough is light enough to have doubled in bulk.—Editor]

If storing the dough in the refrigerator, grease the bowl well. I use butter or margarine and cover with plastic wrap or a tight bowl cover. The best refrigerator temperature is 45° to 50°. Most refrigerator doughs may be kept three or four days with portions removed as desired. Some rising will take place in the refrigerator, but the dough can be punched down if it gets too high.

After refrigeration you can either shape the dough immediately or allow it to come to room temperature—about 1 to 3 hours—before shaping. Then let the shaped dough rise again before baking at the required time and temperature.

When baking bread, if you like a hard crust, set a pan of warm water in the bottom of the oven while baking, and brush the crust when partially baked with ½ cup of water mixed with 1 teaspoon of salt. For a soft crust, brush with melted butter before and after baking.

[A loaf of yeast bread is done when it slides easily from the pan and gives off a hollow sound when you thump the bottom. For information about flour, see Preface, page xiii.—Editor]

YEAST BREADS

꽃 Reader's Request

WHITE BREAD
2 1-pound loaves or 1 2-pound loaf

5½ to 6 cups flour [divided use]
2 packages dry yeast
1 cup milk
1 cup water
2 tablespoons sugar
2 tablespoons oil
2 teaspoons salt
Oil

Stir together 2 cups flour and yeast. Heat milk, water, sugar, 2 table-spoons oil and salt over low heat until warm (120° to 130°). Add liquid ingredients to flour-yeast mixture and beat until smooth, about 3 minutes on high speed of electric mixer. Stir in more flour to make a moderately soft dough. Turn out onto lightly floured surface and knead until smooth and satiny, about 5 to 10 minutes. Cover dough with bowl or pan and let rest for 20 minutes. For two loaves, divide dough in half and roll out into two 7 x 14-inch rectangles; for one loaf, roll out to a single 8 x 16-inch rectangle. Roll from narrow side, pressing dough into roll at each turn. Press ends to seal and fold

under the loaf. Place in 2 greased 4½ x 8½-inch loaf pans *or* 1
greased 5½ x 9¼-inch loaf pan; brush with oil. Let rise in warm place
(80° to 85°) until doubled, about 30 to 45 minutes. Bake in a [pre-
heated] 400° oven 35 to 40 minutes. Remove immediately from pans
and brush with oil or butter. Cool on wire rack.

*You can make cinnamon bread by spreading each rectangle of dough
with soft butter and sprinkling a mixture of half sugar and cinnamon
over the butter. Roll and bake as directed. This makes a pretty tea
sandwich bread.*

STOLLEN (A CHRISTMAS BREAD)

1 cup raisins
½ cup currants
1 cup mixed candied fruit
Cognac
½ cup lightly toasted slivered almonds
1 White Bread Recipe (2 loaves) [page 72]

Cover raisins, currants and fruit with Cognac for at least 1 hour.
Drain, mix with nuts and knead into bread dough.

SALLY LUNN

1 cake or package [dry] yeast
1 cup milk
3 tablespoons butter
3 tablespoons sugar
2 eggs
3½ cups flour
1¼ teaspoons salt

Soften yeast cake in [or sprinkle yeast over] the lukewarm milk. Set
aside. Cream together butter and sugar. Add eggs and mix well. Sift
flour, to which the salt has been added. Add to shortening mixture
alternately with milk-yeast mixture. Beat well. Let rise in a warm place
until double in bulk. Knead lightly. Put into a well-buttered Sally Lunn
mold or bundt pan. Cover. Let stand and rise again until doubled.
Bake 1 hour [in a preheated 300° oven].

REFRIGERATOR WHEAT BREAD
2 1-pound loaves

3½ to 4 cups white flour
2 packages dry yeast
2 cups milk
¾ cup water
¼ cup vegetable oil
3 tablespoons sugar
1 tablespoon salt
4 cups whole wheat flour
Oil

Mix 2½ cups of white flour with yeast. Heat milk, water, oil, sugar and salt over low heat until warm (120° to 130°). Add liquid ingredients to flour-yeast mixture and beat 3 minutes on high speed of electric mixer. Add whole wheat flour. [You may want to exchange beaters for dough hooks.] Gradually stir in more white flour to make a stiff dough. Turn out onto lightly floured surface and knead [by hand or with dough hooks] for 5 to 10 minutes. Cover dough with bowl or pan; let rest 20 minutes. Divide in half. Roll each out to 7 x 14-inch rectangle. Roll from narrow side, pressing dough into roll at each turn. Press ends to seal and fold under loaf. Place in 2 greased 4½ x 8½-inch loaf pans. Brush loaves with oil or melted butter. Cover with plastic wrap and refrigerate 2 to 24 hours. When ready to use, let stand at room temperature 10 minutes. Puncture any gas bubbles with skewer. Bake in a [preheated] 400° oven 40 minutes. Remove immediately from pans and brush with oil or butter. Cool on wire rack. You could also make this dough into 2 dozen medium-sized dinner rolls.

POTATO BREAD WITH RAISINS
2 loaves

4 to 5 cups flour [divided use]
½ cup sugar
1 teaspoon salt
2 packages dry yeast
1 cup potato water or water
½ cup butter or margarine
2 eggs
¼ cup mashed potato

1 cup seedless raisins (you may omit)
Melted butter

Mix 1½ cups of flour, the sugar, salt and yeast. Heat potato water and butter until lukewarm and butter is melted. Add to flour mixture gradually and beat 2 minutes at medium speed with your electric mixer. Add eggs, potato and more flour to make a thick batter. Beat at high speed for 2 minutes, scraping sides of bowl. Stir in the raisins and enough flour to make a soft dough. Turn out on a floured board and knead until smooth and elastic. Return to bowl and rub top with melted butter. Cover and let rise in a warm place until double in bulk, about 1 hour. Punch down, turn out on floured board. Shape into loaves; put into greased loaf pans. Cover with a towel and let rise again until doubled in bulk. Bake in a [preheated] 350° oven for 35 to 40 minutes. Turn out on racks to cool.

Oatmeal Bread is good hot out of the oven, and toasted it is good enough for the gods.

OATMEAL BREAD
2 loaves

1 cup quick-cooking oatmeal
2 cups boiling water
½ cup molasses
1 tablespoon salt
2 tablespoons melted shortening
1 yeast cake [or 1 package dry yeast]
½ cup warm water
6 cups flour

Place the oatmeal and boiling water in a bowl. Stir and let cool. Add the molasses, salt, and shortening. Dissolve the yeast in the ½ cup of warm water. Add it to the oatmeal mixture, and then add the flour. Cover with a cup towel or wax paper and let rise until double in bulk. Knead down and put into two tins greased with soft vegetable shortening, not butter.

Use a pastry brush to glaze the tops of the loaves with 1 egg beaten with 1 tablespoon milk. Sprinkle 2 tablespoons dry oatmeal over them.

Let rise for 2½ hours and bake in a [preheated] 375° oven for 50 minutes.

Sourdough Bread is the most sought after bread in America. This recipe is good.

SOURDOUGH BREAD STARTER

2 cups flour
1 package dry yeast
2 cups warm water

Combine ingredients in large bowl (not metal); mix together until well blended. Let stand uncovered in warm place (80° to 85°) for 48 hours; stir occasionally. Stir well before use. Pour out required amount and replenish remaining starter by mixing in 1 cup each flour and warm water. Let stand uncovered in a warm place a few hours (until it bubbles again) before covering loosely and refrigerating. Use and replenish every two weeks.

SOURDOUGH BREAD
2 1½-pound loaves

3 cups plus 3½ cups flour
1 cup Sourdough Starter
2 cups warm water
2 tablespoons sugar
1 tablespoon salt
1 teaspoon baking soda
Cornmeal
Melted butter

Measure 3 cups of the flour, starter, water, sugar, salt and soda into a large mixing bowl (not metal); beat until smooth. Cover loosely with wax paper and let stand in warm place (80° to 85°) at least 18 hours. Stir batter down. Mix in more flour to make a moderately stiff dough. Turn onto lightly floured surface and knead until smooth and satiny, about 8 to 10 minutes. Shape dough, place on greased baking sheets that have been sprinkled with cornmeal. Brush with butter. Cover and let rise in a warm place until doubled, about 1½ hours. Bake in [preheated] 400° oven 40 to 50 minutes, or until done. Brush with butter after baking.

This bread makes a wonderful sandwich with the turkey leavin's, Christmas night, and though it sounds impossible, thin slices of ham with this bread and prepared horseradish and butter are wonderful.

CHRISTMAS FRUIT BREAD
2 medium-sized loaves

½ cup minced citron
½ cup chopped raisins
½ cup chopped candied cherries
1 tablespoon grated lemon rind
½ cup chopped blanched almonds
1 teaspoon cinnamon
½ teaspoon ground cloves
½ teaspoon nutmeg
¼ cup water or brandy

Soak the fruit, nuts and spices overnight in the water or brandy.

1 yeast cake [or 1 package dry yeast]
2 tablespoons lukewarm water
1 cup milk
⅓ cup shortening
¼ cup sugar
1 teaspoon salt
1 egg, well beaten
4 cups enriched all-purpose flour
Melted butter

The next morning, soften the yeast in the lukewarm water. Scald the milk, add to it the shortening, sugar, and salt, and cool to lukewarm. Add the yeast, the egg, and 2 cups of the flour. Beat thoroughly, then add the rest of the flour. Allow to rise in a warm place until double in bulk, turn out on a floured board and knead, adding more flour if necessary to make a medium firm dough. Allow to rise again; knead the [drained] fruit into the dough and form into two loaves. Place in well-greased loaf pans and allow to rise again until double in size. Brush tops with butter. Bake in a [preheated] 400° oven for 10 minutes; reduce to 350° and bake for 50 minutes [more]. Cool and frost with a thin icing made with confectioners' sugar and water flavored with almond extract.

❧ Reader's Request

Many people claim the original Monkey Bread recipe. I do not. A customer called me out of the blue one day, read it over the telephone and this is my interpretation. I usually bake it in a bundt pan because it looks attractive. This bread freezes well and can be reheated. Great toasted.

MONKEY BREAD

1½ yeast cakes or 2 packages dry yeast
1 cup milk, heated to lukewarm
4 tablespoons sugar
1 teaspoon salt
½ cup melted butter or margarine
3½ cups sifted flour (about)
Additional butter

Dissolve yeast in lukewarm milk. Stir in sugar, salt and butter. Add flour and beat well. Let rise to almost double in bulk. Punch down and roll out on lightly floured board to ¼-inch thickness. Cut in about 2-inch pieces: round, diamond or square. Dip each piece in melted butter. Pile in buttered pans until half full. Let rise to double in bulk. Bake in a [preheated] 400° oven for 30 minutes or until golden brown.

You serve loaf uncut; let people pull off whatever amount they wish. It is already buttered, so no bread and butter plate is needed. It always is a favorite.

Leftover yeast rolls? They will obtain a fresh-baked taste by being sprinkled lightly with water, covered and rewarmed in a pre-heated 400° oven. Store-bought rolls likewise.

ICEBOX ROLLS

For those who asked:

1 cup boiling water
1 cup shortening
1 cup sugar
1½ teaspoons salt
2 eggs, beaten
2 packages dry yeast
1 cup lukewarm water
6 cups unsifted flour

Pour boiling water over shortening; add sugar and salt. Blend and cool. Add eggs. Let yeast stand in water 5 minutes, then add to mixture. Add sifted flour. Blend well. Set in refrigerator. Make into rolls 1 to 2 hours before baking. Bake in a [preheated] 350°–370° oven for 20 minutes.

PLAIN ROLL DOUGH

6 tablespoons butter
4 tablespoons sugar
1 teaspoon salt
1 cup scalded milk
1 yeast cake [or 1 package dry yeast]
¼ cup lukewarm water
4 cups all-purpose sifted flour
1 egg, well beaten

Add the butter, sugar and salt to the milk. When it has cooled to lukewarm, add the yeast dissolved in the warm water, and 3 cups of flour. Beat thoroughly, cover and let rise until light. Cut down and add the well-beaten egg, and remaining cup of flour. Turn onto a floured board and knead until smooth. Put in a greased bowl, cover with a towel and let rise to double in bulk. If you do not use all the dough at once, brush with melted butter, cover with wax paper and refrigerate.

❧ *Reader's Request*

I know everyone wants the Sticky Roll recipe I have used so many places.

STICKY ROLLS

Roll Plain Roll Dough [see page 79] out in a rectangular sheet, spread with softened butter, sprinkle with brown sugar and roll up like a jelly roll. Cut in ¾-inch pieces and place in a pan that has been heavily greased with shortening, not butter, and completely covered with a layer of dark Karo syrup. Sprinkle a little brown sugar on top of the syrup. Place the rolls, close together, cut side down. Let rise to double in bulk, and bake in a [preheated] 400° oven for 20 minutes. You may vary them by adding cinnamon to the brown sugar you roll with, or add pecans or raisins to the pan with the syrup.

❧ *Reader's Request*

Orange Rolls have had the Number Two place in the gastronomical affections of my customers.

ORANGE ROLLS

    1 cup confectioners' sugar
    ⅓ cup butter
    1 tablespoon grated orange rind
    2 tablespoons orange juice, or enough to moisten

Mix and form into small balls. Form plain roll dough around them and place the rounded side down in a buttered muffin tin. Small rolls are better than large, and should be eaten as they come out of the oven.

Rolls are like biscuits: you can roll anything you like into them, from cheese to candied ginger, spices, herbs, parsley, watercress, jelly or your favorite marmalade. It is only you who stops the ball from rolling.

ONION ROLLS
36 small or 18 large rolls

1½ cups water
1 tablespoon plus 1 teaspoon sugar [divided use]
1 tablespoon butter
1 teaspoon salt
1 package dry yeast dissolved in
    ¼ cup lukewarm water
4½ to 5 cups flour
Melted butter
1 egg yolk
1 teaspoon water
1 cup minced onion
2 tablespoons butter
Coarse (kosher) salt

Heat the water, 1 tablespoon of the sugar, butter and salt to lukewarm and until butter is melted. To the dissolved yeast add 1 teaspoon sugar. Add the butter mixture to the yeast and stir in 4 cups of flour. Turn out on a floured board and knead in ½-to-1 cup more flour to make a soft dough. Put back in bowl, brush with melted butter. Cover. Let rise in a warm place until double in bulk. Punch down and turn out on your board. Form into 1-inch flat rolls. Cut a deep crease in each roll. Place rolls 2 inches apart on a buttered baking sheet. Brush with butter. Let rise again.

Brush with egg yolk beaten with the teaspoon of water. Sauté the onion in the 2 tablespoons butter 1 minute. Pile in the crease and on top. Sprinkle with coarse salt. Bake in a [preheated] 350° oven for 30 minutes or until onion is golden brown.

Dark or dull pans absorb more heat with the result that foods actually bake faster and crusts are browner than in shiny pans that reflect the heat.

QUICK BREADS

[All-purpose flour should be used in all these quick bread recipes except crêpes. See page xiii for further information.—Editor]

?❦ *Reader's Request*

POPOVERS
10 to 12

1 cup sifted all-purpose flour
¼ teaspoon salt
2 eggs
⅞ cup milk [1 cup less 2 tablespoons]
1 tablespoon melted butter

[Preheat oven to 450°.] Heavily butter muffin tins or custard cups and put in the oven to get hot. Mix the flour and salt. Beat eggs until light, add milk and butter and add slowly to the flour. Stir until well blended. Beat 2 minutes with rotary beater if by hand, or 1 minute with an electric beater. Fill the cups one-third full. Bake 20 minutes, then reduce heat to 350° and bake 15 minutes more. Don't peek! Serve hot with marmalade.

A standard muffin recipe serves the same purpose as your basic roll or biscuit recipes.

STANDARD MUFFIN RECIPE
12 medium or 24 minis

2 cups sifted flour
4 teaspoons baking powder
½ teaspoon salt
2 tablespoons sugar
2 eggs, well beaten
1 cup milk
4 tablespoons melted butter

[Preheat oven to 425°.] Mix and sift dry ingredients. Mix the egg and milk and stir into the dry ingredients. Stir in the melted butter. Bake in greased muffin tins, three-fourths full, for 20 to 25 minutes.

Variations:

BLUEBERRY MUFFINS: Fold in carefully 1 cup blueberries, fresh or frozen. If frozen, be sure they are thoroughly defrosted and drained.

ORANGE COCONUT MUFFINS: Fold in 2 tablespoons grated orange peel plus ½ cup Angel Flake Coconut; ½ cup toasted chopped almonds are nice, too, with the orange.

BACON MUFFINS: Fold in 6 strips of bacon, fried until crisp and chopped and dried.

CINNAMON MUFFINS: Sprinkle top with cinnamon and sugar, half and half—a goodly amount, too.

NUT MUFFINS: ½ cup chopped toasted nut meats.

GUAVA JELLY MUFFINS: Put ¼ teaspoon of guava jelly on top of each small muffin before baking.

☙ *Reader's Request*

LEMON MUFFINS
2 dozen

> 1 cup butter or other shortening
> 1 cup sugar
> 4 egg yolks, well beaten
> ½ cup lemon juice
> 2 cups flour
> 2 teaspoons baking powder
> 1 teaspoon salt
> 4 egg whites, stiffly beaten
> 2 teaspoons grated lemon peel

[Preheat oven to 375°.] Cream butter and sugar until smooth. Add egg yolks and beat until light. Add the lemon juice alternately with the flour, which has been sifted with baking powder and salt, mixing thoroughly after each addition (*do not overmix*). Fold in stiffly beaten egg whites and the grated lemon peel. Fill buttered muffin pans three quarters full and bake about 20 minutes. These freeze well, and are nice split and toasted with salads.

ह *Reader's Request*

This was the popular muffin served at morning coffees at the Houston Country Club.

SOUR CREAM MUFFINS

¼ pound butter
1½ cups sugar
½ teaspoon salt

Mix until light, then add:

4 eggs, well beaten
1½ cups sour cream
1 teaspoon soda
2¾ cups flour
⅛ teaspoon grated nutmeg
Additional sugar

[Preheat oven to 450°.] Mix thoroughly. Pour into buttered muffin tins and sprinkle with sugar. Bake for 15 minutes.

ह *Reader's Request*

I like to make small muffins, freeze them and eat them frozen. They taste like candy. These make a good picnic dessert too.

ORANGE MUFFINS
3 dozen small muffins

1 cup butter or margarine
1 cup sugar
2 eggs
1 teaspoon soda
1 cup buttermilk
2 cups sifted flour
Grated rind and juice of 2 oranges [divided use]
½ cup golden raisins
1 cup brown sugar

[Preheat oven to 400°.] Cream butter and sugar, add eggs and beat. Dissolve the soda in the buttermilk, add with the flour to the butter mixture. Add rind and raisins. Fill well-buttered muffin pans two-thirds full and bake for 20 to 25 minutes. Mix orange juice with brown sugar. Pour over muffins while hot and remove from pans immediately. Sometimes I substitute pecans for the raisins.

* *Reader's Request*

REFRIGERATOR BRAN MUFFINS
8 dozen

5 cups All-Bran cereal [divided use]
2½ cups raisins
2 cups boiling water
1 cup white sugar
1 cup corn oil
2 cups molasses
4 eggs, well beaten
1 quart buttermilk
5 cups flour
5 teaspoons baking soda
1 teaspoon salt

[Preheat oven to 400°.] Combine 2 cups of the cereal and all the raisins. Pour boiling water over them and set aside to cool. In a very large bowl, combine sugar and oil. Stir in, one at a time, the molasses, eggs, buttermilk and remaining cereal. Mix together the flour, baking soda and salt and add this to the batter. Lastly, add the cooled raisin-bran mixture. The batter is now ready to use; or you can refrigerate it for future use. To bake muffins, spoon batter into buttered muffin pans (filling each section about two-thirds full) and bake for exactly 20 minutes. Allow to cool slightly in pans, on a rack—the muffins come out of the pans more easily if given a short rest period.

❧ *Reader's Request*

QUICK COFFEE CAKE
2 9½-inch cakes

2½ cups sifted flour
1¼ cups brown sugar
½ teaspoon salt
½ cup shortening
2 teaspoons baking powder
½ teaspoon soda
1 egg, well beaten
¾ cup buttermilk
½ teaspoon cinnamon
½ cup chopped pecans

[Preheat oven to 400°.] Mix the flour, sugar and salt. Cut in the short-ening with a pastry blender until it looks like coarse cornmeal. Take out ¾ cup. To the remaining mixture add the baking powder, soda, and mix well. Stir in the egg and buttermilk. Pour into 2 greased square cake tins. Mix the ¾ cup of flour mixture with ½ teaspoon cinnamon and nut meats. Sprinkle over the top of the batter and bake for 20 to 25 minutes. Serve hot or reheated, but not cold.

❧ *Reader's Request*

HELEN CORBITT'S COFFEE CAKE
(Expensive but worth it)

1¾ cups sugar
¾ cup butter
3 cups sifted all-purpose flour
4 teaspoons baking powder
1 teaspoon salt
1 cup plus 2 tablespoons milk
4 egg whites

[Preheat oven to 350°.] Cream the sugar and butter until soft and smooth. Add the milk alternately with the flour, baking powder and salt sifted together. Fold in the egg whites beaten stiff.

Pour into a buttered baking pan and cover with topping made from:

2 cups chopped pecans
1 cup plus 2 tablespoons brown sugar
2 tablespoons cinnamon
¾ cup flour
¾ cup butter

Mix together until it looks like cake crumbs [use the steel blade in your food processor to crumble it]. Spread over the top and bake for 40 to 50 minutes. Cut in squares. If any are left over, roll balls of vanilla ice cream in the crumbs and serve with Butterscotch Sauce [page 319].

You can make any filling go much further in a small cream puff than in a sandwich—and for some reason guests think fewer calories.

CREAM PUFFS

1 cup boiling water
½ cup butter
1 cup flour
½ teaspoon salt
4 eggs

[Preheat oven to 375°.] Put water in a saucepan, and as it boils add butter. Continue heating until butter is melted. Add flour and salt all at once. Stir until dough forms a ball. Remove from heat. Add 1 egg, beat, let stand 5 minutes. Add remaining eggs one egg at a time, beating after each addition. Let stand 10 minutes. Drop on ungreased baking sheet by level teaspoonfuls for small puffs—2 inches apart. Bake 20 to 25 minutes. The surest way to test is to remove one, and if it collapses, it is not done. When cold, split and fill with salad, or cottage cheese and red caviar is delicious too. Dip stuffed edge into chopped parsley.

Choux designates a cream puff mixture. Why? It looks like a cabbage or chow.

🌿 Reader's Request

A better than best corn bread comes from a Texas ranch, straight from the pretty wife of a West Texas lawyer who ranches on the side. She makes it for the ranch hands. I have adapted it for my own use and yellow cornmeal sales have increased.

TEXAS CORN BREAD

1 cup yellow cornmeal
½ cup flour
1 teaspoon salt

Mix [dry ingredients] thoroughly; then add without mixing:

1 cup buttermilk (half sour cream and milk)
½ cup sweet milk
1 egg
1 tablespoon baking powder
½ teaspoon soda
¼ cup melted shortening

[Preheat oven to 450°.] Grease muffin pans or corn-stick pans well and heat. Stir up the mixtures thoroughly and pour into the hot pans. Bake until done. The bread will be moist and brown on the bottom.

[Baked corn bread freezes well and can be reheated successfully in the microwave.—Editor]

🌿 Previously Unpublished

FIESTA SPOON BREAD
For 8

1 4-ounce can whole green chiles
2 eggs
¼ cup milk
1 cup cornmeal
½ teaspoon soda
1 teaspoon salt
1 20-ounce can "cream style" corn
⅓ cup margarine
½ pound grated sharp Cheddar cheese

Preheat oven to 350°. Drain and seed the green chiles before mincing them. Set them aside while you make the cornbread batter. Beat the eggs with the milk. Sift the cornmeal, soda and salt together into a large mixing bowl. Quickly stir the liquid ingredients into the cornmeal. Use as few strokes as possible to mix in the canned corn and melted margarine. Pour half of the batter into an oiled 1½-quart casserole. Sprinkle all of the chiles and half of the cheese over the batter. Pour the rest of the batter over them and top with the remaining cheese. Bake for about 45 minutes. This makes a soft textured bread that should be served with a large spoon.

ORANGE NUT BREAD
2 loaves

Outer peelings from 4 to 5 oranges
1 cup water
2 teaspoons soda

Boil until tender, drain and mash. Add:

¾ cup water
1 cup sugar

Cook until consistency of thick applesauce—almost crystallized. Set aside. Mix:

1 cup sugar
2 eggs, well beaten
1 cup milk
3¼ cups flour
3 teaspoons baking powder
2 tablespoons melted butter
½ teaspoon salt
1 cup broken nutmeats

[Preheat oven to 325°.] When mixed thoroughly, combine with the peel mixture. Mix well but do not beat. Pour into two well-buttered loaf tins and bake for 35 to 40 minutes or until a cake tester comes out clean.

BANANA BREAD
1 loaf

1 ¾ cups sifted flour
2 ¾ teaspoons baking powder
½ teaspoon salt
⅓ cup soft shortening
⅔ cup sugar
2 eggs
1 pound ripe bananas (3 or 4)

[Preheat oven to 350°.] Sift together flour, baking powder and salt. Beat shortening in mixer bowl until creamy consistency. Add sugar and eggs. Continue beating at medium speed for one minute. Peel bananas; add to egg mixture. Mix until blended. Add flour mixture, beating at low speed about 30 seconds, or only until blended. Do NOT OVERBEAT. Scrape bowl and beaters once or twice. Turn into buttered loaf pans and bake about 1 hour and 10 minutes, or until bread is done.

Variations:
BANANA NUT BREAD: To egg mixture add 1 cup coarsely chopped nuts.

BANANA RAISIN BREAD: To egg mixture add 1 cup seedless raisins.

BANANA DATE BREAD: To egg mixture add 1 cup finely chopped dates.

HOLIDAY BANANA BREAD: To egg mixture add ¼ cup seedless raisins and 1 cup mixed candied fruit.

To convert between self-rising and all-purpose flour or cornmeal, remember that every cup of the self-rising product contains exactly 1 ½ teaspoons of baking powder and ½ teaspoon of salt, which must be added or deleted from the recipe, depending on which way you are converting.

CRÊPES
24-30 crêpes

I have found I have a consistently more tender crêpe if I use cake flour, but there is no law that says you must.

    2 cups sifted cake flour
    2 cups milk, whole or skim
    4 eggs, separated
    ½ teaspoon sugar
    10 tablespoons butter or margarine
    Additional butter

Put flour in a bowl, add the milk and stir with a French whip until smooth. Add 4 egg yolks and 2 of the unbeaten egg whites, and beat until well blended. Add sugar and melted butter, not hot, just melted. Let batter stand at least 1 hour before cooking. Fold in the 2 remaining egg whites beaten to soft peak stage. Pour about 1 tablespoon butter into a hot crêpe pan. Swish around until pan is completely covered. Pour off excess butter. Add 1½ tablespoons of batter, more or less. Tilt pan until bottom is covered. (If you find yourself with a hole in the crêpe, simply add more batter while the crêpe cooks. Who will know?) Cook about ½ minute, turn with a spatula, cook ½ minute. Remove from pan and repeat. You do not need to add more butter to pan. Pile crêpes on top of one another; it is not necessary to put paper in between crêpes.

If you prefer a thinner crêpe, add more milk. If making ahead of time, wrap in clear plastic or foil. Crêpes freeze satisfactorily. To use after freezing, defrost at room temperature. Do not put in a hot oven or they will melt into one big glop. Regardless of what you put into a crêpe, the important thing to remember is to roll it loosely. Both the crêpe and the filling will have better flavor and texture.

I use the same formula for dessert crêpes, but I add more sugar.

Do you bake with your oven light on? If so, the light throws extra heat into that corner of the oven, possibly causing uneven baking.

HOT BISCUITS
2 dozen small biscuits

2 cups flour, sifted
3 teaspoons baking powder
1 teaspoon salt
⅓ cup shortening
¾ cup milk

[Preheat oven to 450°.] Sift flour, baking powder and salt together; cut in shortening until mixture resembles coarse cornmeal. Add all of milk and mix into a smooth dough. Turn out on lightly floured board. Knead lightly. Roll or pat out to ½-inch thickness. Cut with biscuit cutter. Place on an ungreased cookie sheet. Bake for 12 to 15 minutes.

With this as a basic recipe, you may do many variations:
CHEESE BISCUITS: Add ½ cup grated sharp cheese to dry ingredients.

PINEAPPLE FINGERS: Add 1 cup diced candied pineapple. Cut the biscuits into fingers and brush with melted butter and sprinkle with granulated sugar.

RICH TEA BISCUITS: Increase the shortening to ½ cup and add 1 beaten egg.

HERB BISCUITS: Add ½ teaspoon of dried herbs for each cup of flour. I add poultry seasoning or sage for cocktail biscuits.

CINNAMON PINWHEELS: These are nice to keep in your icebox and bake as you need them. Roll biscuit into an oblong sheet. Brush with melted shortening and sprinkle it heavily with a mixture of 1 cup sugar and 1½ tablespoons of cinnamon. Roll tight as a jelly roll, wrap in wax paper and chill. Slice thin and bake in a [preheated] 350° oven until brown.

ONION BISCUITS: Add ½ cup French-fried onions, chopped fine, to recipe. Really good with chicken and for brunches or cocktail parties with a slice of ham between.

BLUEBERRY DROP BISCUITS

2 cups flour
3 teaspoons baking powder
1 teaspoon salt
4 tablespoons butter
1 cup milk
1 cup blueberries, fresh or drained, if frozen

[Preheat oven to 375°.] Sift flour twice, add baking powder and salt. Sift again and work in the butter with a fork or pastry blender. Add the milk and berries and drop by tablespoons onto a greased baking sheet. Bake for about 12 minutes.

Biscuits take on a light brown color if the tops are brushed with milk or butter before baking.

BUTTERMILK BISCUITS
12 large or 24 small biscuits

2 cups sifted flour
½ teaspoon baking soda
2 teaspoons baking powder
1 teaspoon salt
¼ cup cold shortening
1 cup cold buttermilk or sour milk

[Preheat oven to 450°.] Sift dry ingredients together and cut in shortening until mealy. Add milk and mix quickly. Knead very lightly on a floured board. Pat to ½-inch thickness and cut with floured biscuit cutter. Place in greased pan close together for crust on top and bottom only; put far apart if crust is desired on sides also. Bake at once for 12 minutes or until brown.

Here's a biscuit recipe that calls for only two ingredients: 2 cups enriched self-rising flour and 1 cup sour cream [not reduced-fat]! Blend the two together, knead slightly, cut and bake at 450° for 15 minutes. It's a light, tasty biscuit.

Pancakes have become a national institution. I use thin rolled ones in place of vegetables with meats, for example—orange pancakes with chicken; lemon pancakes with lamb; blueberry with ham and so on. Try it!

PANCAKES

1½ cups milk for thin ones, ¾ cup for thick ones
3 tablespoons melted butter
2 eggs, whites beaten separately
¾ teaspoon salt
3 tablespoons sugar
2½ teaspoons baking powder
1½ cups all-purpose flour

Heat an ungreased griddle or heavy skillet while you mix the batter. Have the milk at room temperature and add with butter to egg yolks. Add dry ingredients sifted together and stir, adding more milk, if necessary, to make batter just thin enough to pour. Do not overbeat: lumps do not harm. Fold in beaten egg whites.

When you want to serve pancakes family-style and serve them all at once, keep them warm until serving time by placing them between cloth towels in a 200° oven until all are cooked.

Sometimes dress up your pancakes with:

ORANGE BUTTER
1 cup powdered sugar
¼ cup butter
Juice and grated rind of 1 orange

Whip together until light. Roll inside pancake. You may substitute lemon for the orange. When I use blueberries, I add them to the pancakes then use lemon butter—and thickened blueberry sauce on top—or buy blueberry syrup.

BROWN BUTTER FRENCH BREAD:
Make Brown Butter as directed on page 234. Cut French bread into thin slices. Spread lightly on the bread. Form the bread loosely into a loaf again. The flavor is especially good with lamb.

I like to remember my Aunt Laura's Caraway Twists that she served with fricasseed chicken. These are superb with chicken salad, or just "as is."

CARAWAY TWISTS

1 cup grated Swiss cheese
2 tablespoons caraway seeds
Your favorite pie crust recipe [or packaged pie crust mix]
1 egg
2 tablespoons coarse salt

[Preheat oven to 375°.] Add the cheese and caraway seeds to the pie crust before adding the liquid. Roll the crust out on a board until it is as thin as you can handle. Cut into strips ½ inch wide and 6 inches long or longer. Brush lightly with beaten egg. Sprinkle with the coarse salt and twist two strips into a stick, pressing both flat ends together to keep them twisted. Bake on an ungreased cookie sheet for 8 to 10 minutes.

French Toast can be heavenly or awful. I think this recipe extra good. Use it with broiled mushrooms on top—or fresh asparagus—or for creamed entrées.

FRENCH TOAST

2 eggs
½ cup cream
⅛ teaspoon salt

[Preheat oven to 325°.] Mix and beat thoroughly. Cut bread in ¾-inch-thick triangular pieces. Saturate in mixture. Fry in pure butter until golden brown. Drain on a paper towel. Then put in oven for a few minutes to obtain a crusty surface. Sprinkle with powdered sugar—or serve with maple syrup or your favorite marmalade or jam.

Salads and Dressings

There is nothing quite as cool as a shimmering molded salad. Every kitchen, regardless of size, should support a few molds of various shapes, inexpensive or otherwise, but decorative. You may turn out some works of art as your imagination runs riot. Just give everything enough time: allow at least 3 hours for gelatin to "set"—six hours is better—and when making a large mold for a summertime meal, make the day before you use it.

A few things to remember:
Before unmolding, moisten both the plate and the molded salad with *wet* fingers. The moist surfaces make it easy to slide the mold into the center of the plate after unmolding.

To unmold salads quickly, dip the molds in hot water, then loosen sides with a silver knife. Tap it with your hand and the salad will come out easily.

Remember that everything shows in a molded salad, so when adding fruit, bear in mind that:
These Fruits Sink: Canned apricots, Royal Anne cherries, canned peaches and pears, whole strawberries, prunes and plums, fresh orange sections, grapes.

These Fruits Float: Fresh apple cubes, banana slices, grapefruit sections, fresh peach or pear slices, raspberries, strawberry halves, marshmallows, broken nutmeats.

Jello and gelatin are not the same, so watch your recipes and use whichever is called for.

Add whatever you are adding to the gelatin mix ONLY when the mixture is thoroughly chilled or even partly congealed. If you are making a pattern, allow a thin layer of gelatin to "set" before you begin.

Never boil gelatin and never add fresh pineapple to it.

When you make a large mold (over one quart) use 1¾ cups of liquid for every 2 cups specified in the recipe, and keep this proportion throughout.

Too much gelatin or a scarcity of seasoning makes molded salads a poor eating experience. Do not add more gelatin to bring it along, as you get the rubbery glue taste that goes with an overdose of it.

If they are good, they are delicious; if they are bad, they are very, very bad.

❧ Reader's Request

I served this to the Duke of Windsor at a luncheon given in Houston, Texas. Molded in a large ring, garnished with clusters of strawberries, fresh pineapple sticks, orange sections, clusters of white grapes, Bing cherries, and sprigs of fresh mint, the center filled with mayonnaise combined with pecans and grated orange peel—it looked like a beautiful garden party hat. The Duke was intrigued by its appearance and taste. We carried on a spirited conversation over it and the pronunciation of "pecan." I won the round when I said living in the United States you could say it any way you wished.

AVOCADO MOUSSE
For 8

1 tablespoon unflavored gelatin softened in
2 tablespoons cold water
3 ounces lime gelatin
2 cups hot water
1 cup mashed ripe avocado
½ cup mayonnaise mixed with
½ cup [heavy] cream, whipped

Dissolve gelatin mixture and lime gelatin in hot water; when partially congealed stir in remaining ingredients. Pour into a mold greased with mayonnaise and allow to set in refrigerator. Unmold on crisp, dark green salad greens. I usually use this with fresh fruits and it's beautiful!

This is a good salad to accompany any fish entrée. I like to make it in a ring mold for a buffet and fill the center with seafood salad.

CUCUMBER MOUSSE

¾ cup boiling water
1 package [3 ounces] lime gelatin
1 cup cottage cheese
1 cup mayonnaise
2 tablespoons grated onion
¾ cup grated cucumber, with peeling left on
1 cup slivered almonds (you may omit)

Pour boiling water on gelatin, cool; add cheese, mayonnaise, grated onion, cucumber and nuts. Pour into a wet mold and refrigerate.

⅊ *Reader's Request*

Tomato Jelly Salad is gay and can be used with anything as it adapts itself easily to fish, fowl or vegetable.

TOMATO JELLY SALAD
For 8

2½ cups tomato juice
1 bay leaf
¼ cup celery, diced
⅛ cup chopped onion
3 peppercorns
6 cloves
1 sprig parsley
1 tablespoon sugar
1 teaspoon salt
1 teaspoon vinegar

Cook until vegetables are soft; remove from heat and add:

2 tablespoons unflavored gelatin, softened in
½ cup cold water

Stir until completely dissolved, then combine with the first mixture; strain, pour into molds and chill.

If you wish to vary it, drop in a ball of cottage or cream cheese mixed with chopped chives, or finely minced onion, or jumbo cooked shrimp that have been marinated in French Dressing [page 120]. My favorite, which is expensive, of course, is to stuff a canned artichoke heart with a mixture of cream and Roquefort cheeses and drop it in the aspic just as it begins to congeal. It is a nice first course for an entrée of any kind of sea food, or for a main dish luncheon with a fresh crabflake salad roll or sandwich.

Serve with a good mayonnaise or any variety of mayonnaise-base dressing.

❧ *Reader's Request*

This salad is such a nice change from tomato aspic. I really think it is worth the effort to chop the fresh vegetables by hand, but if you don't, use your blender [or food processor].

MOLDED GAZPACHO SALAD
For 8 or 10

6 large ripe tomatoes, peeled and seeded
1 cucumber, peeled
⅓ cup diced green pepper, chopped and blanched
1 tablespoon plus 1 teaspoon unflavored gelatin dissolved in
¼ cup cold water
1½ cups hot tomato juice
⅛ teaspoon Tabasco
4 tablespoons olive oil
1½ tablespoons wine vinegar
1 teaspoon salt
¼ teaspoon white pepper
1 tablespoon chopped green onion

Chop the tomatoes and cucumber fine. Add the green pepper and seasonings. When the gelatin is partially congealed, add the rest of the ingredients. Pour into individual molds lightly rubbed with mayonnaise. Chill until firm. Turn out on salad greens and serve with:

½ cup mayonnaise mixed with
½ cup sour cream
1 cup finely diced celery

FRUIT RING WITH APRICOT DRESSING

½ pound dried apricots
½ cup water
¼ cup sugar

Simmer apricots in water until tender. Remove [from heat] and add sugar. Mix (in blender) until fruit is a pulp. Set aside ¼ cup for dressing.

3½ cups boiling water
6 ounces lime gelatin
1 cup canned crushed pineapple
½ cup slivered [blanched] almonds
Salad greens

[Pour water over gelatin.] Let cool and when it begins to congeal, add puréed apricots, pineapple and almonds. Pour into [a lightly oiled] salad mold. Let set in refrigerator. For dressing:

6 ounces cream cheese
¼ cup reserved apricot purée
1 cup heavy cream [divided use]
1 tablespoon sherry
⅓ cup powdered sugar
¼ teaspoon vanilla
¼ teaspoon almond extract

Beat cream cheese with the reserved apricot purée, ¼ cup of cream and sherry until smooth and fluffy. Whip remaining cream, add sugar, vanilla and almond extracts, and cream cheese mixture. If you like a thinner dressing, add more cream. This dressing is good on any fruit salad, congealed or otherwise.

PEAS IN ASPIC
For 8 to 10

1 tablespoon plus 1 teaspoon unflavored gelatin
⅓ cup dry white wine or water
2 cups chicken broth
Salt and pepper
2 cups cooked frozen petite peas
2 tablespoons mint leaves
2 cups cooked julienne carrots

Soften the gelatin in the wine or water. Heat the chicken broth to the boiling point, remove from heat and add gelatin. Correct seasonings. Coat the bottom of a [lightly sprayed] 1½-quart mold with the gelatin mix. Refrigerate. Add the peas and pour in enough gelatin mixture to hold them in place. Refrigerate to set. Chop the mint very fine (no stems), add to the carrots and arrange over the peas. Add rest of gelatin mixture as it begins to congeal. Refrigerate overnight. Unmold and surround with fresh mint leaves on Boston lettuce. Serve with Mint Dressing:

MINT DRESSING
Makes 2 cups

½ cup vegetable oil
¼ cup red wine vinegar
½ cup fresh mint leaves, finely chopped
1 garlic bud, crushed
½ teaspoon cracked pepper
1 teaspoon salt

Put in a container and shake.

A simple rule for any kind of meat salad is to divide the ingredients into fourths. For one quart, use 2 cups diced cooked chicken (or other meat), 1 cup diced celery and 1 cup mayonnaise or other dressing. The meat should be in medium or large dice so one knows what one is eating; the celery fine, but not minced; the dressing of whipped-cream consistency. The seasoning is up to you.

The usual proportions for making Shrimp Salad are ⅔ shrimp to ⅓ celery or fruit. Sometime try diced red apple or fresh peaches instead of celery. You will need enough mayonnaise or cream to moisten, with salt added to taste. Serve this on red leaf lettuce.

Chicken Salad should be served on cold, crisp salad greens. You can let your imagination run wild on the accompaniments. If you stuff a tomato with the salad, it should be peeled, chilled and stuffed just before serving; if served with fresh fruit as a garnish, likewise. A few things like capers, toasted slivered almonds, chopped chives, or chopped hard-cooked egg if you are from the Carolinas, are good in the mixture; count them as the celery or add them on top just before combining and serving. My favorite garnish and extender is fresh pineapple, or white grapes—and fresh strawberries when they are at the height of the season.

Turkey is a bit better, I think, if you marinate it first in a tart French Dressing [page 120], or add a dash of wine vinegar to the mayonnaise.

ɋ❦ *Reader's Request*

CHICKEN SALAD SUPREME
For 8

2½ cups [cooked and] diced cold chicken
1 cup celery, chopped fine
1 cup white grapes, halved
½ cup slivered almonds, toasted
2 tablespoons minced parsley
1 teaspoon salt
1 cup mayonnaise
½ cup heavy cream, whipped

Combine and serve in lettuce cups with thin slices of chicken on top, garnished with stuffed olives, sliced thin, or chopped ripe olives.

This same mixture can be made into a mold that is delicious. Use the same eight ingredients, plus:

1½ tablespoons [unflavored] gelatin
¼ cup water
½ cup chicken stock

Mix the chicken, celery, grapes, almonds, parsley and salt. Soak gelatin in the cold water for 5 minutes and dissolve in hot chicken stock. When cool, add to mayonnaise and whipped cream. Fold the chicken mixture into it. Pack in individual molds or a large ring. Serve garnished with your favorites—artichoke hearts, for instance.

For a classic sandwich, top my Chicken Salad with a generous topping of crisply cooked crumbled bacon served up on a freshly baked Onion Roll [page 81].

❧ *Reader's Request*

ORIENTAL CHICKEN SALAD
Serves 6 to 8

2 cups fried Chinese rice noodles
[Peanut oil for frying noodles]
6 8-ounce chicken breasts, boned and skinned
Soy sauce to cover
4 tablespoons butter
4 tablespoons vegetable oil
2 heads iceberg lettuce, shredded as fine as possible and crisped
2 teaspoons additional soy sauce
2 tablespoons additional peanut oil
2 tablespoons vinegar
Mayonnaise
[Salt to taste]
Chopped parsley

Rice noodles may be purchased in any Chinese-type grocery store and
are prepared by frying a few seconds in deep hot oil. Remove as soon
as they puff and before they take on any brown color. [Drain on
paper towels and set aside.] Cover the chicken breasts in soy sauce
and marinate for 20 minutes.

Sauté chicken breasts in butter and vegetable oil, 5 minutes on each
side. Keep warm. Cut chicken into thin strips and toss with the shredded lettuce, additional soy sauce, peanut oil, vinegar and fried
noodles. Add just enough mayonnaise to blend and season to taste
with salt. Garnish with chopped parsley and a few additional fried
noodles. I like to surround the salad with snow peas, steamed 60
seconds, and dressed with Sesame Dressing [page 119].

Combining chicken and lobster meat in aspic for a summer luncheon or supper is truly different; but good!

CHICKEN AND LOBSTER RING
For 8

1 ½ tablespoons unflavored gelatin [2 envelopes]
2 cups cold chicken broth [divided use]
1 cup cooked lobster pieces
1 cup diced cooked chicken
½ cup diced cucumbers (omit if cucumber allergic)
½ cup diced celery
1 tablespoon lemon juice
½ teaspoon onion juice
½ teaspoon dry mustard
Salt and pepper to taste

Soften the gelatin in ¼ cup of the cold chicken broth. Heat remaining broth to boiling point and add to the softened gelatin. When cool, add rest of the ingredients. Chill until firm and turn out on a bed of curly bleached endive. Fill the center with cottage cheese and sliced black olives; and serve with mayonnaise whipped up with avocado.

PAPAYA ORIENTAL
For 8

3 cups cooked tiny shrimp or diced shrimp
2 cups freshly grated or Angel Flake Coconut
2 teaspoons grated fresh ginger
4 ripe papayas, peeled and cut in half
½ cup fresh lime juice
Preserved ginger

Mix the shrimp, coconut and ginger. Pile into papaya cavities. Pour lime juice over. Decorate with thin slices of preserved ginger. Chill. This makes a nice luncheon salad also.

In making fresh fruit salads, there are only a few "musts" that should be observed. Fruit should be ripe, but not too ripe; it should be cut into large enough pieces to be able to tell what it is, at least; and should be served cold—really cold. If combined with cheese, or meats of any kind, they should be cold, also, and easily identified—and sherbets are good with them. Mushiness has no place in a salad. The greens that are served with it should be crisp and fresh—and watercress puts the finishing touch to any salad plate.

It's easy to section grapefruit, so they should be sectioned. It is difficult to get perfect sections from an orange, so why not slice them? Melon cut in ball-shaped pieces or slices is more attractive than cubed; whole berries of any kind look and taste better than cut up. Last, but not least, a salad plate should look as if it had been made with a light and airy touch—do not flatten it out or follow a too definite pattern.

The following combinations are thought out as far as availability is concerned. For main course salads:

Orange slices, grapefruit sections and melon balls, with creamy cottage cheese in a bed of romaine in the center of the plate; dates stuffed with ripe olives. Watercress and cinnamon bread finger sandwiches to serve with it.

Cantaloupe slices, fresh peach halves, whole strawberries, orange slices and fresh green grapes left in clusters; balls of cream cheese rolled in freshly chopped mint on well-bleached curly endive or chicory, depending on how you say it.

Canned hearts of artichokes cut in half, with grapefruit sections (pink ones and white ones) arranged in a sunburst fashion with thin slices of oranges. Dust all lightly here and there with chopped chives and serve with it a sandwich made of whole wheat bread with cooked carrots and peas mixed into mayonnaise for a filling.

Orange slices and avocado quarters piled hit or miss on a bed of center pieces of lettuce and sprinkled with watermelon balls and any fresh berry in season, especially raspberries.

Slices of white meat of chicken, pink grapefruit sections, hearts of palm sliced thick, and thin slices of orange piled high on fresh romaine is a meal in itself. Serve with it?—salty rye Melba toast.

Grapefruit sections alternating with ripe tomato quarters, topped with a generous portion of guacamole and served with rolled thin pancakes, filled and covered with grated Cheddar cheese and run under the broiler the last minute.

Sliced oranges, thin slices of fresh pineapple (prepared the day before and mixed with fresh mint and powdered sugar and refrigerated overnight), long slices of honeydew melon, and fresh apricot halves arranged helter-skelter in a bed of watercress, and topped with a ball of lime sherbet rolled in granulated sugar. You can fix your lime sherbet balls the night before, roll in wax paper and put in your deep freeze.

Texas Pink or Ruby Red grapefruit with generous crumbles of Roquefort and a simple vinegar and oil dressing is both beautiful and tasty. Grapefruit sections and thin slices of sweet onion with Poppy Seed Dressing [page 122].

The salad to complement shrimp is made of grapefruit sections left whole, combined with slices of avocado. A good French Dressing [page 120] combined half and half with chili sauce, gives the spiciness desired with the piquant flavored shrimp.

A molded salad with a different twist to serve with shrimp or any seafood dish is made with lemon gelatin, using half hot water and half heated chili sauce and served with mayonnaise, to which has been added a dash of hot mustard.

[Lightly spray your salad molds with cooking oil or] grease your salad molds with mayonnaise before pouring your molded salads; they come out more easily and the mayonnaise gives them an extra nice flavor.

FROZEN FRUIT SALAD
For 8

½ cup Royal Anne cherries, cut in halves and pitted
½ cup Bing cherries, cut in halves and pitted
½ cup [canned] pears, diced and drained
½ cup [canned] peaches, diced
½ cup [canned] pineapple, diced
2 tablespoons powdered sugar
½ cup pineapple juice
½ cup mayonnaise
¼ teaspoon lemon rind, grated
1 cup whipping cream, whipped
½ cup marshmallows, diced (optional)

Mix [cherries and] diced fruits and set aside to drain. Drain pineapple, reserving juice. Dissolve sugar in it. Mix pineapple juice, mayonnaise and lemon rind. Fold in whipped cream, fruit, and marshmallows. Put in molds and freeze.

AVOCADOS WITH SHRIMP MAYONNAISE

Avocados cut in large dice, dipped in Fruit Fresh or lemon juice to keep their color, arranged around a bowl of Shrimp Mayonnaise, adds both color and interest to your table. I find I can count on about 18 pieces to a large avocado. Be sure it is ripe, but not soft. Sometimes I mix it with chunks of cantaloupe. The dressing, good for both, is made merely by adding cooked shrimp, chopped fine (buy the broken pieces), to homemade mayonnaise (1 cup shrimp to ½ cup mayonnaise), a little onion juice, lemon juice, Tabasco and a bit of anchovy paste.

Since I have been in the restaurant business for many years, I am tired of seeing lettuce used for luncheon salads go to waste. So I have designed a salad lunch without lettuce and called it a potpourri of salads. The menu would be a good suggestion if you were entertaining in a club or restaurant, too, as it is pretty to look at and uncomplicated for the cook.

Use three small coquilles (or scallop shells) per guest, or small dessert dishes. The coquilles can be china, foil or the shells you buy from any kitchenware counter. In one coquille I put an assortment of fresh fruit; in another, chicken salad with capers added to the mayonnaise; and in the third, a seafood or Rice Salad [facing page]. Sometimes I make a hot Crab Imperial [page 208] for one coquille while I'm assembling the other dishes. I place the round edge of the coquilles to the outside of the plate so there is room in the center of the plate for a wine glass or parfait glass filled with citrus ice or sherbet. I like to use pink grapefruit ice. You may tuck sprigs of watercress or parsley between the shells. I usually serve a thin Melba toast or toasted crackers and coffee. Do not forget to pass the Poppy Seed Dressing [page 122] for the fruit. Sometimes I use large artichoke bottoms to hold the seafood and the chicken salads, and fill a scooped out orange or papaya with the fruit. You may also use an orange shell to hold the sherbet. This is such a pretty luncheon with no jumping up for dessert; it is all there.

RICE SALAD

4 cups cooked chilled rice
1 cup cooked chopped crab, lobster, shrimp or crayfish
½ cup slivered cooked ham (Virginia, if available)
1 cup *finely* chopped celery
3 hard-cooked eggs, finely diced
2 tablespoons chopped chives
⅓ cup chopped parsley
2 tablespoons olive oil
2 tablespoons wine vinegar
½ cup mayonnaise
Salt and freshly ground pepper

(Try Uncle Ben's Wild Rice Mix.) Combine by tossing lightly the first 7
ingredients [rice, shellfish, ham, celery, eggs, chives and parsley].
Sprinkle with oil and vinegar. Add mayonnaise and season. Let stand
in refrigerator a few hours for a more tangy flavor. (Better made the
day before; however, salt and pepper just before serving.) Try as an
unexpected entrée with sliced cantaloupe and honeydew.

*Potato salad will have more flavor if you add your dressing and
seasonings while the potatoes are hot. The French do.*

WATERCRESS AND POTATO SALAD
For 4

1 potato [a large red one works well]
1 bunch watercress
¼ cup green onion, sliced thin
2 tablespoons Vinaigrette Dressing [page 121]
Salt and freshly ground pepper

Boil potato in skin. Cool and peel. Slice thin. Trim watercress of stems
and toss with the potato, onion, and dressing. Correct seasoning.

BEAN AND EGGPLANT SALAD
For 8 or more

Step Number 1:

3 cups canned Great Northern beans, drained [and rinsed]
3 cups canned or cooked pinto beans, drained [and rinsed]
3 cups canned red kidney beans, drained [and rinsed]
1 cup minced green onion or chives
½ cup finely minced parsley
2 garlic cloves, crushed

Mix beans, onion, parsley, and garlic together. Cover with:

MUSTARD FRENCH DRESSING
⅓ cup olive oil
⅓ cup vegetable oil
⅓ cup wine vinegar
1 tablespoon Dijon mustard
Salt and pepper

Refrigerate for several hours.

Step Number 2:

2 cups diced eggplant
Flour, salt and pepper
¼ cup olive oil
1 cup diced, peeled and seeded tomatoes

Lightly dust eggplant with flour, salt and pepper and sauté in the olive oil until a light brown. Drain and cool. Add the eggplant and the tomatoes to the beans a few hours before serving. I serve this salad in an earthenware crock. Sometimes I add broiled, lightly smoked sausage in place of eggplant. Never, never any leftovers.

My favorite of all low-calorie salads. Fennel looks like an overgrown bunch of celery and smells like anise. Keep it around as an in-between snack! No calories!

FENNEL SALAD
For 4

2 medium-sized fennel bulbs
2 tablespoons vegetable oil
¼ cup wine vinegar
2 hard-cooked egg whites
2 tablespoons capers
2 tablespoons chopped parsley

Place fennel in ice water for one hour. Remove, dry and slice very thin. Mix oil, vinegar, egg whites chopped fine, capers and parsley. Pour over fennel and toss.

MY FAVORITE COLESLAW
For 4 to 6

1 cabbage, finely shredded
1 Spanish onion, sliced paper-thin
1 raw carrot finely shredded
1 cup white vinegar
2 tablespoons vegetable oil
½ cup diced red sweet pepper or pimentos
    (if no pepper is around)
½ teaspoon sugar subtitute [or 2 ½ teaspoons sugar]
½ teaspoon cracked pepper
Salt to taste

Toss all ingredients together. Refrigerate for several hours. It will keep crisp for several days in the refrigerator.

≈ Previously Unpublished

CRAB AND ARTICHOKE SALAD

1 clove garlic
2 heads romaine lettuce
¼ pound fresh mushrooms
3½ cups canned artichoke hearts
1½ cups cherry tomatoes
2 tablespoons minced chives
1 pound lump crabmeat
4 ounces Roquefort cheese
¾ cup olive or vegetable oil
6 tablespoons white wine vinegar
1 teaspoon chopped fresh tarragon or
    ⅓ teaspoon dried tarragon leaves
½ teaspoon salt
Freshly ground pepper

Rub the inside of a wooden salad bowl with garlic; discard. Break the lettuce in bite-sized pieces. Trim and wash mushrooms and split water-packed artichokes and cherry tomatoes into halves. Sprinkle them and the chives over the lettuce. Sprinkle crabmeat over the vegetables. Mash the Roquefort with the oil and vinegar; add tarragon and salt to taste. Toss the greens with the dressing. Grind pepper over top.

There are probably more opinions given on the subject of salad making than on any other gastronomical feat. . . . Everyone has his own idea of a green salad—I like to say a salad of "everything green," then no one tosses in the refrigerator. Combinations of any greens, and the more the tastier, but definitely, if at all possible, the cool crisp "tanginess" of watercress somewhere; lettuce (head or leaf), escarole, chicory, Belgian endive, if the budget allows; tender leaves of spinach, romaine, a few chives, chopped fine. A fan am I of Bibb or Limestone lettuce! Green peppers, if sliced almost too thin to see; if you like, and if you grow them, young nasturtium leaves; fresh tarragon and sweet basil leaves give intrigue but take them easily. All greens should be thoroughly washed and dried, and chilled. From there you are on your own.

Dressings should be sprinkled rather than poured, and the greens tossed gently until thoroughly coated.

If you are Yankee-minded, at the time of the year when wilted salads are good—young greens like turnip greens, beet greens, spinach, dandelion, and especially curly lettuce you grow in your own yard—a bacon dressing is the best. Good for potato salad, too.

WILTED SPINACH AND MUSHROOM SALAD

½ pound bacon, diced
½ cup sliced scallions [or green onions]
4 tablespoons lemon juice
2 tablespoons vegetable oil
1 pound spinach, washed and trimmed
1 pound fresh mushrooms, washed, trimmed and thinly sliced
Salt and pepper to taste

Cook bacon until crisp. Remove, add scallions and sauté until soft. Add lemon juice and salad oil. Pour over spinach and mushrooms. Toss in bacon and correct seasonings. I sometimes add 1 cup diced avocado for this amount and a few cherry tomatoes or sliced pickled beets and sliced hard-cooked eggs. This is a good basic salad using spinach as the greens.

There are so many good mayonnaise type dressings on the grocer's shelf that few people make their own any more; but this one will not fail if you feel inclined.

MAYONNAISE
1¼ cups

[½ to] 1 teaspoon salt
½ teaspoon dry mustard
½ teaspoon sugar
2 egg yolks
2 tablespoons vinegar or lemon juice [divided use]
1 cup vegetable oil
Whiff of cayenne

Mix the salt . . . mustard, and sugar. Add egg yolks and 1 tablespoon of the vinegar and make a paste. Add the oil very slowly, beating constantly (high speed on a mixer). As it thickens, add the remaining 1 tablespoon of vinegar and the cayenne. Continue beating until stiff. Keep refrigerated—or the raw egg will cause it to spoil. Thin with cream (sweet or sour) or lemon juice, and add any flavor you wish before using.

[Please read safety considerations on page xii.]

These variations of mayonnaise I have found most popular over the years.

RUSSIAN DRESSING

1 cup mayonnaise
2 tablespoons finely diced celery
2 tablespoons finely diced green pepper
2 tablespoons finely diced sweet pickles
1 tablespoon chopped pimento
2 tablespoons chili sauce
1 tablespoon tomato catsup

FOR MOLDED VEGETABLE SALADS

1 cup mayonnaise
½ cup finely diced celery or shredded cucumber
1 teaspoon chopped chives or green onion tops
or
1 cup mayonnaise
½ cup any mixed cooked vegetables
¼ cup finely diced American cheese
or
1 cup mayonnaise
½ cup finely diced fresh tomatoes
1 tablespoon chopped fresh tarragon or basil
or
1 cup mayonnaise
¼ cup finely diced cooked shrimp or crabmeat
1 tablespoon lemon juice

FOR FRESH FRUIT SALADS OR MOLDED FRUIT

1 cup of mayonnaise
¼ cup cubed cream cheese
¼ cup fresh orange sections
Grated rind of 1 orange
¼ cup chopped pecans (omit or add for variation)
And sometimes
2 tablespoons chopped candied ginger

GREEN MAYONNAISE FOR SEAFOOD

1 cup mayonnaise
1 tablespoon finely chopped chives
1 tablespoon finely chopped parsley
1 tablespoon finely chopped fresh tarragon
1 tablespoon finely chopped spinach
1 tablespoon finely chopped capers

RÉMOULADE SAUCE FOR SEAFOOD
1½ cups

1 cup of mayonnaise
2 teaspoons chopped anchovy
½ teaspoon dry mustard
1 tablespoon wine vinegar
1 tablespoon tarragon vinegar
2 tablespoons dry sherry
½ cup chopped parsley
¼ teaspoon garlic powder
4 tablespoons capers
1 tablespoon onion juice

Mix together and keep in refrigerator at least one day before using.

GREEN GODDESS DRESSING FOR ASSORTED SALAD GREENS

1 cup mayonnaise
¼ cup finely chopped parsley
½ cup heavy cream
1 teaspoon chopped chives
½ clove garlic crushed with:
⅛ teaspoon salt and
½ teaspoon dry mustard
4 tablespoons anchovies, chopped fine or
     2 tablespoons anchovy paste

MUSTARD SAUCE

1 cup of mayonnaise
4 tablespoons Dijon mustard
Few drops Tabasco
¼ minced parsley

Mix together and chill before using.

TARTAR SAUCE

1 cup of mayonnaise
2 tablespoons chopped gherkins
2 tablespoons chopped green olives
2 tablespoons chopped onion
2 tablespoons chopped parsley
1 tablespoon chopped capers

Mix and serve.

❧ Reader's Request

Sesame seeds are in to stay! The use of toasted sesame seeds was taught to us by the Chinese cooks. The seeds add a delightful new flavor and texture to salad dressings, breads, cakes, cookies, candies. This dressing will perk up a Green or Avocado Salad.

SESAME SEED DRESSING
3½ cups

1 cup sugar
1 teaspoon paprika
½ teaspoon dry mustard
1 teaspoon salt
1 teaspoon Worcestershire sauce
1 tablespoon onion juice
2 cups vegetable oil
1 cup cider vinegar
½ cup toasted sesame seeds*

Put sugar, seasonings and onion juice in a bowl and beat until thoroughly combined. Add the oil gradually, then the vinegar, a little at a time. Add toasted seeds last. Keep in a covered jar in the refrigerator.

*To toast sesame seeds, place on a shallow pan or baking sheet in 200° oven; watch closely and stir frequently. They should be just golden brown to bring out the flavor, but will become bitter if toasted until they are dark.

BASIC FRENCH DRESSING
1¼ cups

2 teaspoons salt
1 teaspoon cracked [or freshly ground] pepper
1 teaspoon paprika
½ teaspoon powdered sugar
½ teaspoon dry mustard
Few grains cayenne
¼ cup vinegar
1 cup olive or vegetable oil
1 clove garlic (optional)

Mix dry ingredients with the vinegar, then add the oil. Shake or beat before using. If you like the flavor of garlic in your dressing, drop a button of garlic into the bottle you keep it in.

With a good Basic French Dressing you may add your choice to give variety to your salads. You might add:

To 1 cup Basic French Dressing:
    3 tablespoons chopped anchovies
    2 tablespoons capers

or

To 1 cup Basic French Dressing:
    4 tablespoons chutney—Major Grey variety

or

To 1 cup Basic French Dressing:
    4 tablespoons chili sauce
    4 tablespoons chopped watercress

[This variation is called Lorenzo Dressing and it's especially good when you add chilled canned pears to a green salad.—Editor]

or

To 1 cup French Dressing:
    ½ cup coarsely crumbled Roquefort

And whip with a beater, or use an electric blender to mix thoroughly.

or

To 1 cup Basic French Dressing:
>2 hard-cooked eggs, finely chopped
>2 tablespoons chopped pimento
>2 tablespoons chopped green pepper
>¼ cup chopped cooked [or canned] beets

or

Vinaigrette I love on cold cooked asparagus, canned or fresh:
To 1 cup French Dressing:
>2 tablespoons finely minced green pepper
>1 tablespoon finely minced parsley
>2 tablespoons finely minced sweet pickle
>1 tablespoon finely minced chives or
>>1 teaspoon of scraped onion
>1 tablespoon finely minced capers

Roquefort Dressing recipes are numerous. This one is asked for time and again:

ROQUEFORT DRESSING
2 cups

3 ounces cream cheese
⅓ cup Roquefort cheese (blue cheese may be substituted)
¼ teaspoon salt
⅛ teaspoon garlic powder
¼ teaspoon prepared mustard
½ teaspoon Beau Monde seasoning (may be omitted)
½ cup mayonnaise
½ cup light cream

Blend cheeses with the seasonings; add the mayonnaise alternately with the cream. Whip until smooth. Sometimes substitute sour cream for light cream!

❧ Reader's Request

I cannot get by without Poppy Seed Dressing though I'm personally tired of it. Why wouldn't I be? Years and years of watching it consumed by customers. Everyone likes this dressing on practically every kind of a fresh salad. I recommend it for fruit. . . .

Where it originated I have no idea; I remember having it served to me in New York so many years ago I hate to recall. Rumors extend hither and yon that I created it; I hasten to deny this; but I did popularize it when I realized that on the best grapefruit in the whole wide world (Texas grapefruit), it was the most delectable dressing imaginable. Today there is hardly a restaurant or home in Texas that does not have some kind of poppy seed dressing. The recipe I use has been in demand to the point of being ludicrous and, strange as it may seem, the men like it—a few even put it on their potatoes. So here it is!

POPPY SEED DRESSING
3½ cups

1½ cups sugar
2 teaspoons dry mustard
2 teaspoons salt
⅔ cup [white] vinegar
3 tablespoons onion juice
2 cups vegetable oil (but never olive oil)
3 tablespoons poppy seeds

Mix sugar, mustard, salt and vinegar. Add onion juice and stir it in thoroughly. Add oil slowly, beating constantly, and continue to beat until thick. Add poppy seeds and beat for a few minutes. Store in a cool place or the refrigerator, but not near the freezing coil.

It is easier and better to make with an electric mixer or blender, using medium speed, but if your endurance is good you may make it by hand with a rotary beater. The onion juice is obtained by grating a large white onion on the fine side of a grater, or putting in an electric blender, then straining. (Prepare to weep in either case.) If the dressing separates, pour off the clear part and start all over, adding the poppy-seed mixture slowly, but it will not separate unless it becomes too cold or too hot.

[To keep dressing from being grainy, heat the vinegar and sugar together until the sugar crystals dissolve; cool the syrup and proceed as directed above.—Editor]

One of my most popular buffet salad bowls at the Houston Country Club, where I was manager, was finely shredded red cabbage, thinly sliced avocado, and halves of fresh grapes with Poppy Seed Dressing—but then Poppy Seed Dressing fans like it on anything.

LIME HONEY DRESSING

1⅔ cups

⅓ cup lime juice
⅓ cup honey
1 cup vegetable oil
½ teaspoon paprika
½ teaspoon prepared mustard
½ teaspoon salt
Grated peel of 1 lime

Blend all ingredients thoroughly and keep in a cool place.

While I was managing the Garden Room at Joske's of Houston, department store, I had several quarts of cream go sour one weekend. As menus were planned two weeks in advance, I was "stuck with it." From this was born a dressing that I have never been able to stop serving; the public demands it.

STRAWBERRY SOUR CREAM DRESSING

2½ cups

½ cup frozen [sliced] strawberries
1 teaspoon salt
2 cups thick sour cream

Fold the fruit into the salted cream. It is especially good on fruit of any kind, and I like it on chilled canned pears for dessert. But here again, fans like it on anything. . . .

If I have my way, I add sour cream to any mayonnaise for any kind of salad mixing. It provides the "umph" so many salads lack.

HORSERADISH SOUR CREAM DRESSING
1½ cups

1 cup sour cream
½ cup mayonnaise
1 teaspoon lemon juice
¼ teaspoon dry mustard
1 tablespoon prepared horseradish
¼ teaspoon onion juice
2 teaspoons chopped chives (optional)
1 teaspoon anchovy paste (optional)

[Mix together several hours before using to blend the flavors.] Confidentially, I like this dressing on green salad, cold thick slices of tomato, cucumbers, potato salad—oh well, almost anything but vanilla ice cream.

This is a must sometime during the holiday season.

CRANBERRY ORANGE RELISH

1 quart fresh cranberries
2 large seedless oranges
1½ cups sugar

Wash fruit, peel oranges and chop rind in very small pieces. Chop orange pulp and cranberries very fine, [or in your food processor, using the steel blade], or put it all through the meat grinder, using a medium knife. Mix fruits with the sugar. This will keep in the refrigerator for over a week without sealing. . . .

When salad dressings get to be routine, it is time to go back a few years. My mother's kitchen always boasted cooked dressings that I remember today with joy. For potato salads and slaws, they are a delightful change, and worth the time it takes to make them.

BASIC COOKED DRESSING
2 cups

2 teaspoons dry mustard
3 tablespoons sugar
1 teaspoon salt
½ cup flour
1⅓ cups milk
2 eggs, well beaten
½ cup vinegar
2 tablespoons butter

Mix dry ingredients; [gradually] add milk, stirring until smooth. Cook over hot water until thick (about 30 minutes), then add eggs, beating constantly, and continue to cook for 3 minutes. Remove from heat and add vinegar and butter. Stir until smooth and thick. Use as is or combine with mayonnaise or sour cream, or whipped cream for old-fashioned mixed fruit salads.

ONION MINT DRESSING
½ cup

1 large bunch of fresh mint
2 tablespoons minced onion
½ green pepper, sliced paper thin
½ cup Basic French Dressing [page 120]

Chop mint leaves and the onions really fine—tears will flow. Add green pepper, then the French Dressing. Chill. I like this dressing when I'm serving a buffet with cold meats such as lamb, ham, and turkey.

RED RELISH

5 pounds red sweet peppers (weigh after seeds and stems are
    removed and before washing)
3¾ pounds mild white onions peeled and cut in small sections
Small hot red pepper (optional)

Grind the peppers and onions together, using coarse cutter. If liked
hot, grind in a small hot red pepper. Mix well (juice and all). Cover
with boiling water and let stand 5 minutes. Drain off as much water as
possible; then squeeze dry. To this add:

1 quart vinegar
2 cups white sugar
3 tablespoons salt [non-iodized or kosher]

Bring to a boil and cook for 20 minutes. Seal in sterilized jars. (If
peppers are not a dark, pretty red, add a little red food coloring. In
preparing peppers, be sure to cut out any green spots.)

SWEDISH CUCUMBERS
For 4

4 small pickling cucumbers, peeled and sliced very thin
White wine vinegar to cover
6 scallions (green onions), sliced thin
½ teaspoon dill seed or few sprigs of fresh dill
Sugar or artificial sweetener to taste

Place all ingredients in a bowl. Cover and refrigerate for several
hours. [Serve very cold.]

Poultry and Stuffings

"Pot Luck" has become associated with me any place I work. It is a means of using experimental dishes not on the menu, and an intelligent use of leftovers. One of the most popular Pot Lucks has been Broiled Chicken Smothered in Fresh Crab or Lobster Bisque—with usually a dash of sherry added before placing it in the oven.

To cook a chicken (or turkey) to use either for fricasseeing or for salads, creaming, and such, you must remember to cook at low heat. A good rule to follow for:

SIMMERING A CHICKEN

1   4½- to 5-pound fowl, whole or cut up
1 quart hot water
1 piece celery
1 slice of onion
1 sprig of parsley
1 whole carrot
1 tablespoon salt

Clean the fowl and place in a kettle; add the hot water and other ingredients, bring to boiling point, cover tightly and let *simmer* over *low heat* until tender, about 1½ to 2½ hours, depending on the age of the fowl. Anyhow, cook it until it is *tender*, and all the time at *low heat*; turning up the gas won't help. Let the meat of the chicken cool in the liquid. And when you remove the bird, use the stock left (you should have at least 2 cups) for Fricassee or for soup.

Fricassee Sauce for chicken is so easy; why do so many people try to make it difficult?

FRICASSEE SAUCE
For 4

3 tablespoons butter
4 tablespoons flour
2 cups chicken stock
½ cup cream (you may omit and use ½ cup more of the chicken stock)
Meat from a 4- to 5-pound fowl (cooked)
Salt and pepper to taste

Melt the butter, add flour and cook until bubbly. [Gradually] add chicken stock and cook until smooth, stirring constantly. Add cream and continue cooking until thickened and smooth. Season to your taste, pour over the chicken, either removed from the bone and sliced or diced, or cut up in serving pieces. Serve hot, from a deep platter or casserole, with light dumplings or baking powder biscuits baked on top [page 92]. A bit of dried sage added to the biscuits gives it a flavor people talk about. Southerners like rice with a fricassee.

SMOTHERED CHICKEN
For 4

2 1½-pound broilers, cut in half or
    4 6-ounce chicken breasts
Flour
Salt and pepper
Vegetable shortening or butter to make ½ inch in the skillet
    when melted
2 cups Fricassee Sauce (see page 128)

[Preheat oven to 350°.] Wash and dry chicken and dust lightly with flour, salt, and pepper. Fry in hot shortening in a heavy skillet until light brown. Remove and drain. Place in a pan, pour Fricassee Sauce over, cover and bake for 1 hour, or until chicken is tender. Halves of browned almonds or fresh sautéed mushrooms added to the sauce dresses it up for company. I like to serve a slice of broiled canned pineapple on top of each serving, and a medley of peas with white and wild rice.

You may smother chicken in almost any sauce you like, but always brown it first. The baking time is about the same. These variations I have found popular:
Bake in Creole Sauce [page 232] and served with pink rice [page 285].

Bake in Mushroom Sauce [page 232]; serve on a thin slice of broiled or baked ham.

Bake in Barbecue Sauce [page 229]; serve with Au Gratin Potatoes [page 278.]

Bake in Medium Cream Sauce [page 223], sprinkled with grated Parmesan cheese and paprika.

Bake in leftover turkey or veal gravy.

Bake in canned Clam or Crab Bisque, thinned down with cream.

Main course pies are centuries old. Knights of old ate sparrow and singing blackbird pies; nursery rhymes like "When the pie was opened, the birds began to sing" must have had some foundation to inspire the poets.

CHICKEN PIE

[Preheat oven to 450°.] Place in individual casseroles or baking dish large pieces of stewed chicken (remove skin and bones), allowing ½ cup per person. Pour Fricassee Sauce [page 128] over and cover with plain pie crust in which several incisions have been made to let the steam escape as it bakes. Bake 10 minutes (until the crust is well risen), then reduce heat to 350° and bake 20 minutes—or until crust is nice and brown.

To vary chicken pie, you may add all sorts of vegetables, but tiny white stewed onions, cooked baby carrots, and little new potatoes are the accepted. Green vegetables usually turn a bit drab in color if added to the pie before cooking, so it is better to serve them separately.

One variation that is good, and different, is to add sautéed mushroom caps and sautéed tiny sausage balls; or place a thin slice of ham in the bottom of your pie dish.

Then for those of you who like your biscuits, a topping of biscuit mixture rolled ½-inch thick, either completely covering the dish or small biscuits placed on top and baked, is good.

A Yankee, misplaced or not, hesitates to mention Fried Chicken south of the Mason-Dixon Line, but I speak up.

FRIED CHICKEN

[Preheat oven to 350°.] Choose fryers of not over 2 pounds, allowing half a fryer for each person. Wash and dry, and cut into the size pieces you like. (Bite-sized pieces are good for cocktail parties.) Season with salt and pepper, dip in cold buttermilk, milk or cream and dust with flour. I like to add a little curry powder to the flour, about ¼ teaspoon to 1 cup of flour. Fry in hot shortening in a heavy skillet until golden brown, turning frequently. Remove and drain on absorbent paper. Place in a pan with just a few drops of water or stock, cover tightly and place in the oven for about 20 minutes. Serve hot with:

CREAM GRAVY

Pour out all but about 2 tablespoons of the fat from the pan in which the chicken was fried. Add 1 tablespoon of flour and cook until brown and bubbly, stirring the crusty pieces of fat that will cling to skillet into the flour mixture. [Gradually] add 1 cup of cold milk, stirring constantly until the gravy is thickened, about 5 minutes. Season with salt and pepper to your taste.

CHICKEN AND ARTICHOKE HEARTS IN NEWBURG SAUCE

6 tablespoons butter [divided use]
6 cups cooked chicken, cut in 2-inch pieces
3 tablespoons sherry
1½ cups half-and-half [divided use]
4 egg yolks, well beaten
1 tablespoon plus 1 teaspoon lemon juice
½ teaspoon salt
⅛ teaspoon white pepper
2½ cups canned artichoke hearts

Melt 3 tablespoons of the butter, add the chicken and heat. Add sherry and ¾ cup of the cream. Let come to a boil. Add rest of cream mixed with beaten egg yolks, stirring all the time. Add lemon juice, salt and pepper and rest of the butter. Add the artichoke hearts and heat until thickened at low heat. *Do not boil.* This sauce is not as thick as a cream sauce and will take 10 minutes to cook after eggs are added. If you make ahead of time, reheat over hot water.

This could be called a Potluck if you have a sense of humor. At any rate it is a show-stopper when you are entertaining guests.

SUPREME OF CHICKEN, NANETTE
For 6

6 chicken breasts
Salt and pepper
¼ teaspoon marjoram
¼ cup butter
½ cup sherry
2 cups cream
3 egg yolks [lightly beaten]
½ cup crabmeat
1 tablespoon parsley
6 large mushrooms
[Additional butter]
½ cup grated Swiss cheese

Remove skin from chicken breasts. Sprinkle with salt and pepper and rub with the marjoram. Sauté in the butter over low heat until done. Remove, and add the sherry to the pan. Cook until almost evaporated. Add the cream and egg yolks. Cook over low heat until thickened. Take enough of the sauce and mix with the crabmeat and parsley to stick the flakes together. Sauté the mushrooms [in additional butter] and fill with the crab mixture. Place the breasts in a buttered shallow casserole, place a stuffed mushroom on top of each. Pour the remaining sauce over, add the cheese and run under the broiler until brown. With this you might serve Rice with Curried Fruit [page 282].

You hardly need a dessert, but if you do why not buy a pound cake, slice and butter and toast till really brown. Serve with an ice you pick up at the frozen dessert counter.

I like Oriental food, especially Cantonese. I had the great privilege of knowing John Kan of Kan's Restaurant in San Francisco's Chinatown. I had always wished I could work in his kitchen to learn authentic techniques. Finally the day came! At that time, Danny Kaye and I were the only non-Orientals who had been allowed that privilege.

[Corbitt called this next dish "Casserole Chicken and Almonds." I have changed it to "Stir-Fried," because it describes the dish better and because most readers today understand this cooking technique. It was still exotic in Corbitt's day.—Editor]

STIR-FRIED CHICKEN AND ALMONDS
For 4 or 6

3 cups diced raw chicken
1 egg white
1 tablespoon vegetable oil
1 tablespoon butter or margarine
½ cup sliced raw celery
½ cup sliced bamboo shoots
1 cup sliced Bok Choy or fresh spinach (you may omit)
¼ cup sliced water chestnuts
½ cup sliced fresh mushrooms
1 tablespoon cornstarch
2 cups chicken consommé
1 tablespoon soy sauce
Handful of snow peas
¼ cup blanched almonds [toasted]

[Dip the chicken cubes in slightly beaten egg white and sauté in hot] oil and butter until done, about 5 minutes, shaking constantly. Add the vegetables [except snow peas] and cover. Cook 3 minutes—the celery should be tender but not soft. Add the cornstarch mixed with the consommé and soy sauce. Add snow peas. Cover and cook 1 minute. Add almonds and serve at once on rice and Chinese noodles (buy them!). If you use dried mushrooms, follow directions on package for using.

One usually does not need a dessert with this dish. It is especially good for the cholesterol watcher (delete the butter for him). However, sliced apricots over pineapple ice would be a nice ending for those who need one and even those who do not.

ﻪ *Reader's Request*

BREAST OF CHICKEN PIQUANTE
For 8

8 whole chicken breasts, 6 or 8 ounces each
1 cup flour
2 teaspoons salt
¼ teaspoon white pepper
⅔ cup butter or margarine
2 tablespoons vegetable oil
1 teaspoon minced shallots
2 garlic cloves, minced
Juice of 4 lemons
½ cup finely chopped parsley

Remove bone from chicken or buy boneless. Remove skin and flatten chicken with the heel of your hand. Lightly dust with flour and seasonings. Heat butter and oil with the shallots and garlic and add breasts, full side down. Sauté lightly, about 6 minutes. Turn once. Continue cooking [until fork-tender]. Remove to a platter or casserole and keep warm. Add lemon juice to pan and dissolve any cooked brown particles. Boil 1 minute. Correct seasonings, add parsley and pour over chicken. Serve at once.

ﻪ *Reader's Request*

One of the truly delicious luncheon dishes I have eaten is Oriental Chicken served over Cheese Soufflé [page 236]. It is adaptable for any kind of entertaining and would be especially suitable for a wedding breakfast or luncheon when you wish something light and delicious. The men like it, too!

ORIENTAL CHICKEN
For 8 or 10

½ cup butter
½ cup flour
1 tablespoon salt
1 cup cream [or half-and-half]
3 cups milk
2 cups chicken stock

Melt butter in top of double boiler, add flour and salt and cook until bubbly; [gradually] add cream, milk, and chicken stock, stirring until smooth. Cook over hot water for 30 minutes. Just before serving add, and heat thoroughly:

    2 cups chicken, large dice
    ½ cup sautéed mushrooms
    ½ cup blanched almonds
    1 cup sliced water chestnuts
    ¼ cup pimento, cut in strips
    ¼ cup sherry

Serve over Cheese Soufflé [page 236], or in a pastry shell; over rice— or what have you; but over soufflé it is the most delightful thing you will ever taste. You may reserve the mushrooms, sauté them whole and top each service with one. Fresh asparagus served across a grilled tomato half completes a beautiful plate.

♣ Reader's Request

One of my favorite ways to fix chicken is what I call Chicken Hawaiian, although the Islands no doubt would probably make no claim to it.

CHICKEN HAWAIIAN
For 6

    3 1½-pound broilers [split]
    4 tablespoons butter
    Salt and pepper
    1 cup water or chicken consommé
    1 cup shredded pineapple [with juice]
    3 tablespoons chopped green pepper
    1½ cups fresh grated coconut

[Preheat oven to 350°.] Wash, split, and dry the broilers. Rub with the butter, salt, and pepper. Add water or consommé and bake until golden brown and tender. Remove, cover with the pineapple, green pepper and shredded coconut; place a tight-fitting lid on the pan and return to the oven for 20 minutes.

SPECIAL CHICKEN WITH ALMONDS
Serves 4

3 6-ounce chicken breasts, boned and skinless
Salt
½ cup flour
½ cup cornstarch
½ teaspoon soda
1 teaspoon baking powder
1 cup water
½ cup fine saltine crumbs
½ cup [additional] flour or water chestnut flour
Peanut oil
1 head iceberg lettuce, shredded
¾ cup slivered toasted almonds

Sprinkle the chicken with salt and set aside. Mix next 5 ingredients [flour, cornstarch, soda, baking powder and water] and dip breasts in the batter, then in a mixture of the saltine crumbs and additional flour. Fry in deep oil at 375° until a light brown. Remove, let cool and refry at 400° until golden brown. Remove, cut crosswise into ½-inch pieces. Pile on the shredded lettuce and pour either Lemon Sauce or Foo Yung Sauce over and sprinkle with nuts.

LEMON SAUCE
½ cup chicken broth
1 teaspoon lemon juice
½ teaspoon lemon extract
1 teaspoon finely grated lemon peel
2 teaspoons cornstarch
2 teaspoons cold water

Mix and cook until thickened.

FOO YUNG SAUCE
1 tablespoon cornstarch
1 tablespoon soy sauce
¾ cup bouillon or water
¼ teaspoon sugar

Mix and cook until thickened.

❧ Reader's Request

In Oriental cooking, the advance preparation is something, but the results are always worth the effort. I like to use Oriental cooking combined with other food, but keeping the Oriental taste. This chicken recipe does just that.

CHINESE ROASTED CHICKEN

3 or 4 roasting chickens (7 to 7½ pounds total)
2 cups soy sauce
¼ cup gin
3 tablespoons honey
8 cloves garlic, crushed
2 bunches scallions, chopped
3 tablespoons shredded fresh ginger root
2 teaspoons salt [optional]

Mix all the ingredients and rub the chickens inside and out with some of the mixture; then pour rest of the marinade over the chickens. Cover and marinate several hours or overnight, but turn the chickens occasionally. If you like a lighter flavor, marinate for 45 minutes. Roast at 350° for about 1 hour or until the fleshy part of the leg feels soft. Or you may fry in vegetable oil as the Orientals do. Disjoint and serve with any of the remaining hot marinade. [Boil marinade for about 10 minutes before serving.]

P.S. Don't get up in the middle of the night to turn the chickens. Anytime in the morning will do.

A word about ginger root. It is the part of the ginger plant that delights the world. Since it is native to the tropics and semi-tropics, there are only a few places on earth that have suitable soil and climate conditions to produce the aroma, taste and tenderness found in high-grade ginger. It is available at all fresh vegetable counters.

❧ *Previously Unpublished*

CHICKEN LIVERS PROVENÇAL

2 pounds chicken livers
Milk (optional)
1 tablespoon flour
¼ cup butter
1 clove garlic, quartered
4 tablespoons green onion, finely sliced
½ cup dry white wine
1 cup canned consommé
½ cup peeled and seeded fresh tomato
2 tablespoons chopped parsley
Salt and pepper
2 tablespoons cognac

Soak livers in milk for an hour if you wish. Drain and shake them in a plastic bag containing flour. Meanwhile, heat the butter with the garlic pieces for a few minutes. Remove the garlic. Add the green onion slices and sauté until tender and shiny. Add the wine, consommé, tomato and parsley. Simmer for 1 minute, add the livers and simmer until the sauce thickens slightly and the livers are tender. Warm the cognac. Pour it over the livers and ignite. Serve in a circle of buttered hominy with specks of green parsley.

❧ *Reader's Request*

Hash is good for informal entertaining, a Sunday Brunch, or a late supper after football games, and such. Spoon Bread or a Grits Soufflé [page 291] should be somewhere near, too, especially if Texans are present.

CHICKEN ALMOND HASH
For 4

2 cups Medium Cream Sauce [page 223]
1 cup diced cooked chicken
½ cup sautéed mushrooms
½ cup slivered toasted almonds

Mix and heat in a skillet. Serve on rounds of oven-buttered-and-toasted bread spread with a thin layer of deviled or Virginia ham.

CHICKEN AND GREEN CHILES CASSEROLE

1 4-pound chicken or 2 2½-pound frying chickens or
   2 pounds boned canned chicken

[For uncooked chicken] cover chicken with water plus 1 tablespoon
salt. Simmer until tender. Cool, and remove chicken from bones. Cut
in large pieces.

    4 tablespoons butter
    1 cup coarsely chopped onion
    3 tablespoons flour
    2 cups milk
    1 cup chicken broth
    1 4-ounce can green chiles, seeded and cut in strips
    5 ounces canned Rotel tomatoes with green chiles (you may omit)
    1½ teaspoons salt
    10 or 12 tortillas
    4 cups grated sharp Cheddar cheese

[Preheat oven to 375°.] Melt the butter. Add the onion and sauté 1
minute. Add flour, cook until bubbly. [Gradually] pour in milk and
broth and cook until thickened, stirring with a French whip. Mix
green chiles with the sauce, add the Rotel tomatoes. Place a layer of
chicken in the bottom of a buttered shallow 3-quart casserole, then a
layer of tortillas [torn into bite-sized pieces], cheese, then sauce.
Repeat, with cheese on top. Bake until bubbling. This may be prepared ahead and frozen. For myself I make individual casseroles and
freeze to have when I crave a touch of Mexico.

If you like this recipe hotter, add 2 tablespoons slivered jalapeño
peppers.

In Texas one hardly thinks of a potluck supper without a Tamale Pie tucked away somewhere.

TAMALE PIE
For 6 or 8

12 tamales cut in 2-inch pieces (canned)
1 quart diced [cooked] chicken
2 cups chopped corn
2 cups canned tomatoes
½ cup raisins
½ cup sliced stuffed olives
3 slices bacon, fried crisp and crumbled
1 tablespoon chili powder
½ teaspoon salt
1 teaspoon Worcestershire sauce
1 cup chicken consommé
¼ cup of butter
1 cup grated sharp cheddar cheese

[Preheat oven to 300°.] Mix the tamales and chicken with the corn, tomatoes, raisins, olives and bacon. Add the chili powder, salt and Worcestershire sauce to the consommé. Place the tamale mix in a buttered 4-quart casserole. Dot with butter. Pour the consommé mixture over. Bake for 1 hour. Remove. Cover with the cheese and return to oven to brown.

If you are taking South of the Border seriously, you might serve a guacamole salad with this and some canned or frozen pineapple spears, some toasted pecans and a bit of candy as the ending.

GREEN ENCHILADAS
For 8

The day before serving, prepare the following:

1 large white onion
2 4-ounce cans whole green chiles
½ cup parsley sprigs or raw spinach
2 chicken bouillon cubes
1 can mushroom soup
1 green tomato, if available
2 cups whipping cream
Salt and pepper

Put onion, chiles, parsley, bouillon cubes, soup and tomato in blender. When blended, add the cream. Season with salt and pepper.

½ cup vegetable oil
16 soft tortillas or crêpes
1 pound Swiss cheese, grated
Meat from a 3-pound roasted chicken, shredded
Sour cream

[Preheat oven to 350°.] Have 2 small skillets ready. In one heat the oil, in the other ¾ cup of the sauce. Dip each tortilla into the hot oil quickly and drain. Dip into the sauce and stack. When all are ready, put 1 tablespoon of the cheese and some of the chicken on each tortilla and roll. Place in [a single layer across] an 8 x 12-inch casserole. Mix rest of sauce with rest of cheese and any of the sauce left from dipping. Pour over the enchiladas. Bake until hot. Top each serving with sour cream. For a luncheon entrée you could use individual casseroles, serving two enchiladas per person.

If you like the flavor of almonds, grind them in your blender, season with salt and roll boned and skinned chicken breasts in them. Sauté in butter and serve with the nut-flavored butter they have cooked in.

Reader's Request

Leftover chicken and turkey dishes may turn out to be more popular than starting from scratch. And for quick entertaining you can always fall back on canned chicken. For leftovers, I have found these are the most popular:

CHICKEN TETRAZZINI
For 8

2 cups Mornay Sauce [page 226]
2 cups Medium Cream Sauce [page 223]
¼ cup dry sherry
12 ounces spaghetti, cooked, well washed and drained
4 cups chicken meat cut from the bones, in as large pieces as
    possible—or turkey—or shrimp
½ cup sautéed fresh mushrooms (use up your stems this way)
[Grated Parmesan cheese]
[Paprika]

[Preheat oven to 350°.] Mix together and pour into a well-buttered shallow casserole. Cover generously with Parmesan cheese, sprinkle lightly with paprika, and bake until brown and bubbly. Vary it by using toasted almonds in place of mushrooms.

I like to serve this dish with little yellow squash steamed, split, and piled high with cooked frozen peas put through a Foley mill or puréed in your blender [or food processor]. Season with a little nutmeg, butter and salt.

Reader's Request

From the first festive Thanksgiving Day in 1621, turkey has been a symbol of our thanks for our independence, our families, our way of life. Today, three centuries later, the turkey is a far cry from those first wild birds; and so is our way of life—for one thing, we eat turkey more often.

TO ROAST A TURKEY

[Preheat oven to 450°.] Place the cleaned, dry fowl on its back in the roasting pan and rub the entire surface with salt. Mix 3 tablespoons butter with 2 tablespoons of flour until creamy and spread over the breast and legs. Place in oven until flour is brown; reduce heat to 300° and baste frequently with ¼ cup of butter melted in ⅔ cup of boiling water. After this is gone use the liquid in the roasting pan. If you wish a thick crust on the bird, sprinkle flour lightly over its surface two or three times while roasting. And if you think the turkey will be too brown for your taste, cover it with a tent of aluminum foil, but a loose one; or a thin cloth moistened with fat. If you wish a glazed surface, spread only butter on the bird.

Whether a small or a large turkey, the best temperature is 300°, never over 350°. You do not adjust the heat to the size, only the time. The turkey is done when you can move the leg joints easily and the flesh of the legs and breast is soft. [A meat thermometer should read 180° internal temperature.]

The trend today is to buy a ready-to-cook turkey, and after the initial browning at 450°, reduce temperature to 300° and this time chart will do the thinking for you, with the turkey ready to go in the oven.

Pounds	Quarts of Stuffing	Hours
4 to 5	1 to 2	2½ to 3
6 to 12	2 to 3	3½ to 5
12 to 16	3 to 4	5 to 6
16 to 20	4 to 5	6 to 7½
20 to 24	5 to 6	7½ to 9

Plan to have your turkey come out of the oven 20 or 30 minutes before serving; the carving is easier if it waits these few minutes, the meat is juicy, and it gives time to make a good gravy. The turkey will keep its heat for 30 minutes.

To make gravy from a roasted fowl, use the drippings left from cooking. Place 4 tablespoons of the fat in the pan the fowl cooked in, brown with it 4 tablespoons of flour; [gradually] add 2 cups of juice from the pan and stock made from boiling the giblets and neck together. Cook until thick [stirring constantly]; add giblets, finely chopped, if you wish.

[These next two preparations are excellent for a buffet.—Editor]

❧ Reader's Request

SINGAPORE TURKEY BREAST

1   4- to 6-pound turkey breast or whole small turkey
1 tablespoon curry powder
1 tablespoon dried fines herbes
1 tablespoon salt
1 teaspoon paprika
1 onion
1 carrot
1 piece celery
½ orange
1 cup gin
1 cup water

[Preheat oven to 350°.] Wash and dry turkey breast. Mix curry powder, herbs, salt and paprika. Rub turkey inside and out with this mixture. Place in pan with vegetables and orange. Roast uncovered for 3 hours, or until tender. Baste with the gin and water. When done, spoon off all fat from juices. Serve sliced thin with the pan juices unthickened.

Slice smoked or roast turkey in thin slices; place overlapping in either a casserole or on a serving tray. Then pour either a lightly curried cream sauce or mushroom sauce over. This looks like a much more complicated entrée. Somehow when you dice the turkey and add to a sauce, it usually falls into an "oh we had creamed chicken" category.

CURRY OF SMOKED TURKEY
For 10 or 12

½ cup butter
½ cup minced onion
1 clove garlic, crushed
3 to 4 tablespoons curry powder, heated in a skillet before using
8 tablespoons flour
4 cups milk, half-and-half or chicken consommé
3 to 4 pounds boned smoked turkey, cut in large dice
Salt and cayenne pepper
¼ cup sherry

Melt butter, add onion and garlic and cook until yellow, but not brown. Add curry powder, cook 2 minutes; add flour, cook until foamy. . . . [Gradually] pour in milk, cook and stir with a wire whip until thickened. Add the smoked turkey, heat and then season [to taste] with salt and cayenne pepper. The turkey is salted, so do not salt the sauce before adding the turkey. Add sherry. Keep hot over hot water or cool and reheat.

Use the same basic sauce for seafood or whatever curry. However, when I curry shrimp, I start with raw shrimp and sauté them with the onion and garlic, then remove to add later. They will have much more flavor. Sometimes I heat the milk with 2 cups of coconut, cook and strain, then discard the coconut.

We have a tendency to serve curry on rice because we first heard of it served on rice. I like to use fresh, frozen or canned cling peach halves, in this order. Dust the peaches lightly with flour and sauté in butter until a lacy brown. Serve curry over them or use corn bread in place of rice.

With curry, the accompaniments are important. In India each accompaniment is served by a servant boy, so we call curry "Five-boy," "Seven-Boy," or however many accompaniments we use. These are usual, and served in individual bowls:

Chutney, of the Major Grey variety
Diced crisp bacon
Hard-cooked eggs, whites and yolks finely diced separately
Finely chopped salted peanuts, pecans or almonds
Finely chopped [canned] French-fried onions
Shredded coconut, fresh if possible
Shredded Bombay Duck (an Indian fish delicacy)
Tart jelly
Finely chopped sweet pickles
Pappadums (a special wafer from India)
French-fried shrimp
Olives, ripe and stuffed, slivered
Seedless raisins

One of my favorite people in Houston gave me the tip for an accompaniment that I think always makes my Curry Parties successful—a bowl of cold, fine cole slaw [page 113] with tissue-thin slices of onion on top.

One of the most succulent little fowls ever to come across the dinner table is the sensational Rock Cornish Game Hen. . . . Fine grained, the meat is all white, even to the tip of the drumstick. When ready for the oven, they weigh one pound and are plump, pretty little things to taste and to see. . . . They are easy to cook and take only about 40 minutes. This is how I do them.

ROCK CORNISH GAME HENS

4 Rock Cornish hens
Butter and salt
1 carrot
1 teaspoon finely minced onion
1 cup chicken stock, fresh, canned, or made from
    chicken bouillon cubes
1 jigger [1½ ounces] sherry
1 teaspoon cornstarch

[Preheat oven to 350°.] Rub the hens inside and out with butter and salt; place in shallow baking pans small enough so that the hens will touch each other; slice the carrot, add the onion, and place in the pan; roast uncovered, basting several times during the baking with the chicken stock and drippings. When done [meat thermometer reads 180° and thighs are tender], remove from pan to a heated serving dish. Reduce remaining stock in the pan to ½ cup and strain. Add the sherry, mixed with cornstarch, and cook until clear. Pour over the hens.

Dress up for company! Add whole mushrooms, sautéed in butter and a little sherry, and sliced truffles or black olives to the sauce. Serve with wild rice if the budget allows, or converted rice, swished around in the drippings. I like to serve them with their openings filled with crisp watercress and spiced kumquats split and placed over their drumsticks.

Another way for ROCK CORNISH GAME HENS:

[Preheat oven to 450°.] Season with butter and salt, place a small [minced] onion in the pan, and roast uncovered for 10 minutes; lower heat to 350° and roast 25 minutes longer, basting frequently with the stock [or chicken bouillon]. If further browning is necessary, run under the broiler. Remove and add, for each hen:

    1 tablespoon butter
    ¼ cup currant jelly
    1 tablespoon lemon juice

Simmer, strain, and thicken with:

    1 teaspoon cornstarch

Add:

    ½ cup port wine

Recook until hot. Pour sauce over the hens, return to 350° oven for 10 minutes, and serve.

DEVILED ROCK CORNISH HENS
For 8

    8 10- to 12-ounce Rock Cornish Game Hens
    Salt and white pepper
    ½ cup Dijon mustard
    ⅔ cup white bread crumbs
    3 tablespoons minced shallots
    ½ cup butter
    White wine

[Preheat oven to 400°.] Rub each bird with salt, pepper and 1 table-spoon of the mustard. Sprinkle with bread crumbs. Place each hen in a square of foil and fold to center. Add 1 teaspoon shallots, 1 table-spoon butter and 3 tablespoons white wine to each package. Fold the foil over tightly and bake about 50 minutes or until chicken is tender. Carry to picnic in the foil.

Good for informal eat-on-the-floor to watch a television show. No knives and forks. Good cold, too.

There are two schools of thought on roasting duck, depending on whether you like the skin crisp or not. (It doesn't really matter to the duck.)

ROAST DUCKLING AU NATUREL
For 8

Depending on how extravagant you are, there are many ways to estimate how many ducks you will need to prepare. If you serve only half of the breast, you will need 4 ducks; if a quarter, using breast and legs, you will need 2.

2 4- to 5-pound ducks (¼ per serving)
2 teaspoons salt
Juice of 1 lemon or lime
1 teaspoon white pepper
1 orange [halved]
1 medium-sized onion
Dry white wine or chicken broth
Garlic, if you like (then you would be cooking the ducks Niçoise style)
Additional chicken broth
1½ teaspoons arrowroot or cornstarch
¼ cup brandy or Grand Marnier (optional)

[Preheat oven to 450°.] Rub the ducks with the salt, lemon or lime juice and pepper. Place on a rack in a pan. Put one half each of orange and onion in cavities and roast uncovered for 20 minutes. Pour off all melted fat. Return to oven, turn down to 325° and baste with a dry white wine or chicken broth. Roast about 1½ hours or until duck is tender. Wiggle the leg bone! Remove duck. If you wish crisp skin, refrigerate duck until cold or overnight, then return to a 375° oven until thoroughly heated. Baste with juices. Pour off the fat from the juices and for a plain sauce, add enough chicken broth to make 1 cup. Stir in 1½ teaspoons arrowroot or cornstarch. Cook until thickened and clear. Strain and serve with the ducks, or add ¼ cup brandy or Grand Marnier and ignite. I think the sauce should be passed. Most people like to ladle it for themselves. Throw away orange and onion!

An important thing to remember about handling any dressing is to have a light hand. If you are in doubt as to your strength, use a fork to stir and mix.

SAVORY DRESSING

¼ pound bacon
¾ cup chopped onion
2 tablespoons chopped parsley
1 quart white bread crumbs
¼ cup butter
1 teaspoon salt
¼ teaspoon pepper
½ tablespoon Poultry Seasoning (or more if you like)
1 egg [optional]

Dice the bacon and fry with the onions until crisp. Add parsley, crumbled bread, butter [melted], and seasonings. If you like a moist dressing add enough cold water to moisten. Beat and fold in the egg; stuff the fowl with it, or bake in a buttered casserole until brown. I prefer a dry, crunchy dressing, so I do not add any liquid or egg.

CORN BREAD DRESSING

½ cup onion, chopped fine
½ cup green pepper, chopped fine
½ cup celery, diced fine
⅔ cup butter
2 quarts corn bread crumbs (and be sure the corn bread is well
    browned)
6 hard-cooked eggs, chopped
½ cup chopped pimento
Salt and pepper
Chicken or turkey stock (or canned consommé)

[Preheat oven to 350°.] Sauté the onions, green peppers and celery in the butter; add corn bread, eggs and pimento. Season with salt and pepper, and moisten with stock or consommé. Turn into a shallow well-buttered casserole and bake until brown on the top.

Half Corn Bread Dressing and half Cooked Wild Rice make a delightful dressing.

OYSTER STUFFING

1 onion [chopped finely]
½ cup chopped celery
¼ cup butter
1 clove garlic
1 pint small oysters, drained [and rinsed]
2 tablespoons chopped parsley
4 cups soft bread crumbs
1 teaspoon salt
¼ teaspoon white pepper
½ cup light cream

Sauté the onions and celery in the butter with the garlic until soft.
Remove the garlic, add the oysters and parsley, and cook until the
oysters begin to curl. Add the bread crumbs and seasonings. Stir in the
cream; stuff turkey cavity, [which has been] well rubbed with butter.

FRUIT DRESSING

2 quarts white bread, cubed
¼ cup diced onion
¾ cup butter
2 cups chicken broth
1 tablespoon salt
¼ teaspoon pepper
1 teaspoon Poultry Seasoning
2 cups diced apples or prunes or stewed apricots
1 cup sliced Brazil nuts

Use stale bread. Sauté the onion in the butter, add to the bread and
toast in the oven until dry. Moisten with the broth, add the seasonings, fruit and nuts, mix and stuff turkey or chicken. Nice with duck
or goose, roasted veal, or pork.

*Thinly sliced cold turkey, stuffing and cranberry jelly put between
thin slices of white bread is something special!*

This dressing I use for a vegetable at times. It freezes well. In fact, I think it is better if frozen a few days, then baked. Those Texas politicians I fed for three years always thought it was wild rice, so I didn't correct them.

RICE DRESSING

2 cups Uncle Ben's converted rice
3 large onions, chopped fine
4 large stalks of celery, chopped fine
1 green pepper, chopped fine
Ground heart, gizzard, and liver
½ cup butter
1 tablespoon salt
1 tablespoon Poultry Seasoning
2 eggs
1 cup chopped nuts (preferably pecans)
½ cup parsley, chopped
Oysters and mushrooms to taste, if desired

Cook rice according to directions on the package. While rice is cooking, sauté onions, celery, pepper, liver, gizzard and heart together in the butter until thoroughly cooked. Add seasonings and mix [lightly]. Beat eggs until frothy. Remove sautéed onion mixture from heat, add rice and fold in beaten eggs, mixing thoroughly. Add chopped nuts and parsley. Add oysters and mushrooms if desired. Stuff turkey and bake for the last 30 minutes of its cooking, or bake separately in a buttered shallow casserole for 25 minutes at 350°.

Being a wild rice fan, and who isn't, I like to extend it (because it costs so much) as far as I can without losing its identity. This dressing is wonderful with duck or turkey.

WILD RICE STUFFING

1 cup wild rice
Giblets (liver, gizzard and heart)
2 cups hot broth or water
½ cup finely chopped onion
½ cup butter or margarine
2 quarts oven-toasted dry bread crumbs
1 teaspoon salt
¼ teaspoon ground sage
¼ teaspoon pepper
2 eggs, beaten

Cook the rice according to directions on the package. Chop the giblets fine and cook in [hot broth or] water until tender. Sauté onion in the butter until yellow in color, add the bread crumbs with the giblets and broth. Add the seasonings and mix lightly. Cover and let stand until the bread is moist. Add the wild rice and eggs, and mix lightly. Pour into a buttered baking dish and bake at 325° for 25 minutes, or stuff whatever fowl you are roasting and cook during the last 20 minutes of its cooking.

CHESTNUT DRESSING

1½ cups seedless raisins (white ones are best)
1 cup melted butter
2 tablespoons salt
2 cups cream
2½ quarts crumbled white bread
1½ cups finely diced celery
4 cups chestnuts, toasted and broken up

Mix together and stuff into the turkey cavity, or bake in buttered
casserole at 325° for 1 hour. Very rich—and very good!

Meats

Roast beef is a word thrown about loosely. To me it means Prime Ribs, to others just a piece of meat, but when roasting beef you should insist on a rib, top sirloin or top round. . . . The tenderloin, which is smaller and expensive, may also be used for roasting. The best quality you can find in your local market should be used for roasting. . . . Roasted beef can never be any better than the grade of beef you start out with.

A barbecue originally referred to a whole animal roasted or broiled for a feast. Derived from the French "barbe-a-gueve," meaning from snout to tail, the popular version of the word barbecue or cook-out was first known in Virginia before 1700.

Don't forget the secret of barbecuing is a solid bed of glowing coals. Whether charcoal, wood or other fuel is used, light the fire at least 30 minutes ahead of time so that it will burn down to ash-gray coals before cooking starts.

Rub the outsides of pots and pans with soap before using over an open fire. They will be much easier to clean afterward.

BEEF

ک *Previously Unpublished*

[After you've cut beef tournedos or filet mignons from the larger part of a beef tender, what can you do with the smaller end?] *At the Zodiac Room this dish was prepared and served in individual small sauté pans.*

HELEN CORBITT'S BEEF GRENADINS
For 4

Cut 1 pound of 1-inch cubes from the small end of a beef tenderloin and flatten each with the heel of your hand.

½ cup flour
1 tablespoon paprika
1 tablespoon butter
¾ teaspoon salt
¼ cup brandy
1 cup heavy cream

Lightly dredge the meat in a mixture of flour and paprika. Melt butter in a sauté pan and quickly sear the meat. Remove the grenadins to a warm platter and sprinkle with salt. Add brandy to the skillet, allowing it to warm, and then light it to burn off the raw alcohol taste. Scrape the browned bits from the bottom and sides of the pan as you add the cream. Continue cooking over medium heat until it reduces to a rich smooth sauce, but do not boil. Return the grenadins to the sauce to reheat for a moment and serve with boiled noodles or rice. You'll also like this same sauce for cooking 4 boned and skinless chicken breasts. Flavor them with 1 tablespoon of chopped chives and truffles or cooked mushrooms.

BEEF TENDERLOIN IN CLARET
For 6 or 8

1 3-pound piece of beef tenderloin, trimmed for roasting
Salt and pepper
4 young onions or shallots [sliced]
4 tablespoons butter
½ cup claret
½ cup beef consommé
1 teaspoon cornstarch or arrowroot
½ teaspoon lemon juice
Brandy [2 tablespoons]

[Preheat oven to 300°.] Roast the tenderloin, rubbed with salt and pepper, for 1 hour. Sauté the onions in the butter, add the claret and cook until reduced by half. Add the consommé mixed with the cornstarch and simmer until thickened [stirring constantly]. Add the lemon juice and pour over the fillet. Run under broiler until the whole thing is bubbling; add heated brandy at the table and light.

Serve with halves of tomatoes covered with sour cream and baked, asparagus, and mushrooms (fresh or canned) stuffed with chopped, cooked chicken livers. An elegant dish when you feel like celebrating. It calls for an elegant dessert, too!

TOURNEDOS

Tournedos are for informal suppers. For a seated dinner you need a larger filet mignon, 6 to 10 ounces. These are tournedo preparations you could use.

1. Halve lengthwise one clove of garlic and brown in a small amount of olive oil, salad oil, or oil and butter, about 1 tablespoon for each tournedo. [Remove garlic.] Add the meat and brown both sides quickly, turning only once. Add 1 tablespoon sherry for each tournedo and stir the skillet to incorporate all the brown bits of oil and meat. Remove meat and let the sherry reduce a little. Pour the

liquid over the meat and serve. I like to rest tournedos in a freshly cooked artichoke bottom.

2. After cooking meat, deglaze skillet with pale dry Madeira. Spoon over meat.

3. Deglaze with [heated] brandy, igniting same to burn off the raw taste of the brandy, then add ½ teaspoon of Dijon mustard and ¼ cup sour cream for each tournedo. Heat, but do not boil, then pour over meat.

4. Deglaze with red burgundy wine, place a thin layer of Roquefort cheese on top of meat. Spoon sauce over.

5. Deglaze with Madeira, place a slice of pâté de fois gras on top of each tournedo and pour sauce over (called Rossini).

6. Serve with Béarnaise Sauce [page 224].

❧ *Reader's Request*

PRIME RIBS OF BEEF

Three ribs will feed five or six people, depending on how thin you slice it. [Preheat oven to 350°.] Rub the roast with salt, lots of salt, and freshly ground pepper, if possible. Peel one clove of garlic, if you are so minded, and push it between two ribs. If not, add a whole onion to the pan, a carrot, and sprig of parsley. Roast uncovered in a pan. I am amazed at the people who still think you burn up the outside to start with. For a rare roast, allow 15 to 18 minutes per pound; for medium, 20 to 25 minutes. If you are a "well done" addict, 30 minutes per pound, and you shouldn't try to roast less than three ribs for good results. Use the same procedure for other cuts for roasting.

For those who refuse to take cooking seriously, but still want to make an impression, we have the answer.

BEEF FONDUE BOURGUIGNONNE
For 4 or 6

2 pounds tender fillets of beef, cut in ¾- to 1-inch cubes or thin
    slices
1½ cups good grade olive oil or 1 cup oil and ½ cup melted
    butter
A metal fondue pot or chafing dish or electric skillet—but to be
    proper and impressive—the pot, please
Long-tined fondue forks with heat-proof handles

Place uncooked beef on a wooden tray or board; either place on table or pass for guests to help themselves. The oil should be boiling, then placed on the table and kept hot with Sterno during the cooking process. Each guest spears a piece of meat, then cooks it himself in the hot oil. You should also have a variety of sauces or condiments for them to dip the meat into.

For instance, Lawry's Seasoned Salt and Pepper
Or a "Corbitt Special" made with:
    4 tablespoons salt
    1 tablespoon cracked pepper
    ½ teaspoon paprika
    ½ teaspoon curry powder
    Pinch of nutmeg and oregano

Or any preserved spiced fruit juice mixed with enough dry mustard to make a paste (this is good with any kind of meat).

Or 1 cup mayonnaise mixed with ¼ cup chopped capers and ¼ cup chopped parsley.

Or ¼ pound of butter mixed with 2 tablespoons of anchovy paste.

You can really let your imagination run riot for the sauces to dip the meat in.

I have pieces of fresh parsley to fry also, and slices of sweet onion. Your guests are so busy you only need to provide a bowl of relishes, quite hardy ones, hot French bread and coffee.

FILLET OF BEEF WITH LOBSTER
For 8 to 12

3 pounds beef tenderloin
1 teaspoon vegetable salt [optional]
½ cup soy sauce [divided use]
2 tablespoons grated fresh ginger root
½ cup onion, sliced
¼ cup dry sherry [divided use]
3 lobster tails

[Preheat oven to 450°.] Rub the beef with vegetable salt, [half of] the soy sauce and the ginger. Scatter onions in a shallow pan and place the beef on top. Roast for 30 minutes. Remove [baste with half the sherry] and let the roast rest. [Turn the oven down to 350°.]

[Rinse and] split lobster tails in half lengthwise. Loosen the meat from the shell, rub lightly with remaining soy sauce and bake in their shells for 15 minutes. Remove the lobster from shell. Cut a pocket [lengthwise] three-quarters of the way through the roasted fillet; stuff the lobster into the cavity. Return to oven to heat, basting with the pan juices and remaining sherry. [Remove it to a heated serving platter.] Slice and serve with pan juices. The combination of flavors is delicious.

There are still those who like Yorkshire Pudding with their beef.

[These are really just beef flavored popovers.—Editor]

YORKSHIRE PUDDING

[Preheat oven to 450°.] Pour out 6 tablespoons of beef drippings from the roast into a shallow pan [about 9 x 12 inches] and keep it hot. [Have the following ingredients at room temperature when they are mixed.] Beat 2 eggs until light, add 1 cup milk, and beat until frothy. Stir in 1 cup of sifted flour and ½ teaspoon salt and beat until smooth. Pour into the hot drippings and bake for 15 minutes, then reduce the temperature to 350° for 15 minutes more. [Don't open the door during baking!]

a *Reader's Request*

With a leftover roast of beef or veal there is no better dish than

STROGANOFF
For 6

4 cups cooked beef or veal
2 tablespoons olive oil
2 tablespoons butter
1 cup thinly sliced [and coarsely chopped] onion
1½ cups sliced mushrooms
1 cup beef stock or consommé
1½ tablespoons flour
1 teaspoon salt
½ teaspoon whole caraway seeds
A dash of nutmeg
2 cups sour cream

Trim all fat from the meat and cut into strips, about 1-inch long and ¼-inch wide. Heat oil and butter in skillet, add onions and mushrooms and sauté at low heat until soft. Add meat and continue cooking for 10 minutes; add consommé and cook for 30 minutes. Mix flour and seasonings with the sour cream and add it to the first mixture. Cook slowly until thick, but do not boil. Remove from direct heat and keep over hot water. I like to serve Stroganoff with fine noodles, well buttered and seasoned, with chopped parsley and combined with peas; or add potato balls, cooked in consommé, to the Stroganoff just before serving.

Add a can of beer to meat you simmer, braise or roast. It will act as both tenderizer and flavor bud.

A different twist for hash that could be a great Potluck dish is

BEEF HASH AURORA

4 cups ground cooked beef
1 small sweet white onion
1 10½-ounce can beef broth
¼ cup (or more) sour cream
¼ cup catsup
½ teaspoon sugar
¼ teaspoon garlic powder
Salt and pepper

Grind together all trimmings you can cut from bones, and all leftover pieces of beef in a food grinder, using medium blade [or in your food processor, using steel blade]. You should have 4 cups of ground beef for 4 servings. Peel the onion and grind with the beef. Moisten the beef-onion mixture with beef broth, sour cream and catsup. Add sugar and garlic powder; mix thoroughly. Taste for salt and pepper. Add it, if it needs it, for it depends on how the beef was seasoned in the first place. If the mixture is not quite moist, add more sour cream. The best way of mixing this is with your hands; no spoon will do as well. Pile hash in the skillet or casserole. Top with:

2 ripe red tomatoes
½ teaspoon salt
¼ teaspoon pepper
½ teaspoon dried sweet basil
½ teaspoon sugar
4 tablespoons sour cream

[Preheat oven to 425°.] Slice each tomato into 2 thick slices. Arrange these on top of hash. Combine and sprinkle the salt, pepper, basil and sugar over all. Place a tablespoon of sour cream on top of each tomato. Bake in the hot oven until heated through and bubbly. The sour cream should be slightly brown; if it isn't, slide the casserole under the broiler for a moment to finish browning. Serve directly from casserole.

BEEF AU POIVRE

1 rib eye of beef
Olive oil
Salt
¾ cup peppercorns
Burgundy wine [approximately 1 cup]

[Preheat oven to 350°.] Rub rib eye or another boneless beef cut with olive oil and salt. Rub freshly ground or cracked pepper over the entire piece and roast in oven, about 20 minutes for each pound. Dash a cup of Burgundy wine over after the first hour and baste with it frequently. Serve medium rare or rare for best tasting results. Wonderful for a cocktail buffet!—with thin sliced French bread and sweet butter.

This recipe is a hostess-saver, because it should be done the day before you serve it.

RIB EYE EN GELEE

1 whole rib eye of beef, well trimmed
2 cloves garlic, crushed
Salt and pepper
2 tablespoons unflavored gelatin
3 10½-ounce cans beef consommé [divided use]
½ cup dry white wine

[Preheat oven to 450°.] Rub the rib eye with garlic, salt and pepper. Roast for 30 minutes. Reduce heat to 350° and cook 20 minutes longer. Do this the day before serving. Dissolve the gelatin in ½ cup of the consommé. Bring the rest of the consommé to a fast boil. Remove from heat. Add the gelatin and wine. Pour a thin layer in a [lightly oiled] shallow pan or platter. Chill until almost set. Slice beef in thin slices and place overlapping on top of aspic. Pour a thin layer of the gelatin mixture over and chill again. Decorate with thin-sliced canned mushrooms, tiny carrots, julienne of tongue or ham, artichoke hearts, whatever suits your fancy. Pour more aspic over all and chill again. Repeat, but be sure you have a thin layer of the aspic each time. Pour leftover aspic in [another] pan. Let set until firm, overnight.

Take a long spatula and remove the meat to your serving tray. Cut aspic left in pan in small cubes and use as decoration on the tray.

You may prepare a tenderloin of beef the same way, only roast for 25 minutes at 450°. If you wish your meat well done, increase the roasting time. Or a baked boneless ham may be done the same way, adding 1 cup of finely chopped parsley to the gelatin mixture. Leftover ham may be diced, put into a loaf pan and covered with the gelatin. Leftover roasted veal combined with the ham in the parsleyed aspic is delicious.

A well-done flank steak is pretty poor eating, I think, but that is just one gal's opinion.

MARINATED FLANK STEAK
For 8 to 12

1   2½- to 3-pound flank steak
1 tablespoon vegetable oil
½ cup dry white wine
1 or 2 cloves garlic, minced
1 tablespoon onion, minced
Pinch of thyme
1 bay leaf
2 tablespoons chopped parsley or chives

Trim the steak of all visible fat. Place it in a shallow casserole. [Mix the remaining ingredients together and pour over the steak.] Cover and refrigerate overnight, turning once. [Preheat broiler.] Remove the meat, reserving the marinade. [Place steak on a flat pan and slide it 4 inches below broiler for 4 to 5 minutes; turn over and repeat.] Slice thin diagonally and keep it warm while you make a sauce by deglazing the broiler pan with the leftover marinade. You can vary the flavor by using dry red wine or by adding soy sauce, more garlic and slivers of fresh ginger root.

A 3-ounce portion will yield 3 or 4 thin slices. I know that the amount of food we think we see affects our appetites. In fact, I sometimes cannot finish the 3 or 4 thin slices, whereas if the same 3 ounces are served as a solid piece of meat, I can quickly gobble it up and want more. Purely psychological!

I was both amused and flattered a few months ago while riding home in a taxicab. My companion was talking about my job, of course, and the cabdriver stopped the cab, turned in his seat, and said, "Lady, can you cook Corn Beef?" The man with me picked up his lower jaw and said, "Golly, can you? My wife can't!" So from there the fun was on.

CORNED BEEF (THE GOOD OLD IRISH WAY)
For 8

To begin with, I say buy good corned beef.

For eight hungry people you use a 4-pound piece of corned beef. I think the brisket is the best; the streak of fat through it helps the texture and flavor. Wash under running water and cover with cold water; bring to a boil slowly and cook 5 minutes, removing the scum that will come to the top of the pot. Then cover and simmer until the meat is tender—about 3 hours, but it could take longer. Cool in the stock until easy to handle. Slice with a sharp knife the long way of the piece of meat and place on a hot platter with just enough of the stock to keep it moist.

Twelve minutes before you are ready to sit down to eat it, cut a medium-sized head of cabbage in eighths, add to the liquid and boil uncovered. Twelve minutes only! Remove and place around the corned beef and eat at once. Just boiled potatoes is the accepted accompaniment; and horseradish or mustard sauce.

GLAZED CORNED BEEF is good. Cover cooked corned beef with ⅓ cup of brown sugar and stick with whole cloves. Bake at 350° until glazed. Remove the cloves and serve. Really good for a snack with dark rye bread and dill pickles.

CORNED BEEF BRISKET WITH ORANGES

1 4-pound corned beef brisket
2 oranges, sliced
1 lemon, sliced
2 peeled onions, sliced
1 tablespoon pickling spices
¼ cup brown sugar

Cover beef with cold water, bring to a boil and skim. Add rest of ingredients [except brown sugar]. Simmer at medium heat until tender, about 4 hours. Remove, sprinkle with brown sugar and bake at 350° until sugar melts. Slice thin and serve hot or cold.

❧ *Reader's Request*

I have been served short ribs of beef in many homes, surprisingly at dinner parties; at least everyone went in their best clothes. For the most part they have been a sorry dish. So perhaps I'm putting this recipe here in self-defense, because I really like short ribs—but then I like everything.

SHORT RIBS OF BEEF WITH HORSERADISH SAUCE

    6 pounds beef short ribs
    1 tablespoon salt
    1 tablespoon Accent [optional]
    8 peppercorns
    2 sliced onions
    1 diced carrot
    ½ cup parsley [chopped]
    [2 or 3 tablespoons flour]
    Prepared horseradish

Cut the meat only if you have to fit it to a large kettle. Cover with cold water and place over high heat until the water begins to boil; reduce heat to low and simmer for 2 hours. Add the seasonings and vegetables and continue to cook at low heat until the meat is tender, probably 2 hours. Remove the short ribs to a hot platter. Strain the broth and make a sauce of it by slightly thickening with flour and then add enough horseradish (grated, if fresh) to season it well.

And ¼ cup of finely chopped raw peeled apple added to 2 cups of the sauce makes it more interesting. It is good to cook young carrots, boiling onions and new potatoes the last hour with the short ribs. [Sometimes omit the sliced onions and diced carrot from the stock.]

❧ Reader's Request

Meat loaf can be a sorry concoction or a thing of gastronomical delight. The trouble is that most people overcook it, or rather use too hot an oven so it is dry and hard on the outside. Good meat loaf is made from fresh-ground beef.

MEAT LOAF
For 8

2 pounds chopped beef
¼ pound salt pork, chopped fine
2 eggs, slightly beaten
1 cup milk
3 tablespoons melted butter
1 tablespoon prepared horseradish or 3 tablespoons catsup
2 tablespoons minced onion
¼ teaspoon pepper
1 tablespoon salt [scant]
1 cup soft bread crumbs
2 strips bacon

[Preheat oven to 350°.] Mix meat and salt pork with the eggs, milk, butter, horseradish or catsup, onion, seasonings, and bread crumbs. Pack in a buttered loaf tin (8 x 4 inches) and cover with the strips of bacon. Bake for 60 minutes, or until it is well browned and shrinks from sides of tin.

Or dress it up by putting half in the tin and placing 3 hard-cooked eggs end-to-end through center of pan, or slices of aged American cheese; pack the rest of the meat in and bake as above. Remove to a hot platter and slice as served, using any sauce you like, or French-fried onion rings and scalloped or Au Gratin Potatoes [page 278]. Oversized Idaho potatoes baked, split, and topped with thick sour cream salted and peppered, does it well, too. I put this recipe in strictly at the request of many of my men customers!

MEAT CONCERN
For 6

2½ cups canned cream-style corn
2½ cups canned tomatoes
Salt [to taste]
3 tablespoons butter [divided use]
1 package fine noodles
¼ cup chopped onions
¼ cup finely chopped green pepper
½ cup [sliced] mushrooms
½ cup chopped celery
1½ pounds ground beef
Pepper
1 can tomato soup
Worcestershire sauce
[Additional butter]
[Grated cheese]

Put corn and tomatoes in kettle and cook with salt and 2 tablespoons of the butter. Boil noodles, wash and drain. Melt remaining tablespoon of butter in skillet and sauté onion, green pepper, and mushrooms slowly until onion is clear; add celery, meat, and pepper. Cook well [until meat loses its redness]; add to corn, tomatoes, and tomato soup. Add Worcestershire and taste for seasoning. Add noodles and simmer all together for ½ hour. Set back and let stand [in a cold place]—all night, if possible. One hour before serving, put in buttered baking dish, dot generously with butter and grated cheese (any kind you have), and bake at 325° for 1 hour.

BEEF À LA DEUTSCH
For 6

1½ pounds beef top sirloin, cut in 1-inch strips
1 cup sliced mushrooms
½ cup sliced green peppers
½ cup sliced onions
2 tablespoons butter
1 quart stock [beef]
¼ cup flour
1½ cups sour cream
Salt and pepper
¼ cup chopped pimento

Sauté the beef, mushrooms, green peppers, and onions in the butter until meat is brown and the onions soft. Add stock (you can make it with bouillon cubes and water, if you have none, or use canned consommé) and simmer slowly until the meat is tender. Mix flour with a little of the sour cream and add; cook until thick, season with salt and pepper . . . . Add remaining sour cream and pimentos and bring [almost] to a boil. Remove from heat and keep hot [place over hot water] for 15 minutes before serving—to catch the flavors. This is a good do-the-day-before dish, as it really tastes better the second day.

SPICY ROAST BEEF WITH GINGERSNAP GRAVY
For 6 or 8

5 pounds rump or round of beef
2 cups vinegar
1 ripe tomato, peeled and chopped
4 bay leaves
½ teaspoon whole cloves
½ teaspoon peppercorns

Place in container [glass or plastic] and add enough water to cover the meat. Refrigerate overnight or longer if you like a spicier meat. Remove the meat, saving the marinade.

¼ cup flour
½ teaspoon pepper
1 teaspoon salt
½ teaspoon allspice
4 tablespoons soft vegetable shortening
½ cup sliced onions
12 gingersnaps
Additional salt and pepper.

[Rub the meat with a mixture of flour, seasonings and allspice. Heat shortening and onions in a covered skillet or Dutch oven. Brown the meat on all sides.] Add 3 cups of liquid the meat has soaked in and cook, covered, over low heat for 2 or 3 hours, or until the meat is tender. Add crumbled gingersnaps and cook until thick. Season to your taste; remove to a hot serving dish, and strain the gravy. Serve with dumplings or boiled potatoes.

A good meat sauce is one thing you can keep in your icebox or deep freeze, and this one I like because it is gentle with my taste buds.

MEAT SAUCE
For 6 or 8

¼ pound salt pork, diced
½ cup minced onion
1 cup minced celery
½ cup minced carrots
1 tablespoon butter [or olive oil]
2 pounds ground lean beef
¼ cup white wine
1½ cups peeled chopped fresh tomatoes
2 cups light cream [or half-and-half]

Sauté the salt pork until brown. Add the onion, celery, carrots and cook until they are transparent. Add the butter, meat, wine and tomatoes. Simmer for 1½ hours. Add cream and continue cooking until thick.

Combine this sauce with any pasta and sprinkle with Parmesan cheese. Why be in a rut though for pastas? At least change the shape. Try mostaccioli for a change. Serve a salad of greens and fennel with oil and vinegar dressing.

The following recipe was brought to me by my favorite wine merchant from one of his many trips to Europe. An Italian-American, he recognized its worth.

LASAGNA VERDE AL FORNO

BOLOGNESE SAUCE
½ pound ground salt pork
1½ pounds ground top round of beef
½ pound ground lean veal
2 cups thinly sliced onion
2 carrots, thinly sliced
2 stalks celery, diced
2 cloves
2 cups beef consommé
2 tablespoons tomato paste
1 teaspoon salt
Few twists from pepper grinder
1 cup water
½ pound mushrooms, diced
4 chicken livers, diced
1 cup heavy cream

Put salt pork into a large deep skillet and fry until brown. Pour off the melted fat. Put in beef and veal, onions, carrots, celery and cloves. Brown over low heat. Add the consommé and cook until it evaporates. Add tomato paste, salt, pepper and water. Cover skillet and cook at low heat for 1 hour. Add mushrooms and chicken livers and cook 15 minutes longer. Just before assembling lasagne, add cream and reheat.

BÉCHAMEL SAUCE
4 tablespoons butter
3 tablespoons flour
2 tablespoons finely chopped onion
2 cups chicken broth or milk
Salt and pepper
¼ cup heavy cream

Melt the butter. Add flour and cook until bubbly. Stir in onion and cook 1 minute. [Gradually] pour in broth or milk, stirring constantly with a French whip until thickened. Season to taste. Add cream and simmer until thoroughly heated. Strain.

1 pound spinach lasagna noodles
2 cups grated Parmesan cheese
2 cups grated Gruyère cheese

[Preheat oven to 375°.] Cook noodles in boiling salted water until just tender, but not soft. Drain, but do not wash. Place a layer in a shallow 3-quart oblong casserole. Cover with a layer of the Bolognese meat sauce, then a layer of the Béchamel, then grated cheeses mixed together. Continue layering in the same order, ending with grated cheese on top. Bake until brown and bubbling. Let stand outside of oven 10 minutes before serving. Prepare ahead of time and it freezes well.

A wok is not necessary for Chinese cooking but if you like to talk about it, by all means use one. A heavy-bottomed skillet will do as well, but be sure it is clean and dry.

SAUTÉED BEEF WITH LEEKS AND MUSHROOMS
For 4

¾ ounce dried Chinese mushrooms
4 tablespoons peanut oil [divided use]
1 cup leeks, white part only, thinly sliced diagonally
1 pound beef tenderloin, sirloin or flank, sliced thin
1 tablespoon soy sauce
1 teaspoon cornstarch
¼ cup water
Few drops sesame oil
1 tablespoon sherry

Soak the mushrooms in cold water for 30 minutes. Drain, trim and slice them. Preheat skillet or wok to a very high temperature. Swirl 2 tablespoons of oil into skillet and add leeks and dried mushrooms. Cook 1 minute, stirring constantly. Remove from skillet and keep warm. Rub skillet with paper towels, being careful not to burn your fingers. Add remaining 2 tablespoons of oil and the sliced beef. Cook 2 minutes stirring constantly. Add the cooked vegetables and the soy sauce and cook 1 minute more. Mix cornstarch and water and add to skillet. Add sesame oil and sherry just before removing from heat.

BEEF PATTIES MADEIRA
For 4

2 pounds ground lean beef
4 tablespoons butter [divided use]
1 teaspoon salt
½ cup Madeira
Cracked pepper
4 slices toast, cut to fit the patties
1 7-ounce container liver paté
4 mushroom caps, browned in additional butter

Mix beef with 1 tablespoon of butter and 1 teaspoon salt. Form into 4 patties. Marinate the patties in the Madeira for at least 1 hour. Remove [and save marinade]. Sprinkle with cracked pepper and sauté in the butter over high heat for 3 minutes on either side. [Remove and keep warm.] Place toast in the remaining butter and sauté. Place a patty on each slice and cover with a slice of the liver paté. Top each with a mushroom cap. Pour the remaining marinade from the steaks into the pan and boil for 3 minutes. Pour over steaks and place in a 400° oven for 3 minutes. Do tenderloin steaks the same way.

Backyard chefs come into their own with outdoor cooking, and for the most part, these brothers of the skillet do a fine job, especially at kibitzing each other's techniques. However, I must admit that they do their best with a steak 2-inches thick—but you can't always afford a 2-inch-thick steak.

For those who can, this sauce will make the steak extra good. With a good charcoal fire, it takes about 15 minutes on each side to cook a two-inch steak that is charred on the outside, and has a redness on the inside. Then put the steaks in a shallow pan, shake on salt and pepper (fresh ground, of course), and spread with a thin layer of dry mustard and a generous amount of butter, softened—not melted—and sprinkle with Worcestershire sauce. Swish the steak around until the sauce is well blended.

HUNGARIAN GOULASH
For 4

2½ pounds beef, rump or round, or veal
⅓ cup chopped suet [or vegetable oil]
½ cup chopped onions
½ clove garlic, crushed
2¼ cups water [divided use]
1 cup catsup
½ teaspoon dry mustard
1 tablespoon paprika
2 tablespoons brown sugar
1 tablespoon salt
1 teaspoon Worcestershire sauce
1 teaspoon vinegar
2 tablespoons flour
1 package fine noodles

Cut meat into 1-inch cubes. Brown in suet [or oil] with onion and garlic. Add 2 cups water, catsup, and seasonings [mustard, paprika, sugar, salt, Worcestershire and vinegar], cover and cook at low heat until the meat is tender, about 2 hours. Mix flour with remaining ¼ cup of water and add to the hot mixture, stirring constantly, and cook until thick. In the meantime cook noodles in boiling salted water. Drain, mix with part of the sauce from the meat, and serve with the meat over them. This recipe is also at the request of a favorite customer—a man, of course!

Hearty casserole dishes are good for parties where you know appetites will be keen, like after a football game, merry elbow-lifting, skiing or whatever. This you may do ahead of time, and bake while socializing—or complete and reheat.

BEEF ROULADE
For 4 or 8

8 thin slices beef, about 4 inches square (round or bottom butt)
Salt and pepper
2 dill pickles
1 cup thinly sliced onion
2 tablespoons butter
4 slices bacon
Vegetable oil
2 cups leftover brown gravy. . . . I have seen brown gravy in cans on the grocer's shelf. What next?
¼ cup red Burgundy wine, or not

[Preheat oven to 350°] Lay beef flat on a meat board, flatten with a cleaver or edge of a china plate. Sprinkle with salt and pepper. Quarter the pickles lengthwise. Sauté the onions in the butter until yellow, but do not brown. Cut bacon in half crosswise. Place a piece of pickle and bacon and 1 tablespoon of sautéed onion in center of the beef. Roll and secure with a toothpick. Brown in a skillet in hot cooking oil or fat. Place in a shallow casserole. Cover with the brown gravy and wine. Cover and bake for 1 hour. Uncover and bake 1 hour longer, or until tender. Serve with noodles. Teen-age boys and girls like this! Serve 1 or 2 depending on how generous you are.

❧ *Previously Unpublished*

This is one of my favorite dishes. It is inexpensive, goes a long way and is good for informal entertaining and picnics.

CHALUPAS

2 tablespoons butter or vegetable oil
1 cup chopped onion, divided use
1 pound lean ground beef
2 tablespoons flour
3 tablespoons chili powder

1 cup water
1½ cups canned tomato soup
1½ cups half-and-half cream
1½ cups grated American cheese
12 corn tortillas

Preheat oven to 325°. Heat the butter or oil in a skillet and sauté half of the onions until limp and transparent. Add meat and continue to cook until brown. Drain fat and return to the heat. Mix flour and chili powder together, add to meat and continue to cook. Add water, cover the pan and simmer until sauce is thick. Mix soup, cream and remaining onion, and stir into meat. Cut tortillas into strips and place a layer in the bottom of an oiled casserole. Cover with a layer of meat and then one of grated cheese; repeat the layers, ending with cheese over the top. Bake uncovered until steaming hot and browned.

ROAST LOIN OR RACK OF VENISON

2 loins or racks of venison
Red wine or half wine and half water
2 bay leaves
2 onions, sliced
Few juniper berries
8 peppercorns
8 sprigs parsley
Salt and pepper
½ cup melted butter
1 cup [additional] red wine
1 cup currant jelly
2 tablespoons arrowroot

Cover meat with red wine; add bay leaves, onions, berries, peppercorns and parsley. Cover and refrigerate for at least 24 hours. Remove, drain and dry [saving marinade]. Sprinkle with salt and pepper and roast uncovered in a 400° oven for 45 minutes. Baste with the strained marinade and butter. Use a meat thermometer and cook until medium rare (140°). Remove meat and let rest. Add 1 cup wine and the jelly to juices to make 1 pint or more of sauce. Add the arrowroot mixed with a little cold water to make a paste and heat until thickened. Slice meat in thin slices and serve with unstrained sauce.

VEAL

❧ *Reader's Request*

Killing and cooking the fatted calf has been the symbol of hospitality since the beginning of time. How we do it is the only change.

VEAL BIRDS OR ROLLS
For 6

1½-pound veal cutlet, sliced ¼-inch thick and cut in 6-inch
    squares
2 cups Savory Dressing [page 149]
Flour, salt and pepper
2 tablespoons butter
1 cup Thin Cream Sauce [page 223]
1 cup leftover meat gravy
1 teaspoon horseradish

[Preheat oven to 350°.] Pound cutlet until thin, place dressing in center of each, roll and secure with a toothpick. Roll in seasoned flour and brown carefully in the butter. Arrange in baking dish, add cream sauce, gravy and horseradish; cover and bake for 1 hour, or until tender.

❧ *Reader's Request*

VEAL PICCATE
For 8

2 pounds thinly sliced veal cutlets
1 cup flour
1 tablespoon salt
½ cup butter
¼ cup olive oil
1 cup chicken broth
¼ cup lemon juice
2 lemons, sliced very thin
½ cup finely chopped parsley

Place cutlets between two pieces of foil [or wax paper] and pound until they are thin, but not torn. Dredge in the flour and salt; shake off all excess flour. Heat the butter and oil and sauté the veal about 5 minutes over medium heat, turning the meat only once. If skillet is not large enough, as soon as first slices are done, pile on a plate and keep warm. Then return all veal to the skillet, add the chicken broth. Simmer until the liquid is reduced by one-half. Add the lemon juice and the thin slices of lemon. Heat only until lemons are hot. Correct seasonings. Add parsley at the last minute. Serve with the sauce poured over and garnish with the hot lemon slices.

❧ Reader's Request

One gets a feeling the French see Americans coming and say, "Give them the sauce." However, the French sauces are delicious, and all generously doused with wine. I must say I think veal dishes are better with a spot of wine added.

VEAL À LA CRÈME
For 6 or 8

1 teaspoon sugar
¼ cup thinly sliced onion
3 pounds lean veal stew meat
1½ cups chicken stock or water
2 tablespoons butter
2 tablespoons flour
½ cup dry white wine
½ cup whipping cream
Salt and white pepper
½ teaspoon grated lemon peel

Melt the sugar in a heavy skillet and brown onion in it. Add the meat and chicken stock (or water). Cover and simmer until fork-tender. Melt the butter, add the flour and stir in the wine and cream. Add salt if needed, then add to the veal with the lemon peel and cook 5 minutes. This is a delicately flavored dish, so the vegetables served with it should not overshadow it. Rice or noodles cooked in chicken stock, new potatoes, little white onions, baby zucchini with chives in the butter or fresh carrots would be good with it, but lightly seasoned. Again a chilled white wine would go well. For dessert, a combination of canned fruits sprinkled with brown sugar and butter and baked until hot. Run under broiler for the glisten you like.

*Veal chops make a dinner fit for a king, especially when done with
sour cream.*

VEAL CHOPS IN SOUR CREAM
For 4

4 veal chops ½-inch thick or more
Salt
Flour
¼ cup butter or margarine
1 cup sour cream
Finely slivered rind of 1 lemon [the zest]
2 tablespoons lemon juice

Sprinkle the chops with salt and dredge them lightly in flour. Shake
off all you can. Sauté lightly in butter for 15 minutes. Turn once. Add
the sour cream to the skillet you cooked the chops in and cook over
very low heat until the sauce is yellow. [Do not allow to boil.] Add the
lemon juice and rind and simmer a minute. Serve at once.

Green beans (fresh) cooked underdone and dressed with chopped
dill and parsley are nice with it. . . .

VEAL ROAST WITH HERBS
For 8 to 12

3 pounds boneless leg of veal
1 tablespoon vegetable oil
[2 teaspoons salt]
½ teaspoon dried tarragon
½ teaspoon dried rosemary
½ teaspoon oregano
1 teaspoon paprika
2 tablespoons chopped parsley
2 tablespoons minced shallots
1 cup chicken broth
1 cup dry white wine
Canned artichoke bottoms (optional)

[Preheat oven to 350°] Remove any visible fat. Rub the veal with oil.
Mix the salt, tarragon, rosemary, oregano and paprika with fresh parsley
and shallots and rub over the meat. Baste frequently with a mixture of

broth and wine. Roast uncovered for about half an hour, or until 170°
[on meat thermometer. Remove to a heated platter to rest for about 10
minutes.] Slice thin and serve with the pan juices. Slice a few artichoke
bottoms into the juices—so few calories you don't need to count them.

*Morels are edible wild mushrooms with spongy oval caps. They must be
carefully cleaned and cooked for a long time if fresh or dried. Very
expensive, but worth it at times, I think.*

VEAL ROAST WITH MORELS IN CREAM

6-pound boned and tied loin or leg of veal
½ cup thinly sliced onion
¼ cup small-diced carrots
¼ cup small-diced celery
Few sprigs parsley
1 clove garlic (you may omit)
Salt and white pepper
1 cup dry white wine

[Preheat oven to 450°.] Place veal in a shallow pan, uncovered, large
enough to hold the veal. Put in oven for 15 minutes. Remove from
oven [reduce heat to 350°] and put vegetables around the veal.
Sprinkle with salt and white pepper. Return to oven. Pour some of the
wine around the veal after 15 minutes. Baste frequently with the rest
of wine and drippings. Roast about 1 hour if a loin roast, about 1
hour and 20 minutes if cut from the leg. The temperature on a meat
thermometer should be 170°. Do not overcook. Remove strings and
transfer to a warm serving platter or tray. Serve with the juices and:

MORELS IN CREAM
½ pound dried morels
3 tablespoons butter
1 tablespoon flour
1 cup whipping or sour cream

Rinse morels thoroughly many times until all sand is removed and let
soak for several hours in cold water.

[Slice the mushrooms and pat dry.] Melt butter, add morels and sauté
until they are shiny. Add flour and cook 1 minute. Add cream and
simmer for 5 minutes. You may use canned morels, chanterelles or
fresh mushrooms in place of morels.

❧ *Previously Unpublished*

STUFFED RACK OF VEAL
For 6

Allow a half-pound of meat and bones per person. Ask the butcher to "French" the ends of the rib bones, cut away the chine bone and remove the layer of fat over the ribs, and ask for a pocket to be cut into the top side of the rack.

> 3-pound rack of veal
> 2 tablespoons minced onion
> 2 tablespoons butter
> ¼ cup minced parsley
> ¼ cup pine nuts
> 1 cup finely chopped cooked ham
> ¼ cup mozzarella cheese
> Salt and pepper
> 1 cup dry white wine
> Butter

Preheat oven to 350°. Sauté the onion in butter until it is transparent, but not browned; add parsley and cook 1 minute. Stir in the nuts and ham. Cool and mix in the grated cheese. Stuff into the veal pocket, distributing it evenly over the ribs. Salt and pepper to taste. Tie securely and place in a shallow roasting pan and roast for 1 hour. Baste with white wine and a little butter, since veal is so lean. Remove to a hot platter. Skim fat from pan juices and pass them in a heated sauce dish.

This stuffing would be good in Rock Cornish Game Hens or chicken. Or baked inside small pastries to serve with cocktails.

Over the years my cooks have greeted me with "What do we scallopini today?" Since I like the flavor, I really do scallopini almost every cut of meat and poultry. These have been among my most popular luncheon entrées.

VEAL PATTIES SCALLOPINI
For 8

2 pounds ground veal
½ cup finely minced onion
1 small clove garlic, finely minced
2 teaspoons salt
½ teaspoon white pepper
2 eggs
½ cup flour
½ cup grated Parmesan cheese
½ cup butter
¼ cup olive oil
1 cup Marsala wine
½ cup chicken broth

Mix the first six ingredients [veal, onion, garlic, salt, pepper and slightly beaten eggs] and form into patties, 2 inches in diameter. Flatten with palm of your hand. Dust lightly with mixture of flour and Parmesan. Let stand at least 1 hour. Sauté in butter and olive oil until brown. Remove from pan. Add Marsala and chicken broth to pan. Cook until slightly thickened [stirring and scraping the bits of meat into the sauce]. Correct seasonings. Pour over patties. Allow at least two patties for each serving.

Meatballs for a gourmet dinner, for a cocktail tidbit, and especially for Potluck—these have taken top priority for all meatballs.

VEAL AND PORK MEATBALLS
For 6

1½ pounds ground veal
¼ pound ground fresh pork
3 tablespoons butter [divided use]
1½ hard rolls or 1½ slices dry bread
2 tablespoons grated onion
½ teaspoon grated lemon peel
3 eggs, beaten
½ teaspoon pepper
1 teaspoon salt
1 tablespoon lemon juice
1 teaspoon Worcestershire sauce
Chopped parsley
1½ quarts stock or bouillon

Mix meats with 2 tablespoons butter [butter should be soft, not melted]. Moisten rolls with water; when soft, squeeze water out and mix bread with meat. Cook onion in remaining butter until browned. Add to meat mixture with lemon peel, eggs, pepper, salt, lemon juice, Worcestershire and parsley. Mix thoroughly. Shape in 12 balls (or 48 small ones for a cocktail tidbit). Heat bouillon or stock to boiling; drop balls in and simmer, covered, 15 minutes. Remove from stock with slotted spoon to a warmed dish and make:

GRAVY
2 tablespoons butter
2 tablespoons flour
2 cups stock in which the meatballs cooked
2 tablespoons chopped parsley
2 tablespoons capers
½ cup buttered crumbs

Stir the butter and flour mixed together into hot stock [or form into small balls and drop into hot stock]; cook and stir until smooth and boiling. Add parsley, capers and crumbs. Serve the meatballs on noodles or with Späetzle [page 290].

OSSO BUCO
For 4

10 pounds veal knuckles (each knuckle could weigh ½ pound,
    so allow 2 per person)
1 cup flour
1 tablespoon salt
½ teaspoon white pepper
½ cup butter
½ cup olive oil
3 cups sliced onion
4 or more garlic cloves
8 ripe tomatoes, peeled and quartered
2 bay leaves
1 cup chopped parsley
12 peppercorns
Rind of 3 lemons
2 cups dry white wine
Chicken broth to cover
[Small boiling onions]
[Lemon]

Dredge knuckles in the flour, salt and pepper. Melt the butter in a
skillet, add the olive oil and brown each knuckle. Place in a large
roasting pan. Add the onion and garlic to skillet and cook until onion
is soft. Add to meat with butter left in skillet. Stir in the remaining
ingredients [tomatoes, bay leaves, parsley, peppercorns, lemon rind,
wine, and broth] and cover. Use foil if you do not have a cover.
Simmer at low heat until meat is tender and bone is soft. Add more
liquid if necessary. Remove meat, strain the sauce. Correct seasonings.
Pour sauce over the meat and let stand in the liquid until ready to
serve. Allow about 3 hours for this preparation. You may simmer
(covered) in the oven also. Add thin slices of lemon just before
serving—and I add boiled little white onions. Serve a cocktail fork
along with it so the marrow inside the knuckles can be eaten. My
men's cooking class sure did like these.

PORK

The "little pig who goes to market" saw America first some 400 years ago with the Spanish explorer, De Soto. Since then there has been more controversy over how to cook it; when, or IF you should eat it, than time allows to tell. By all means eat it.

PORK LOIN [HERBED]
For 10 or 12

5 pound boneless pork loin
2 cups dry white wine
Fresh thyme, rosemary and tarragon
2 tablespoons salt
2 tablespoons Dijon mustard
4 tablespoons brown sugar
Garlic clove, crushed
Celery stalk, sliced
Onion
Carrot

Marinate a boned pork loin in wine mixed with fresh herbs overnight in the refrigerator. I like a bit of thyme, rosemary and tarragon. Remove the herbs, save marinade. [Preheat oven to 450°.] Rub pork on either side with salt, mustard, brown sugar. Place in roasting pan with garlic, and celery, onion, carrot. Bake covered for 30 minutes. Remove cover, baste with marinade, reduce heat to 350°. Roast uncovered, basting frequently, about 2 hours [or until meat thermometer shows 160° internal temperature]. Remove meat and pour off excess fat. Add:

1 tablespoon of flour mixed with
1 tablespoon of soft butter

Cook until brown. Add pan juices to half water, half beef consommé, to make 1 cup for this amount of flour. Season with more salt and white pepper, if necessary. I like to add a little apple or currant jelly, about 1 tablespoon for each cup of sauce.

The easiest way to remove fat is to pour all the drippings into a glass. The fat comes to the top so you can see it.

≈ Previously Unpublished

From France comes this luscious

PORK LOIN STUFFED WITH PRUNES
For 4 to 6

3 to 3½-pound boneless pork loin
1   12-ounce package pitted cooked prunes
1 onion, sliced
1½ teaspoons dry mustard
½ teaspoon dried thyme
Salt and pepper
3 tablespoons butter
Dry white wine and water
Cornstarch or arrowroot for gravy

Cut a lengthwise slit into the center of the pork loin, carve out a triangle of meat lengthwise down the center of each half, removing enough meat so that the prunes can stand on edge when the loin is put back together into a roll. When it is carved, each circle of pork should have a slice of prune in its center.

Trim the loin of visible outside fat. Prepare the prunes according to package directions, undercooking them. Insert about 12 to 15 prunes in the trench. Push the onion slices in beside them. Put the roast back into its original shape and tie with clean kitchen twine. Refrigerate for a few hours or overnight. Preheat oven to 425°. Lay the loin in a shallow roasting pan and rub with a mixture of mustard and thyme. Melt butter and pour over the meat; roast uncovered in oven for 50 to 60 minutes. Sprinkle with salt and pepper to taste. Reduce the oven heat to 300° and roast for an additional hour or to 160° internal temperature, basting frequently with white wine laced with water or chicken bouillon. Remove to a heated plate to rest for about 15 minutes before slicing.

Skim off the fat from the pan drippings. Allow ½ teaspoon of corn-starch or arrowroot to each cup of meat juices. Mix a little cool water into the thickener and stir into a thin paste before you add it back into the hot pan juices; continue to stir while the gravy thickens. Serve with Sautéed Apples [page 274].

Pork has an affinity for fruit and especially for citrus fruit.

FLORIDA PORK LOIN
For 4 to 6

3-pound pork loin, boned or not (there is always more flavor if
    the bone is left in)
2 teaspoons salt
½ teaspoon Tabasco
¼ cup finely chopped onion
½ cup orange juice
½ cup water
1 lemon sliced thin
Cornstarch or arrowroot

[Preheat oven to 300°.] Rub the pork with salt and Tabasco. Place in a
skillet with the onion and brown on both sides. Remove and pour off
the fat, and return meat to skillet. Baste frequently with the orange
juice and water, and bake uncovered for 2 hours at 300° or until done
[160° internal temperature]. Add the lemon slices on the top side the
last 30 minutes. Drain off the excess fat and thicken the [pan] juices
with a very little cornstarch or arrowroot—about ½ teaspoon to 1 cup
of liquid.

Serve with thick slices of tomato baked until soft, and covered with
mayonnaise flavored with garlic and run under the broiler, and
broccoli undercooked and sprinkled with Parmesan cheese and
poppyseeds—no butter is necessary. This pork is good cold also—
and cold roast pork sandwiches made on raisin bread are terrific.

❧ *Previously Unpublished*

CHAR SIEU
For 12

4 pork tenderloins
1 teaspoon salt
½ teaspoon pepper
½ teaspoon ground ginger
2 teaspoons sugar (white, brown or 1 tablespoon honey)
2 tablespoons sherry
½ cup soy sauce

Rub the tenderloins with a mixture of salt, pepper, dried ginger and sweetening. Let them stand in the refrigerator several hours or overnight. Mix sherry and soy sauce and pour over the tenderloins; marinate for at least 20 minutes, or even several hours if you want a stronger Oriental flavor. Preheat oven to 350°. Drain the meat, reserving the marinade to use as a baste. Lay the meat on a lightly oiled baking pan and roast uncovered for 20 minutes. Turn and continue to roast for another 20 minutes, basting frequently. Remove to a warm plate and slice across the grain into ¼-inch thick pieces. You can serve it plain or with Hot Mustard Sauce [page 227].

Stuffed pork chops are always company fare. You should engage your butcher in flattering conversation and have him cut the pockets for the stuffing.

STUFFED PORK CHOPS
For 8

2 cups frozen corn
2 cups white bread crumbs
1 teaspoon salt
¼ teaspoon pepper
1 tablespoon chopped onion
2 tablespoons chopped parsley
1 tablespoon butter
1 egg, beaten
1 cup chopped [and peeled] fresh apple
¼ cup cream
1 teaspoon poultry seasoning
8 pork chops [cut extra-thick]
Salt and pepper
1 cup stock or water

[Preheat oven to 325°.] Mix corn, crumbs, salt and pepper. Sauté onion and parsley in butter, add to corn mixture with the beaten egg and apple. Stir in the cream with a light touch; add poultry seasoning, stuff pockets in pork chops, and brown on both sides in a heavy skillet. Sprinkle with salt and pepper, pour 1 cup stock or water in pan, cover, and bake for 1½ or 2 hours. Add more liquid, if necessary. Please do these; they are so good!

The young fry of today are the gourmets of tomorrow, and that goes for some of them right this minute. I am thrown for a recipe every so often for the under-twelve set, who are bored with the same old thing. Let's face this interest of theirs with foods that are different both in appearance and in taste.

FRUITED PORK CHOPS
For 6

3 strips bacon
2 tablespoons chopped onion
1 cup soft bread crumbs
1 cup peeled chopped raw apple
¾ cup chopped cooked prunes
6 pork chops, cut 1-inch thick
Salt and pepper
Flour
½ cup pineapple juice
½ cup Sauterne

Mince bacon and cook until almost crisp. Add onion and cook 3 minutes (medium heat). Add crumbs, apple and prunes. Cut a slit in each chop and fill with the stuffing and fasten with a toothpick. Sprinkle with salt, pepper and flour. Brown in a heavy skillet, pour off fat and add the pineapple juice and wine. Cover and either bake at 325° or cook on top of the stove at low heat until tender, about 1 hour. Add more juice if necessary, or water.

HAM STEAK À LA BOURGUIGNONNE

I would suggest you buy a whole bone-in ham and have the butcher cut two 2-inch steaks through the center. You can use the rest of the ham for baking or boiling. Rub the steaks with Dijon mustard, cover with honey and dry red wine and marinate for several hours or overnight. [Save marinade.] Place ham on your broiling rack and broil for 20 to 30 minutes, 5 inches from heating element, basting frequently with marinade. Slice thinly and serve. You may do ahead of time and reheat. Cover with mushrooms sautéed in butter and red wine. I use the entire mushroom, split in half; allow 3 mushrooms per person. I also like to stuff prunes with sharp Cheddar cheese and marinate with the ham; broil the prunes with the ham the last 5 minutes.

The smell of home cooking is always a welcome sign, especially on a
cool night, and this one I like to do in a casserole.

HAWAIIAN HAM
For 4 or 6

Slice of ham, 2 inches thick [Center is best]
1 tablespoon honey
½ cup water
½ cup sugar
½ cup sherry
½ cup raisins
½ cup canned pineapple chunks

[Preheat oven to 325°.] Place ham, honey and water in casserole and
simmer on top of stove until water has evaporated. Add the rest of the
ingredients [sugar, sherry and fruit]. Cover and cook in oven until
tender, about 1 hour. Remove cover and continue cooking until the
sauce is transparent looking. Cut in thin slices and serve it with a
Corn Pudding [page 254]—I like to do the puddings in individual
soufflé cups—then spill buttered peas over them. Same old thing, but
they look pretty. Or you could bake it in a ring mold and fill the
center with any green vegetable.

HAM STEAK WITH ONION GRAVY
For 8

6 tablespoons butter
8 6-ounce ham steaks, horseshoe cut ½-inch thick
¼ cup hot [strong] coffee
2 cups thinly sliced onion
1 tablespoon flour
1 cup sour cream

Melt the butter in a skillet, add ham steaks and pan fry at medium
heat until lightly browned. Baste with the coffee. Remove and keep
warm on serving platter. Add the onion to the pan and sauté at low
heat until soft and yellow. Add the flour and cook until bubbly. Add
the sour cream, and thoroughly heat, but do not boil. Pour over the
ham steaks; run under broiler for a few seconds.

❧ *Previously Unpublished*

CHOUCROUTE GARNI
For 10 to 12

¼ pound salt pork
2 pounds (5 cups) sauerkraut, in chilled plastic bags or canned
1 medium onion
Freshly ground pepper
Dry white wine
2- to 3-pound boneless ham
2 tablespoons honey
1 teaspoon dry mustard
2-pound boneless pork loin
Apple cider
6 Polish sausages
Dry red wine
6 knockwurst
12 small new or red potatoes
¼ cup butter
½ cup minced parsley

Dice the salt pork, leaving the bottom attached to the heavy rind for easy removal before serving. Empty sauerkraut into a colander and run cold water through it; drain. Place salt pork and kraut in the bottom of a deep kettle. Bury a whole onion in the kraut and grind some black pepper over the top. Mix equal parts of white wine and water to cover the kraut. Bring rapidly to a boil, then reduce the heat to low, cover and simmer for 4 hours, or place the covered pan in a 325° oven for about the same length of time. Occasionally stir the kraut off the bottom of the pot.

Bake the ham according to your favorite method. Rub a mixture of honey and mustard over the pork loin and roast uncovered in a 325° oven until a meat thermometer registers 160°. Baste with cider or water during roasting. Poach the Polish sausage in red wine for 20 minutes; simmer the knockwurst in water for 10 minutes. Boil or steam the potatoes until tender. Dress them with melted butter and parsley, correct seasonings and turn them into a heated vegetable bowl.

Drain sauerkraut and pile it in the center of a large heated platter. Slice the ham and pork into thin slices, alternating and overlapping them around the kraut. Cut the sausages into easily handled portions and arrange them over the sauerkraut. Serve with boiled potatoes, prepared horseradish and both mild and hot mustards.

HAM LOAF
For 6

2 eggs
4 cups ground ham
1 teaspoon baking powder
1 teaspoon Worcestershire sauce
1 cup light cream [half-and-half]
1 cup bread crumbs

[Preheat oven to 375°.] Beat eggs, add ham and rest of ingredients; mix thoroughly. Butter a 2-quart loaf pan and line with waxed paper. Fill and spread with:

½ cup brown sugar
1 teaspoon flour
1 teaspoon prepared mustard
Vinegar to moisten

Set pan in hot water and bake for about one hour.

For a cool evening supper, glazed ham balls and baked beans.

GLAZED HAM BALLS
For 8

1½ pounds ground cured ham
1½ pounds ground fresh ham
1¼ cups milk
2½ cups bread crumbs
1½ cups brown sugar
¾ cup vinegar
¾ cup water
1½ teaspoons dry mustard

Mix first four ingredients [ham, milk and crumbs] and let stand for 1 hour. Form into balls. Melt brown sugar in skillet, add vinegar, water, and mustard. Boil 15 minutes and pour over the ham balls. Cover and bake at 350° for 30 minutes. Uncover and bake 30 minutes longer.

HAM CRÊPES

16 thin slices baked or canned ham or prosciutto
16 thin slices Gruyère cheese
16 thin crêpes [page 91 or purchase ready made]
4 tablespoons butter
4 tablespoons flour
4 cups milk or half-and-half
¼ cup cognac
Salt and white pepper
Grated Parmesan cheese
Paprika

[Preheat oven to 350°.] Place a slice of ham and cheese the same
length on each crêpe and roll. Place crêpes in a shallow casserole.
Melt butter, add flour and cook 1 minute. [Gradually] pour in milk;
cook until thickened. Heat cognac, ignite, add to sauce and cook 5
minutes. Season to your taste. Pour sauce over crêpes. Sprinkle with
Parmesan cheese and paprika. Bake until brown. You may prepare
the day before and reheat, or freeze for a few days. A thin slice of
chicken may also be added to the crêpes. Substitute sour cream for
the sauce sometime!

LAMB

*Spring Lamb is an overworked expression, but if it makes everyone feel
better, more power to the lamb. However, facts about lamb are good to
know. The meat from lambs three to five months old is known as
"spring lamb," and is in season from April through June. Because of
the preference for the taste of lamb, rather than mutton, most of the
sheep are killed before they are a year old, as the younger the animal,
the more delicate the flavor. The flesh of both lamb and mutton should
be fine-grained and smooth, the color of lamb should be deep pink,
and of mutton a dark red. The fat of lamb should be white and firm,
and of mutton the fat is pink and really hard. Lamb for the most part
is cooked well done except for lamb chops, which are better if broiled
until medium done. Of course, some strange characters like me like
them burnt rare—burned black on the outside and rare on the inside.
When you feel adventurous sometime, try them.*

My favorite lamb dish is

STUFFED LAMB CHOPS

Have the butcher cut lamb chops thick—at least 2 inches. Split the
lean part of the meat in half, cutting to the bone. [For each chop you
will need]:

    2 fresh mushrooms
    2 chicken livers
    Butter
    Salt and pepper
    Olive oil
    Garlic salt

Chop mushrooms and chicken livers and sauté in butter until done,
but not brown. Season with salt and pepper and stuff in the chop.
Rub [chops] with olive oil and sprinkle with garlic salt. Repeat for as
many chops as desired. Broil under a high heat on both sides until
brown. Turn only once. Serve with fresh under-cooked spinach that
has been finely chopped in an electric blender, if you have one [or
food prcessor with steel blade], and dressed with heavy cream and
Parmesan cheese.

LEMON ROASTED LAMB
For 8 to 12

6-pound leg or shoulder of lamb, trimmed
4 cloves garlic
1½ teaspoons salt or salt substitute
½ teaspoon white pepper
½ teaspoon paprika
1 tablespoon fresh or dried mint leaves
2 tablespoons lemon juice

[Preheat oven to 400°.] Cut 16 tiny pockets, 1 inch deep, all over the lamb. Cut garlic into fourths and stick one into each pocket. Mix remaining ingredients [salt, pepper, paprika, mint, and lemon juice] and rub over surface of lamb. Place fat-side-up on a rack in an open pan. Do not cover. Insert a meat thermometer in flesh, away from bone. Roast for 15 minutes. Reduce heat to 325° and cook for 1½ hours or until meat thermometer registers 170° for medium rare (best for flavor) or 180° for well done. Remove from oven and remove garlic. Let stand at least 10 minutes before carving. Slice thin; strain any fat from juices left in pan before serving. Good cold, too.

Any picnic is elegant with:

LEG OF LAMB IN PASTRY

1 boned leg of lamb, 5- to 6-pound size or smaller
2 cloves garlic
Salt and pepper
2 teaspoons dried or 2 sprigs of fresh rosemary
2 tablespoons melted butter
White wine or consommé
1 [double] Pie Crust [page 358]
1 egg mixed with
2 tablespoons cold water

[Preheat oven to 450°.] Rub leg with garlic, salt and pepper. Cut a few slivers of the garlic and insert into slits here and there in the flesh. Sprinkle with the rosemary and butter. Roast uncovered for 15 minutes. Reduce the heat to 350° and roast about 10 minutes for each pound or to 140° on your meat thermometer. Baste frequently with the wine or consommé. Remove from oven and cool. Shape the meat as well as you can to look like original leg. Roll out pie crust about ⅛ inch thick, large enough to cover the meat; allow 3 inches in length and 2 inches in width to overlap. Place seam side down on an ungreased cookie sheet. Roll out some of the dough and cut into decorative pieces and fashion over the pastry. Bake at 425° for 10 to 15 minutes. Brush with egg and cold water and return to oven. Continue to bake until pastry is brown, brushing once more during baking with the egg wash.

LEG OF LAMB, MUSLIM-STYLE

2 tablespoons grated fresh ginger
3 cloves garlic, crushed
1 cup [plain] yogurt
1½ teaspoons salt
¼ teaspoon black pepper
Juice of 2 limes
4- to 5-pound leg of lamb, boned
1 tablespoon ground coriander
½ teaspoon cayenne pepper
½ teaspoon ground cinnamon
½ teaspoon ground cloves
½ teaspoon ground cardamom

Mix ginger, garlic, yogurt, salt, pepper and lime juice. Make several gashes in the lamb and spread mixture over the surface. Marinate overnight [in the refrigerator. Preheat oven to 450°.] Mix spices and put into a small skillet on medium heat. Cool, sprinkle over lamb. Roast for 15 minutes. Reduce heat to 350°, and roast for 40 minutes longer, for medium rare (150° on your meat thermometer), longer if you wish it well done (165° on your thermometer). Remove, let rest. Slice thin and serve with strained juices from roasting pan.

LAMB DIJON
Serves 10

3 tablespoons Dijon mustard
3 teaspoons salt
2 cloves garlic, minced
⅓ cup olive oil
3 single racks of lamb, trimmed
1½ cups dry red wine
2 tablespoons honey

Mix mustard, salt, garlic and oil. Rub over the racks and let stand for several hours. [Preheat oven to 375°.] Roast for 40 minutes, basting with the wine and honey. Serve with juices. Cook longer for well done, but I think you will enjoy lamb pink—at least give it a try.

LAMB CURRY

¼ cup butter
¾ cup diced onion
1 teaspoon sugar
1 teaspoon salt
3 pounds lean lamb, cut in 1-inch pieces
¼ cup diced preserved ginger
2 tablespoons curry powder
1 teaspoon chopped mint, fresh or flakes
1 tablespoon flour
2 cups chicken broth
1½ cups half-and-half [or cream, divided use]
¼ cup shredded coconut
2 tablespoons lime juice

Melt the butter, add the onion, sugar and salt. Sauté until yellow. Add the lamb and cook at medium heat until lamb is tender. Add ginger, curry powder and mint. Cook 1 minute. Add flour and cook 1 minute. [Gradually] pour in chicken broth and cook until liquid is reduced by one-half. Stir in 1 cup of the half-and-half and coconut. Cook until thickened. Add lime juice and rest of half-and-half. Heat thoroughly, but do not boil. You may prepare ahead and freeze.

[A list of suggested condiments will be found on page 145.—Editor]

The elegant look of a Crown Roast of Lamb can never be lauded enough. Fill the center with a Mushroom Soufflé and your taste buds and your eyes will love this entrée.

CROWN ROAST OF LAMB
For 8

1 crown roast of lamb, consisting of 16 well-tied chops
Salt and pepper
1 clove garlic, slivered

[Preheat oven to 400°.] Sprinkle lamb inside and out with salt and pepper. Trim all fat. Insert garlic here and there. Place an empty can in center to make a smooth well to hold the Mushroom Soufflé. Cover the chop ends with foil. Roast for 20 minutes. Remove from oven. Remove can. Pour off all fat. Cut out a circle of foil to cover bottom of roast and place the roast on it. Fill the center with Mushroom Soufflé [page 261] and sprinkle Parmesan cheese over the filling. Return to oven and bake at 350° for 40 minutes. Slide onto a heated platter and remove foil and strings.

When serving lamb, place a dish of spiced or minted fruit near it. Sometimes drain canned peach halves and fill with Major Grey's chutney; bake them on a lower oven rack with the lamb for the last 20 to 30 minutes.

The following sauce may be passed with the Lamb and Soufflé: Add 1 cup beef consommé to roasting pan, and cook for 5 minutes. Add 1 tablespoon currant jelly, 1 tablespoon red wine vinegar. Cook until jelly is melted. Carve 1 double chop for each guest, including some of the Soufflé. Pass the sauce. There will be more than enough Soufflé to fill the lamb. Put the rest in a buttered soufflé dish and bake along with the lamb.

A lamb chop grill is a good company dish.

LAMB CHOP GRILL

For each serving, you will need:

 1 lamb chop (1 rib)
 1 tablespoon butter
 2 links pork sausage
 1 chicken liver
 1 bacon curl
 2 mushroom caps
 [Additional butter]

[Position oven rack 3- to 4-inches below broiler unit and preheat.] Brush the chop with butter and place under broiler for 5 minutes on each side. Pan-fry sausage and chicken liver. Roll bacon into a curl and sauté until crisp. Sauté mushroom caps in butter. Arrange on a hot platter and serve with thin Blueberry Pancakes with whipped Lemon Butter [page 94].

Loin lamb chops are less expensive than rib chops as a rule. Those people who do not like lamb like them this way.

LAMB CHOPS À LA SUISSE
For 4

 4   8-ounce loin lamb chops
 Salt and pepper
 ½ cup chopped mushrooms or stems
 2 tablespoons butter
 2 tablespoons sherry
 4 thin slices Swiss or Muenster cheese

[Position oven rack 3- to 4-inches from broiler unit and preheat.] Broil seasoned chops under low heat about 10 minutes on each side. Place in a casserole or heat proof platter. Sauté the mushrooms in the butter and sherry. Pour over the chops. Cover with the cheese, and run under the broiler. In fact, you can cover up many not-so-good-looking meat dishes by adding Swiss or Muenster cheese on top and melting under the broiler. Good for left over stew!

Fish and Seafood

I like fish. But when I suggest fish to housewives as a way to add variety to their menus, I usually am met with "I hate fish!" The Dutch theologian, Erasmus, said of fish on Fridays, "My heart is Catholic; my stomach is Lutheran."

Delectable fish dishes can be served from the . . . kitchen—if the desire is great enough. But fish should be treated with respect; never overcooked, and always eaten when ready. It is not a "keep hot in the oven" dish.

And they say it is good food for thinking! Anyhow, catch (or buy) it and cook it; don't keep it. Quick-frozen fish has the original flavor but as soon as it comes into the kitchen, cook it.

In buying fish, allow from ½ to ¾ pound per serving with the bone in—or ¼ pound boned. Wash it well inside and out and wipe dry.

When buying a whole fish in the market, be sure the fish looks you in the eye with a healthy stare. You cannot tell about one that has been skinned and boned, so smell it and cook as soon as possible after you buy or catch, or freeze it. Don't overcook.

SALMON MOUSSE

1 tablespoon unflavored gelatin, softened in
¼ cup cold water
1 cup hot sour cream (do not boil)
1 pound canned or 2 cups leftover cooked salmon or fish
¼ cup mayonnaise
1 tablespoon grated onion
¼ cup finely chopped celery
1 cup whipping [or heavy] cream
Salt and white pepper to taste

Add softened gelatin to hot sour cream. Cool. Add the salmon, mayonnaise, onion and celery. When mixture begins to congeal, fold in
the cream, whipped. Correct seasonings and pour into a wet mold [or
lightly oil it]. Chill. Decorate with slices of pimento and black olives.
[See molded salads, page 97].

*This lovely light entrée is perfect for lunch or as an appetite teasing first
course.*

FILLET OF SOLE MOLD
For 8

4 fillets of sole
Juice of 1 lemon
1 cup finely chopped mushrooms
4 tablespoons whipped butter
1 pound white crabmeat or any white fish, flaked
½ cup soft white bread crumbs
¾ cup skim milk
4 eggs, beaten
3 tablespoons melted whipped butter
2 tablespoons lemon juice
Salt and white pepper

[Preheat oven to 350°.] Line a lightly buttered 2-quart ovenproof bowl
or soufflé dish with the sole fillets sprinkled with the lemon juice.
Lightly sauté the mushrooms in the butter. Mix with the crabmeat or
white fish. Soak the bread in the milk and squeeze dry. Add to the
crab mixture. Pour in the eggs and butter. Blend in the 2 tablespoons

lemon juice and season with salt and white pepper. Pour into the fish-lined mold. Cover with foil or wax paper. Place in a pan of hot water and bake for 1 hour. Unmold on a heated serving tray and serve with:

SHRIMP AND DILL SAUCE
2 tablespoons whipped butter
1 cup uncooked small shrimp
2 tablespoons flour
2 cups skim milk
2 teaspoons lemon juice
1 teaspoon dill weed
Dash of cayenne

Melt butter; add shrimp and sauté until pink (about 1 minute). Add flour; cook 1 minute. [Gradually] pour in milk and cook until thickened. Add lemon juice, dill and cayenne.

RED SNAPPER WITH COCONUT

[Preheat oven to 300°.] Dip fillets of red snapper in pineapple juice. Dot generously with butter, sprinkle with salt and paprika. Bake [in a single layer] until partially done. Cover with fresh grated or canned coconut. Return to oven until done. Baste frequently [with pan juices]. Serve with fresh lime slices.

OVEN BAKED FRESH SALMON STEAKS
For 4

¼ cup lemon juice
1 teaspoon grated lemon peel
1 clove garlic, crushed
½ teaspoon paprika
4   6-ounce salmon steaks
1 teaspoon chopped chives
Thin lemon slices

[Preheat oven to 350°.] Mix lemon juice, peel, garlic and paprika. Rub over salmon and place on oven broiling pan. Bake for 20 minutes. Baste [with pan juices]. Then turn on broiler and brown. Sprinkle on chives just before serving. Serve with a twist of lemon and Swedish Cucumbers [page 126].

Stuffed fish of any kind makes it a company dish! You may use this for trout, snapper, or flounder.

STUFFED FISH
For 8

2 cups cooked shrimp or crabmeat, chopped
2 eggs [lightly beaten]
1 cup cream [divided use]
2 tablespoons butter
½ cup chopped canned or fresh mushrooms
2 teaspoons chopped chives
1 tablespoon flour
1 3- to 4-pound trout or snapper, split and boned
Salt and paprika
4 tablespoons sherry
2 limes

[Preheat oven to 350°.] Mix the shrimp [or crab], eggs and ½ cup of the cream together. Melt butter, add mushrooms and chives and sauté until soft; add flour and cook until bubbly. Add shrimp mixture and cook until thick. Place fish in a buttered baking dish and spread the mixture between the two sides of the fish. Pour the remaining cream over, sprinkle with salt and paprika. Add sherry and bake for 45 minutes. Serve with fresh lime quarters. When stuffing small flounder (and the ½- to ¾-pound size are best), slit along the backbone and cut the flesh of the fish away from the bone but leave intact. Spoon as much stuffing into slit as possible.

Rub fresh pineapple spears or those canned in their own juice with curry powder and then bake. They are good with any fish when you are not serving a sauce.

Mild-flavored fish, like flounder or red snapper, have an affinity for grapefruit, and especially when combined with white wine.

FLOUNDER
For 4

4 ½-pound flounders
Salt
2 tablespoons butter
2 tablespoons olive oil
1 tablespoon chopped onion
1 tablespoon chopped parsley
1 cup dry white wine
12 grapefruit sections
[1 lime]

[Preheat oven to 450°.] Sprinkle the flounder with salt. Melt the butter with the olive oil; add the onion, parsley and wine. Lay the flounder in and simmer for 5 or 10 minutes. Place the grapefruit sections on top; put in oven and bake until the top is brown—about 15 minutes. Serve at once with a wedge of fresh lime in place of the usual lemon.

TROUT AMANDINE
For 4

4 6- to 8-ounce fillets of Gulf trout
Salt and flour
½ cup butter [divided use]
½ teaspoon onion juice
¼ cup blanched, finely slivered almonds
1 tablespoon lemon juice

Wash and dry the fish. Dust lightly with salt and flour. Heat half the butter and onion juice in a heavy skillet and cook fish until a light brown. Remove and place on a hot serving dish. Pour off the grease left in pan and add remaining butter to the same pan. Add the almonds and brown slowly. Add lemon juice and when the mixture foams, pour it over the fish. Garnish with something green.

POACHED RED SNAPPER
For 8

1 6-pound red snapper
Salt and white pepper
1 bay leaf
½ onion, sliced
1 stalk celery, sliced
¼ carrot, sliced
Few sprigs parsley
Few slices of lemon

Sprinkle fish cavity with salt and pepper and fill with rest of ingredients [bay leaf, vegetables, parsley and lemon slices]. Wrap in foil, shiny side in, with foil overlapping on top. Place in a roasting pan on a rack. Pour boiling water over until top of rack is reached. Cover and steam for 30 minutes; water should simmer. Test with a fork for fish to flake. (That is why you have the foil overlapping on top of fish.) Remove fish to serving platter, and slip foil out. Remove vegetables and with a sharp knife strip off the skin from the gills to the base of the tail. When serving, cut in portions to the backbone, then remove bone and cut lower half. Use the same method for poaching whole salmon—that is if you do not have a fish poacher. I personally like a cold sauce with the hot fish—this one especially:

CUCUMBER SAUCE
3 cups chopped cucumbers, peeled and seeded
⅓ cup chopped green onion
1 ½ teaspoons lemon juice
1 ½ cups sour cream
2 tablespoons mayonnaise
Few drops Worcestershire sauce
Salt and white pepper

Mix and season to taste.

Being a fish eater, I am interested in ways of broiling fish. These methods I have found to my liking and to that of my customers:

BROILED FISH

Whether for a whole or filleted fish, I start it in a 350° oven with salt and butter sprinkled over and a little water in the bottom of the pan. If it is a "pale" fish, I sprinkle it lightly with paprika, but no pepper. (George Rector told me a long time ago not to pepper fish. I was convinced, and have never done so since.) When the fish is tender (it will take from 15 to 20 minutes, depending on its thickness), add more butter and place 2 inches below the broiler heat to crisp on top. Remove and serve at once with more melted butter and lemon or lime.

Variations:
Cover the fish, especially flounder, with light cream [or half-and-half] and proceed as above, or

Cover fish with a mixture of half mayonnaise and half Thick Cream Sauce [page 223], and proceed as above, or

Cover with Imperial Sauce [page 222] and proceed as above.

To pep up melted butter for any broiled fish, add to each ½ cup of butter:

1 teaspoon anchovy paste
   or
2 tablespoons chopped chives
   or
¼ cup of any finely diced shellfish
   or
1 tablespoon grated onion browned in additional butter
   or
½ cup browned finely chopped almonds
   or
2 teaspoons prepared mustard
   or
1 tablespoon lemon juice and 1 teaspoon of grated lemon peel
   or
2 tablespoons finely chopped parsley or watercress.

If you are in Texas over a reasonable time you will, no doubt, find yourself frying fish. Those fishermen think they know how, too. Some insist the fish must have been swimming on its right side going down the left side of the water, but be that as it may, FRY it!

FRIED FISH
For 4

4 Gulf trout or red snapper fillets or small whole fish
1 egg white, lightly beaten
1 cup corn meal, salted to suit your taste
1 cup vegetable shortening or peanut oil

Wash and dry the fish, dip in egg white, then in salted corn meal. Heat oil in heavy skillet and fry fish in hot fat until brown. Turn once. Serve with lemon and Tartar or Peppy Cocktail Sauce [pages 119 and 225].

Lump crabmeat is a delicacy you should cultivate. Expensive but worth it. . . . The delicate flavor and texture of lump crabmeat has an affinity for both fruits and vegetables, and especially so with white meat of chicken and the flavor of smoked meats.

CRABMEAT CASSEROLE (OR SOUFFLÉ)
For 8 or 10

4 tablespoons butter
4 tablespoons flour
1¼ cups milk
1 teaspoon salt
Freshly ground black pepper
1 tablespoon Madeira (you may omit)
1 tablespoon lemon juice
4 eggs, separated
6½ ounces canned crabmeat
1 cup cooked finely slivered ham
1 cup cooked finely slivered white meat of chicken
Parmesan cheese

[Preheat oven to 350°.] Melt the butter, add the flour and cook until bubbly. [Gradually] add the milk and cook until thick. Add seasonings, Madeira and lemon juice. Add egg yolks and crabmeat, ham and chicken. Beat egg whites until stiff. Fold in cooled crab mixture and pour into an unbuttered 3-quart casserole. Sprinkle with Parmesan cheese and bake for 45 minutes (in a warm water bath). Serve with Newburg sauce or a Thin Cream Sauce with slivers of pineapple added to it [pages 225 and 223].

With it, canned or fresh pineapple fingers sprinkled with brown sugar and fresh mint or flakes and baked at the same time. A tray of thick slices of avocado and tomato quarters, and hot bread sticks would make an interesting supper, with a tray of homemade cookies.

The delicate subtle flavor of crabmeat is always an addition to any table—and I like this for many occasions.

CRABMEAT LORENZO
For 8 to 10

½ cup finely chopped green onions
1 cup finely chopped mushrooms
½ cup butter
½ tablespoon Dijon mustard
½ cup dry white wine
1 cup Thin Cream Sauce [page 223]
½ cup half-and-half
½ tablespoon Worcestershire sauce
1 pound lump crabmeat
¼ cup minced parsley
Salt and white pepper

Sauté onions and mushrooms in butter until soft. Add mustard, wine, Cream Sauce, cream and Worcestershire. Heat, add crabmeat and parsley, correct seasonings and keep warm over hot water until served. King crab, shrimp or mixed seafood may be substituted.

Frozen fish poached in cider and butter takes on a better flavor. The Scots like to soak frozen seafood in salted ice water to restore its "freshly caught" taste.

CRABMEAT RAVIGOTE
For 4

Cover ½ pound cooked crabmeat with tarragon vinegar and let stand for 15 minutes. Squeeze out the vinegar and season to your taste with salt and white pepper. Add:

½ cup mayonnaise
1 tablespoon chopped sweet pickles or green pepper
    (or leave out)
1 teaspoon chopped chives
1 teaspoon chopped pimento

Mix well. [Use a fork]. Serve either on toast rounds as an appetizer or in hollow tomatoes. I like to mask it with a little mayonnaise and garnish with capers and pimentos. It should be served very cold. For luncheons, it is especially good served in avocado halves.

CRAB IMPERIAL

¼ cup butter
1 tablespoon finely chopped shallots or onion
1 cup sliced mushrooms
¼ cup flour
1½ cups milk
½ cup sherry
1 teaspoon salt
2 teaspoons Dijon mustard
1 pound crabmeat, fresh, frozen or canned
2 tablespoons mayonnaise

[Preheat oven to 300°.] Melt butter, add shallots or onion, sauté 1 minute. Add mushrooms and sauté until limp. Add flour and cook until foamy. [Gradually] pour in milk, stirring constantly until mixture is thick. Mix in the sherry and seasonings. Cook until thickened again. Add crabmeat, cool and stir in mayonnaise. Correct seasonings. Spoon into lightly buttered coquilles or a 1½-quart shallow casserole. Return to oven to heat. Run under broiler to brown. May be prepared ahead of time.

BROILED OYSTERS
For 6

3 dozen large plump oysters
1 clove garlic, minced
2 tablespoons minced parsley
Olive or vegetable oil

Mix garlic and parsley with oysters in a bowl and cover with cooking oil (olive oil is best, but not necessary). Let them stand in the refrigerator for several hours, the longer the better. Place on a flat pan with the oil they have soaked in and broil under direct heat until the edges curl. Don't ever overcook this little bivalve—when his body puffs and his edges curl, he is done; take him out quick. Serve at once on bread sautéed in butter, or on a thin slice of ham or Canadian bacon. They are wonderfully good eating. You can also stick a toothpick in them and serve as an hors d'oeuvre, but have plenty of them—they catch on.

BAKED OYSTERS
For 4

1 cup small white bread cubes
½ cup butter
1 bud garlic, minced
2 dozen large oysters
Salt
Nutmeg
Light cream [or half-and-half]

[Preheat oven to 375°.] Sauté the bread cubes in butter with the garlic until golden brown. Remove the garlic. Cover the bottom of 4 individual casseroles with a layer of the sautéed bread; place 6 oysters on top, sprinkle with salt and a few grains of nutmeg, cover with cream and sprinkle with remaining bread cubes on top. Bake for 15 minutes. Serve at once.

Specially special if the night is cool, the spirits high!

CELESTIAL OYSTERS
For 8

2 dozen large oysters
1 teaspoon salt
¼ teaspoon cayenne pepper
24 thin slices cooked turkey
24 thin slices bacon
Toothpicks
2 tablespoons butter

Drain oysters, season with salt and cayenne; wrap each in a slice of turkey, then in bacon, and secure with a toothpick. Melt butter and pan-broil rolled oysters until the bacon is cooked, turning frequently. Serve with a dish of sparkling cranberry sauce.

TO COOK SHRIMP

1½ pounds shrimp
3 quarts boiling water
3 teaspoons salt
3 slices of onion

Boil for 5 or 8 minutes (depending upon the size of the shrimp), or until the [shrimp curl and] shells turn pink. Drain, rinse with cold water to chill; remove shells and dark intestinal vein running along the back.

You may also clean the shrimp before cooking [but they seem to shrink more]. Drop them into the salted, boiling water and simmer until they curl. Cleaned shrimp take less time to cook.

You really have to watch them or they will overcook, and what is worse than a tough old shrimp?

ᕽ *Previously Unpublished*

[For real authenticity, spread an outdoor table with several layers of newsprint and furnish each diner lots of paper napkins and a paper bib. Cold beer and good French bread are the only accompaniments needed. Boil the shrimp just before you are ready to serve them.—Editor]

PASCAGOULA SHRIMP BOIL
For 6

3 ounces purchased "Shrimp Boil"
1 small onion, sliced
1 lemon, sliced
1 clove garlic, sliced
1 gallon water
½ cup salt
5 pounds raw shrimp, fresh or frozen

Tie Shrimp Boil, onion, lemon and garlic loosely in a piece of cheese-cloth. Put the water in a large pot and add the salt and seasoning bag. Cover and bring to the boiling point over a hot flame or burner. Add the shrimp and return to the boiling point. Simmer until the shrimp curl and turn pink. Drain and pile the shrimp in a big bowl in the center of the table and let everyone peel his own. Serve hot with Peppy Cocktail Sauce [page 225].

ᕽ *Previously Unpublished*

BUTTERED SHRIMP AND PEACHES

12 peach halves, fresh, frozen or canned
¼ cup flour
⅓ cup butter
2 cups tiny croutons
3 cups tiny cooked shrimp
¼ to ½ cup additional butter

Sprinkle peaches lightly with flour. Sauté in butter until lacy brown. Put a layer of croutons on a tray, then peach halves filled with the shrimp heated in additional butter. Sprinkle with rest of croutons. Nice as a first course done individually.

*Shrimp cocktails are overworked, but baked or broiled shrimp are not.
I like this recipe either as a first course or as an entrée.*

BAKED SHRIMP (SHRIMP SAKI)

[Preheat oven to 350°.] Use as large shrimp as you can obtain in the
shell. Remove small legs and then split the shrimp over the black
intestinal tract and down the back shell as far as the tail. Rinse and
remove black tract but do not remove the shrimp from the shell.
Flatten shrimp meat with palm of hand. Put shell side down on a
baking sheet, sprinkle with salt and a little white pepper and brush
with melted whipped butter or margarine. Bake 15 minutes. The best
way I know to tell when shrimp is properly cooked is to observe the
shell; when it changes from an opaque to a translucent appearance
the shrimp is cooked enough. Overcooking shrimp is far worse than
having them slightly underdone. Arrange shrimp on a plate with the
tails to the outside and halves of fresh limes for a garnish—and lime
juice and melted whipped butter for a sauce. It depends on the size
of the shrimp how many you serve: if very large, 5; if smaller, 7. An
odd number on the plate looks better than an even one.

❧ *Reader's Request*

FRIED SHRIMP
For 4

2 eggs
1 cup milk
1 pound large shrimp, uncooked
1 cup flour
1½ teaspoons garlic salt
36 saltines, smashed with fingers
[Vegetable oil for frying]

Beat the eggs and add the milk. Clean the shrimp [remove the black
vein] and split down the backs to "butterfly." Dip in the flour seasoned with garlic salt, then the egg and milk, then in the smashed
saltines. Fry in deep hot fat until golden brown. Serve with a good
cocktail sauce or Rémoulade [page 222]. The smashed saltines give
them a rough pretty appearance and somehow they "eat" better.

STIR-FRIED SHRIMP WITH SNOW PEAS

1 pound raw shrimp, fresh or frozen
2 teaspoons cornstarch
1 egg white
1 teaspoon soy sauce
1 tablespoon dry sherry
½ pound snow peas
2 tablespoons peanut oil
2 scallions, slivered
1 tablespoon fresh ginger root, slivered

Remove the black or white intestinal vein of the shrimp by making a
shallow slit down the round side of the shrimp. Wash in cold water
and dry on paper towels. Split in half lengthwise. Mix cornstarch, egg
white, soy and sherry into a light batter and coat shrimp with it. Wash
and sliver the snow peas. Pour boiling water over and drain. Heat the
oil in a hot heavy skillet or wok. Add the scallions and ginger root.
Stir-fry for 1 minute, then remove from oil. Drain shrimp, reserving
liquid, and stir-fry for 1 minute. Add snow peas and stir-fry for 30
seconds. Add leftover cornstarch mixture. Stir and cover for 30 seconds. Serve at once.

*The Chinese cuisine does not, I think, include refreshing desserts. I like
to end a dinner with very cold peach halves, stewed or canned. Serve
in shallow dessert bowls and pour thin threads of caramelized sugar
over. In fact it is a delightful ending for any occasion.*

*Vol-au-Vent is a patty shell filled with a creamed mixture, usually
seafood or fowl, and covered with a tiny pastry lid. Literally
means "windward flight," so be sure the patty shells are light and
be sure to heat them.*

When I want my guests to watch me cook, which isn't often, the watching I mean, I do a Paella. This could be a one-dish supper with salad and bread, and can be made as expensively as you wish or as cheaply. I recommend it to young brides who want to make their party food appear ample. I always recommend it be brought to the table in the pan it was prepared in, preferably a paella pan, which can be used for other things. I like to use a patchwork quilt for my table (it looks full already), a whole loaf of bread to slice or hard rolls, and perfect peaches used as a centerpiece. Then I tell my guests peaches are the dessert. I find my guests either eat them or take them home, sometimes both.

PAELLA

3 tablespoons olive oil
1 cup diced onion
1 clove garlic, minced
½ pound fresh lean pork, cut in cubes
2-pound broiling chicken [uncooked], meat cut from bones, or
    1-pound uncooked [boneless] turkey meat
1 cup uncooked white rice
1 pound mild smoked sausage, sliced
1 cup peeled sliced tomato, fresh or canned
3 cups chicken broth
½ cup dry white wine
Pinch of saffron
1 pound raw shrimp, peeled [and deveined]
1 uncooked lobster tail, sliced
2 dozen mussels or littleneck clams in shells
2 tablespoons chopped pimento
Salt and pepper
¼ cup minced parsley

Heat the oil in the paella pan. Add the onion and garlic, sautéeing them until soft and yellow, not brown. Remove. Add pork and chicken and sauté at medium heat until brown. Remove from pan. Add rice and sausage and stir until lightly toasted. Stir in tomatoes, the cooked chicken, pork, broth, wine and saffron; cook covered about 25 minutes. Add shrimp, lobster and mussels or clams; cook 6 minutes, stirring with a fork. Add pimento and stir. Correct seasonings. Add parsley and serve at once. Paella is best when eaten immediately. Leftovers freeze well, but the seafood will be soft—sorry! You can use whatever proportions of meat, fish and rice you like, but this recipe is the one I find everyone likes.

JAMBALAYA
For 8

½ cup salt pork
½ cup diced ham
½ cup chopped onions
1 garlic clove
2 cups canned tomatoes
1 cup raw rice
1 teaspoon salt
1 pint [raw] oysters
2 cups raw shrimp, peeled and cleaned

Dice the salt pork, add the ham, and fry slowly until crisp. Add the onions and garlic, cook until soft. Remove garlic, add the tomatoes and simmer slowly until thick. Add the raw rice, 2 cups water, and salt. Cover and cook for 10 minutes. Add the oysters and shrimp and cook until the rice is done. If you don't like sea food? Add 2 cups of slivered lean ham or chicken.

Lobsters make inroads in the housewife's budget. Strictly on the extravagant side, but one can hardly resist their delicate flavor after once tasting this intriguing crustacean. You have to work hard to cook them, harder to eat them, but once you succumb you will become an addict and then everything about them becomes worthwhile. . . .

There is one thing to remember when you buy a lobster: buy only the best. Lobsters, if they are bought alive, should be alive, and you will know by the prancing they do; if they are sleepy, leave them alone. If buying a cooked lobster, test it by straightening out the tail. If the tail springs back into a curled position, the lobster was alive when it was cooked. When buying a frozen lobster, be sure you know the reliability of the concern from whom you buy it. Frozen lobsters should remain in perfect condition for several months. . . .

No one knows how to prepare lobster better than the natives around the lobsters' habitat. This is how they say to do it—and they know.

TO BOIL MAINE LOBSTERS

Place live lobsters in a kettle of briskly boiling salted water, boil for 15 to 20 minutes (depending upon number and size of lobsters), remove from water, place on drain board or wipe dry. Serve whole lobster either hot or cold, with a side dish of melted butter.

All of the Maine lobster is edible *except* the bony shell structure, the small crop or craw in the head of the lobster, and the dark sand vein running down the back of the tail meat. The green is the liver (tomalley) and the white is the fat—both are highly seasoned and should be saved. The red, or "coral," is actually the underdeveloped roe or spawn of the lobster.

The liver of the lobster. . . can be taken out and mixed with a little mayonnaise and you have the best hors d'oeuvre you ever ate. Natives dunk the lobster meat in the tomalley or spread it on bread in place of butter. Anyhow, eat it.

LOBSTER THERMIDOR
For 2

1 2-pound lobster
4 tablespoons butter, divided use
2 tablespoons flour
1 cup cream or milk [or half-and-half]
¼ teaspoon salt
½ teaspoon dry mustard
4 tablespoons sherry
1 egg yolk
1 cup fresh mushrooms, quartered
½ cup grated Parmesan cheese
Paprika

Boil the lobster [according to directions above] and split lengthwise.
[Take care to save the shells.] Remove all the meat and cut in 1-inch
cubes. [Preheat oven to 375°.] Melt 2 tablespoons of the butter in a
skillet, add flour and cook until bubbly, then [gradually] add cream,
salt, and mustard; cook until thick; add the sherry and egg yolk,
stirring thoroughly. Keep warm over hot water. Sauté mushrooms in
remaining 2 tablespoons of butter and add the lobster meat. Swish
around, then add the sherry sauce to it. Sprinkle part of the cheese in
the bottom of the lobster shells, add the mixture and sprinkle remaining cheese on top. Sprinkle with a little paprika and brown in oven.
You could do these ahead of time and freeze them, then brown when
ready to serve.

BROCHETTE OF LOBSTER AND CHICKEN

2 8- to 10-ounce lobster tails
2 8-ounce boneless chicken breasts [skinless]
1 cup sherry wine
½ cup melted butter
Salt and white pepper

Cut shells of lobster tails lengthwise. Place your thumb under the
lobster meat at the large end of the tail and loosen meat. Pull the
meat out. It will come out easily. Cut tail meat in ½-inch slices. Cut
chicken breasts in half lengthwise and slice in ½-inch pieces. Thread
alternately with the lobster onto a buttered or oiled skewer. (I use
bamboo and throw away.) Place in a shallow pan, pour wine over
and refrigerate until ready to cook. Bake in a preheated 350° oven for
10 minutes, then slide under the broiler for about 5 minutes. Baste
with the wine and butter. Correct the seasonings; serve either on the
skewer (I do not like) or slip off but retain shape. A lemon cup filled
with red caviar would be a pretty garnish.

*You can buy 1-pound packages of frozen crayfish in the market today.
No fuss, no cleaning and fairly low in calories. If you do not have
crayfish, use any other shellfish.*

SCOTCHED CRAYFISH
For 8 to 10

6 tablespoons unsalted butter [divided use]
½ pound diced fresh mushrooms (you may omit)
2 pounds crayfish
2 ounces Scotch whisky
1½ pints whipping cream
2 tablespoons flour
½ teaspoon salt
¼ teaspoon Worcestershire sauce
Dash of Tabasco

Melt 4 tablespoons of the butter, add the mushrooms and sauté for 1
minute; add crayfish and cook until hot. Pour in the whisky and
ignite. Add cream and stir while heating, but do not boil. Make a

paste (beurre manie) of flour, remaining butter, salt and Worcestershire and Tabasco. Add to the cream mixture. Cook for 5 minutes or until thickened. Serve in pastry cups or on rice as an entrée.

CLAM PIE

Pastry for 9½-inch 2-crust pie
2 tablespoons minced parsley
6 tablespoons butter
⅔ cup chopped onion
6 tablespoons flour
3 cups half-and-half
Salt and pepper
¼ teaspoon Worcestershire sauce
4 cups chopped clams (fresh, frozen or canned)
1 egg yolk mixed with
1 teaspoon water

[Preheat oven to 425°.] Line a pie tin with one half the pie crust, rolled thin [page 358]. (I use a Pyrex pie casserole for this.) Sprinkle bottom with parsley. Melt the butter, add onions and sauté until soft, but not brown. Add flour and cook until bubbly. [Gradually] pour in half-and-half and cook until thickened, stirring constantly. Season with salt, pepper and Worcestershire sauce. In alternate layers put the clams and sauce into the pastry-lined tin. Cover with a top crust thinly rolled. Crimp the edges to seal. Decorate top with pastry cutouts, leaves, flowers or shells. (It depends on how good an artist you are.) Brush with the egg and water and bake for 35 to 40 minutes. Brush once more during baking with the egg wash. Serve very hot.

FROGS' LEGS

8 pairs frogs' legs
2 tablespoons lemon juice
Flour
¼ cup butter
2 tablespoons olive oil
1 clove garlic, crushed
2 tablespoons chopped chives
2 tablespoons dry white wine
Salt and white pepper
[Minced parsley (optional)]

Cover the frogs' legs in water mixed with the lemon juice [for 30 minutes]. Dry and dust lightly with flour. Shake off excess. Melt butter, add oil and garlic. Sauté 1 minute. Add chives and frogs' legs. Shake pan while cooking to prevent sticking. Turn once. When golden brown, add wine, season with salt and pepper, and parsley if you wish. Use the same ingredients for shrimp or chicken, especially the wings, which make a good cocktail morsel.

Entrée Sauces

The sauce to meat is ceremony, according to Lady Macbeth. But what would the ceremony be without the sauce? I'm sure the hostess who serves a really superb sauce feels at times that she is playing god to the mortals who partake of it. And why not? It takes patience to make a sauce that will enhance, not disguise.

Any sauce, whether simple or complex, takes time—to blend the proper proportions of fat, flour or egg yolks, and whatever liquid goes into it. A good rule in blending is to follow your sauce recipe, and carefully; but let your imagination inspire your seasoning.

⊱ *Reader's Request*

A sauce to make a fish dish a delectable entrée any day, and especially for company.

IMPERIAL SAUCE
2½ cups

2 tablespoons finely chopped onion
¼ cup finely diced mushrooms
1 tablespoon butter
1 cup Thick Cream Sauce [opposite page]
1 cup mayonnaise
1 teaspoon lemon juice
2 tablespoons finely chopped sweet mustard pickles
1 tablespoon finely chopped pimento
¼ teaspoon Worcestershire sauce

[Preheat oven to 300°.] Sauté onion and mushrooms in butter; add cream sauce, mayonnaise, lemon juice, pickles, pimento, and Worcestershire. Completely cover any boned fish like red snapper, sea trout, fillet of sole, and similar fish, and bake for 40 minutes. Part of the sauce cooks into the fish and part stays on top. I use it also combined with shrimp, lobster, and crabmeat, and baked in individual casseroles for a luncheon dish and find it popular as a hot hors d'oeuvre served with pastry scoops: pie crust molded on a table-spoon, placed close enough to touch on a baking sheet and baked at 400° until light brown and crisp.

YOGURT RÉMOULADE
1⅓ cups

1 cup yogurt
¼ cup chopped parsley
½ teaspoon dried tarragon
2 tablespoons finely chopped onion
1 teaspoon prepared mustard
1 tablespoon chopped capers

Mix and refrigerate. Good with all seafoods.

Trite as it may seem, every cook should know how to make a smooth cream sauce—thick, thin, or medium. It is the foundation of many a sauce, soup, scallop and casserole—and can save many a hostess an embarrassing moment when a planned meal for two must be stretched for more.

BASIC CREAM SAUCE

Thin Sauce	**Medium Sauce**	**Thick Sauce**
Use for soups, etc.	Use for au gratin, gravies, etc.	Use for croquettes, etc.
1 tablespoon butter	2 tablespoons butter	4 tablespoons butter
1 tablespoon flour	2 tablespoons flour	4 tablespoons flour
1 cup milk	1 cup milk	1 cup milk
¼ teaspoon salt	¼ teaspoon salt	¼ teaspoon salt

Melt butter in top part of double boiler, add flour and cook until bubbly. Slowly add milk and stir briskly. Add salt and cook over hot water until thick and smooth, stirring occasionally. (A French whip or wire whisk is, or ought to be, a must in the kitchen drawer, especially for stirring sauces of all kinds.) With the new type heavy-base sauce-pans it is not necessary to use a double boiler if low heat is maintained. But all cream sauces should be cooked until there is no starchy taste remaining [for about 20 minutes].

A sauce less expensive than Hollandaise or Maltaise, which are both elegant but expensive, is:

LEMON SAUCE
1¼ cups

2 egg yolks
1 tablespoon flour
1 cup liquid from fish poaching or chicken broth
1 tablespoon fresh lemon juice
2 tablespoons chopped parsley
Salt and white pepper

Mix egg yolks with the flour, add liquid and [cook over low heat] stirring with your French whip until thick. Add lemon juice and parsley and correct seasonings. Add more lemon juice if you desire.

HOLLANDAISE SAUCE
½ cup

½ cup butter
2 egg yolks, slightly beaten
1 tablespoon lemon juice
Dash of cayenne

Divide butter in half and put half in a small saucepan [or double boiler] with the slightly beaten egg yolks and lemon juice. Hold the pan over hot water (do not allow water to boil) and stir constantly until butter is melted. Add remaining half of butter and stir until thick. Remove and add cayenne pepper. Serve at once with any vegetable or fish. (If the sauce curdles, beat in 1 tablespoon of cream.) If left over you may reheat. Set in a pan of warm water and stir until ready to serve. If it breaks again, add the cream again. This can go on indefinitely.

Variations:
MOUSSELINE SAUCE: After sauce is thickened, fold in ¼ cup whipped cream. Serve on fish, asparagus or Brussels sprouts.

LOBSTER OR SHRIMP HOLLANDAISE: Add ¼ cup finely chopped cooked lobster or shrimp to finished sauce. Serve over poached fish of any kind.

VERONIQUE: Combine ½ cup Medium Cream Sauce [previous page] with 1 cup Hollandaise. Add ½ cup seedless grapes (white is usual) cut in half. Serve over poached fish, or white meat of turkey, or chicken and ham. Run under broiler to brown.

MALTAISE SAUCE: Whip 2 tablespoons of orange juice plus ½ teaspoon grated orange rind into ½ cup Hollandaise. I like this with salmon.

BÉARNAISE SAUCE: Substitute 2 teaspoons tarragon vinegar for lemon juice; add a dash of mushroom catsup (if you have it), 1 tablespoon minced parsley, ¼ teaspoon freshly ground pepper and 1 teaspoon snipped chives. Serve with beef fillets or prime rib roast.

NEWBURG SAUCE
2½ cups

2 tablespoons butter
2 tablespoons flour
¾ teaspoon salt
A dash of cayenne
2 cups thin cream (or half milk, half cream)
4 egg yolks, well beaten
¼ cup dry sherry (or half brandy)

Melt butter, stir in flour, salt, and cayenne. When well blended [gradually] add the cream and cook over low heat until smooth and the mixture boils. Stir a little of the sauce into the egg yolks and add [back into] the rest of the sauce. If using for lobster or shrimp or other seafood, sauté the seafood, or what you have, in a little butter and the sherry. [For other uses, add sherry to sauce and heat.] This amount will serve 6 or 8 people.

ネ *Previously Unpublished*

PEPPY COCKTAIL SAUCE
1½ cups

½ cup chili sauce
½ cup ketchup
3 tablespoons lemon juice
1 tablespoon horseradish
1 tablespoon mayonnaise or salad dressing
1 teaspoon Worcestershire sauce
½ teaspoon grated onion
¼ teaspoon salt
3 drops Tabasco
Dash pepper

Combine all of the ingredients and chill thoroughly. Make this sauce the day before you plan to serve it so it can meld.

Mornay Sauce has as many definitions as there are people who make it. If you must be technical, it is a "cheesed" sauce. Start or finish how you wish, but "cheese" it you must. This one is easy, keeps well, and can be used for many things.

MORNAY SAUCE
1½ quarts

¼ pound butter
1 cup flour
4 cups milk
2 pounds Velveeta cheese
1 can beer

Melt butter, add flour and cook until bubbly. [Gradually] add milk and cook until smooth. Boil 1 minute. Cut cheese in small pieces and beat into hot cream sauce. I recommend an electric beater and beat at medium speed over heat for a minimum of 15 minutes; longer beating improves the sauce. Add beer a little at a time to obtain consistency desired. Pour over whatever vegetable, fowl, fish or meat you wish, put a level teaspoon of Hollandaise on top, and run it under the broiler until brown. Or sprinkle with grated Swiss or Parmesan cheese before browning. If you make the sauce and keep it several days, beat it again before using to restore its light consistency.

Using the cheesed sauce as a base, you can add all sorts of things to make it interesting:
RAREBIT SAUCE: Add 1 egg yolk and ½ teaspoon dry mustard.

ALMOND SAUCE: Add 2 tablespoons blanched slivered almonds, lightly toasted. For fish.

FRESH TOMATO CHEESE SAUCE: Add ¼ cup finely diced fresh tomatoes and serve over toasted seafood sandwiches or croquettes.

SHERRY SAUCE: Add 2 tablespoons sherry.

I like Mustard Creams for carrying various foods: ham, seafood, leftover roast beef, artichoke hearts, green beans, carrots—oh, many things—and especially to serve over a Cheese Soufflé Pie [page 236]. Cut the Soufflé Pie, then spoon the sauce over it.

MUSTARD CREAM
2 cups

4 tablespoons butter or margarine
2 shallots or green onions, finely minced
3 tablespoons flour
2 cups half-and-half
½ teaspoon salt
2 tablespoons Dijon mustard
2 tablespoons dry white wine

Melt butter, add the shallots or onion. Cook until yellow. Add the flour; stir and cook until bubbly. [Gradually] pour in the half-and-half. Cook and stir with a French whip over low heat until smooth and thickened. Add salt, mustard and wine. Cook about 5 minutes more. For a thinner sauce, add a little more half-and-half or chicken broth. To the sauce I add 1½ cups of slivered ham, chicken, sliced shrimp or crabmeat. This method may be used as a basis for making any sauce, i.e., in place of mustard, add capers, parsley, chives, mixed herbs, slivered vegetables, chopped eggs, seafood—you name it.

HOT MUSTARD SAUCE

2 cups light cream, heated
4 tablespoons dry mustard
1 cup sugar
1 cup vinegar
Salt to taste
2 egg yolks, well beaten
2 tablespoons flour

Mix thoroughly and cook in double boiler for at least an hour. When cold, drained horse-radish may be added; or whipped cream.

SAUCE LOUIS
3½ cups

2 cups mayonnaise
½ cup chili sauce
2 tablespoons lemon juice
6 drops Angostura bitters (you may omit)
½ cup whipping cream

Mix mayonnaise, chili sauce, lemon juice (1 lemon normally yields 3 tablespoons of juice) and bitters. Whip cream and fold into the mixture. Chill. Good with any kind of seafood.

What do you mean by a brown sauce? Everyone agrees on one thing— you make it from meat stock. So, brown gravy, brown sauce, Espagnole, are all basically the same.

BROWN SAUCE
1 cup

2 tablespoons butter or meat drippings
1 tablespoon minced onion
1 tablespoon minced carrot
½ bay leaf
2 tablespoons flour
1 cup meat stock
Salt and pepper

Melt the butter or drippings; add onion, carrot and bay leaf and cook over low heat until butter is brown. Stir in flour and cook until bubbly. [Gradually] add stock and cook until thick and smooth. Strain and season.

Variations:
Add 1 cup sliced mushrooms, sautéed, and 1 tablespoon sherry. Serve with roasts, meat loaf or cutlets.

Substitute ½ cup orange juice for ½ cup stock from roasting ducks. After sauce is strained, add 2 tablespoons slivered orange rind. Serve with duck.

Barbecue Sauce should be among a housewife's prized possessions, especially if she is south of the Mason-Dixon Line. This one I like to keep on hand and use, especially for barbecuing chicken and pork ribs:

BARBECUE SAUCE
1½ cups

1 cup chicken bouillon or stock
¼ cup vinegar
½ teaspoon prepared mustard
½ teaspoon Worcestershire sauce
2 tablespoons chili sauce
1 tablespoon lemon juice
Grated rind of ½ lemon
½ clove garlic, finely minced
¼ cup finely minced onion
¼ cup butter
¼ teaspoon Tabasco
1 bay leaf
¼ teaspoon whole cloves
2 tablespoons sugar
2 tablespoons flour

Mix all ingredients except flour and cook until onion is soft and it smells heavenly. Add flour moistened with water and cook until thick. For barbecuing chicken, I oven-roast them until nearly done, cover with the barbecue sauce, cover and cook at least 45 minutes at 325°; uncover and bake another 15 minutes at 400° or run them under the broiler until crisp on top.

Pour the sauce over a turkey or ham and use it to baste for the last hours of its cooking.

Mix it with prepared barbecue sauce, half and half, and use for beef short ribs or chuck roast, increasing the time for cooking after the sauce is added to 2 hours. It will keep indefinitely if refrigerated.

I think this is the best barbecue sauce for chicken. Prepare it ahead and keep in your deep freeze.

FRUIT BARBECUE SAUCE
1 quart

2 cups chopped onion
2 cloves garlic, minced
4 cups catsup
½ cup vinegar
1 tablespoon plus 1 teaspoon dry mustard
2⅔ cups butter
2 cups raisins, chopped
2 teaspoons dried basil
1 teaspoon dried tarragon
1 teaspoon dried rosemary
2 teaspoons dried marjoram
¾ cup brown sugar
1 tablespoon plus 1 teaspoon salt
Juice of 2 lemons
1 cup dry Burgundy wine
2 cups seedless grapes (you may omit)

Mix all the ingredients together except the wine and grapes. Bring to a boil and simmer for 45 minutes. Stir in wine and cook 10 minutes longer. Add the grapes as a garnish when ready to serve. Allow ½ chicken per person and proceed as directed in the previous recipe.

The hot, smoky sauce used by the Texans for outdoor picnics may be used as a steak sauce or for oven barbecuing.

TEXAS BARBECUE SAUCE
3 cups

1 tablespoon salt
½ teaspoon pepper
3 tablespoons brown sugar
¼ cup catsup
3 tablespoons prepared brown mustard
2 tablespoons Worcestershire sauce
1 teaspoon Liquid Smoke sauce
1 cup water
2 tablespoons chili sauce
½ cup vinegar
1 cup melted butter or cooking oil

Mix in order given, using rotary egg beater as oil is added. Simmer slowly until slightly thickened. This makes enough sauce for 6 pounds of meat. Keep hot.

HORSERADISH SAUCE
1 cup

1 tablespoon chopped onion
3 tablespoons butter
2 tablespoons flour
1 cup milk or light cream [half-and-half]
¼ cup prepared horseradish

Brown onion slightly in butter; add flour, then [gradually stir in] milk or cream to make a sauce. [Continue to cook.] When thick, add horseradish. This is especially good on boiled brisket of fresh beef—and corned beef, without saying.

Variation: In place of the horseradish, substitute 3 tablespoons of prepared mustard and ½ teaspoon of Worcestershire sauce. Serve over fresh pork, spareribs, pork butts and regular hams.

Use the following sauce over meat loaf, cutlets and with cooked shrimp over rice. Leftover sauce may be poured over canned green beans, okra, eggplant, and like vegetables.

CREOLE SAUCE
3 cups

½ cup chopped onion
1 clove garlic, crushed
½ cup diced celery (may be omitted)
¼ cup diced green pepper
2 tablespoons olive oil
2½ cups canned [diced] tomatoes
1 bay leaf
2 teaspoons salt
2 teaspoons sugar
2 teaspoons chopped parsley
4 cloves
1 teaspoon flour

Sauté the onion, garlic, celery, and green pepper in olive oil until soft, but not brown. Add tomatoes, bay leaf, salt, sugar, parsley and cloves and cook over low heat until thick. Remove cloves and add flour, dissolved in a little water. [Continue cooking until raw flour taste disappears.]

MUSHROOM SAUCE
1 cup

½ cup sliced mushrooms
2 tablespoons butter
2 tablespoons flour
¾ cup chicken stock
½ cup cream [or half-and-half]
Salt
Sherry (may be omitted)

Sauté the mushrooms in butter until soft. Add flour, [and gradually stir in] stock, and cream to make a cream sauce. Season with salt and sherry, if you like.

Variation: Add ½ cup slivered toasted almonds and ½ cup grated sharp cheese to serve over asparagus or broccoli as an entrée.

Lamb, of all kinds, calls for a variety of sauces. There is nothing the matter with Mint Jelly—it's just overworked.

FRESH MINT SAUCE
1 cup

1 cup lamb pan drippings
1 tablespoon vinegar
¼ cup currant jelly
2 tablespoons fresh minced mint

Cook drippings, vinegar, and jelly together until jelly is melted. Add the fresh mint just before serving.

A delicious and easy sauce to serve with ham or cold turkey (you can keep it on hand in the refrigerator and take it out a few minutes beforehand to serve at room temperature) is

CUMBERLAND SAUCE
½ cup

3 tablespoons grated orange rind
3 tablespoons red currant jelly
2 tablespoons port
2 tablespoons orange juice
1 tablespoon lemon juice
1 teaspoon dry mustard
½ teaspoon ground ginger
1 teaspoon paprika

The orange rind should be finely shredded and white part removed, covered with cold water and brought to a boil and drained. Melt jelly over low heat until liquid. Cool and add rest of ingredients.

A rather hot sauce, delicious with lamb is

LAMB SAUCE ANITA
1 cup

½ cup brown sugar
½ cup currant jelly
1 tablespoon dry mustard
3 egg yolks
½ cup vinegar

Mix brown sugar, jelly, mustard and egg yolks and cook in double boiler until thick. Add vinegar slowly, beating after each addition.

❧ *Previously Unpublished*

BUTTERS

CLARIFIED BUTTER: Melt butter over hot water. Pour off the butter and discard the sediment left in the pan. If you make a large amount, cool and chill in the pan; you will be able to remove a cake of solid clarified butter.

BROWN BUTTER (Beurre Noisette): Melt butter over low heat, shaking it to prevent burning, until it is lightly browned. Serve over fish or vegetables. Allow 1 tablespoon per serving. The butter flavor is enhanced, so you can use less.

BLACK BUTTER (Beurre Noir): Melt ½ cup butter until it becomes dark brown, but do not let it smoke. (Don't brown it too much since it turns dark as you add the juice.) Remove from the heat and add 2 tablespoons of minced parsley and 1 teaspoon of lemon juice. Pour over vegetables, eggs, sweetbreads, brains, etc.

THICKENED BUTTER (to keep on hand): Blend ¾ cup of all-purpose or blending flour with 1 cup of soft (not melted) butter. [The plastic blade in your food processor will make quick work of this chore.] Store in a covered container in the refrigerator to use as a quick thickener for making sauces.

ORANGE BUTTER AND LEMON CREAM BUTTER can be found on pages 94 and 309.

Cheese and Eggs

In the sixteenth century a Bishop of Paris was authorized by a bull from Pope Julius III to permit the use of eggs during Lent. The Parliament took offense and prevented the execution of the mandate. From this severe abstinence from eggs during Lent arose the custom of having a great number of them blessed on Easter Eve, to be distributed among friends on Easter Sunday.

SWISS CHEESE SOUFFLÉ
For 8 to 10

[If you plan to serve this with Oriental Chicken [page 134], use American (Cheddar) cheese rather than Swiss and add ¼ teaspoon of White Wine Worcestershire sauce.]

½ cup butter
6 tablespoons flour
2 cups milk
2 cups grated Swiss cheese
8 eggs, separated [at room temperature]
1½ teaspoons dry mustard or 1 tablespoon prepared Dijon
    mustard
⅛ teaspoon cayenne pepper
1 teaspoon salt
Parmesan cheese (may be omitted)

[Preheat oven to 350°.] Melt the butter, add the flour and cook slowly until mixture foams. Do not brown. [Gradually] add the milk, [stirring constantly], and bring to a boil; use low heat to ensure the flour and milk being thoroughly cooked. The sauce should be smooth and thick. Remove from heat. Add the [Swiss] cheese and stir until blended. Cool slightly. Beat the egg yolks and add to the mixture. Add the mustard, cayenne and salt. Let mixture cool until you can place your hand on the bottom of the container without feeling any heat. Beat the egg whites until stiff but not dry. (Tip the bowl and if the whites do not slide out, they are ready.) Stir gently about one third of the egg whites into the mixture, then fold in remaining egg whites until well distributed. Pour into a 2½- or 3-quart buttered soufflé dish sprinkled lightly with Parmesan cheese or into two 1½-quart ones. Bake for 30 minutes if you are going to eat at once, or place in a pan of hot water and bake 1 hour, and it will hold awhile.

You may substitute grated Cheddar, Gruyère or any other hard cheese. I do think Swiss or Gruyère makes a better soufflé.

There are many things you can do with soufflé besides baking it in a soufflé dish. I like to pour it into a partially baked pie crust for a Cheese Soufflé Pie; bake in a preheated 350° oven until set, about 30 minutes. Use it as a carrier for any creamed food, or you may serve it simply as a soufflé pie. It is delicious topped with broiled mushrooms or broiled shrimp for a less caloric item. You can bake a soufflé in individual casseroles for a luncheon. Use your basic soufflé recipe and put on the bottom a layer of one of the following: sliced sautéed mushrooms, sautéed thinly sliced onions, shrimp, or a layer of spinach or ham soufflé and bake together. Use the new see-through glass soufflé dishes and watch your soufflé come to life with the added color. Before cooking, ring the dish with buttered bakers' parchment paper for a higher soufflé (do not use foil). Bake in a shallow casserole for a buffet and cut in serving portions. Use a soufflé in place of a vegetable. Serve it with cold boiled salmon, and pass the melted sweet butter, as the Danish do. With cold baked ham it is divine. Use the leftovers in an omlette, in macaroni and cheese, in an oven-toasted cheese sandwich. Just use soufflés for they are delicious.

Being a career woman, I am many times caught with the emergency shelf bare. Scrambled eggs I can always do, and everyone has asked me to include them in my book.

SCRAMBLED EGGS
For 2

2 tablespoons butter
4 eggs
¾ cup cottage cheese (dry)
½ teaspoon salt
Freshly ground or cracked pepper

Melt the butter in a skillet and remove from the heat. Break the eggs into the skillet and beat with a fork. [For dry cottage cheese, place regular cottage cheese in a strainer, run under cold water and drain thoroughly.] Add the cottage cheese and salt. Return to the heat and cook over low heat, stirring constantly. Sprinkle with fresh-ground or cracked pepper as served.

When scrambling eggs, let your sophisticated imagination run riot. Toss in things like diced avocado, orange sections and grated orange peel. Toss in lobster, shrimp, or crabmeat with a whiff of garlic. Toss in Matzo crackers. Toss in anything. Toss in the Better Half!

HOW TO PREPARE AN OMELET

*It really isn't difficult. If you have an omelet pan reserved for omelets,
fine, if not, any 8-or 9-inch skillet will do. Be sure it is very clean and
dry. Two or three eggs make a better omelet than one. Melt 2 tablespoons butter in the pan, swirl it around so that the bottom and sides
are completely covered. Beat the eggs lightly with ½ teaspoon salt and
1 tablespoon of cold water or milk, pour into the hot pan. Butter should
be sizzling. Cook at high heat. As the omelet begins to cook, swirl it and
pull edges of the mixture toward the center of the pan. The liquid part
will fill the space. Repeat until all of the egg is cooked, but soft. With a
spatula fold toward center of pan. Lift pan up to edge of plate so that
the omelet slides out. If you wish to add anything to the omelet such as
jelly, sour cream, strawberries, cheese, mushrooms, add just before you
fold. Don't let your omelet stand around!*

*Then there is the Fluffy or Angel Omelet. [Preheat oven to 375°] You
separate the eggs; beat the whites until stiff. Beat the egg yolks with 1
tablespoon of cream and fold into the whites. Pour into the pan coated
with melted butter. Cook 1 minute at medium heat. Fold in half gently
and put in oven for about 4 minutes. I usually sprinkle a little
Parmesan cheese on top before putting it in the oven.*

*When you have conquered the omelet you can add anything to it and
get away with it. For instance, the PEASANT OMELET is wonderful for
a Sunday morning after a big Saturday night, or for any supper to fill
up the hungry.*

*For two servings, you simply brown 1 cup of sliced cooked potatoes in
butter and add to 4 eggs, mixed with ¼ cup of chopped chives or
spring onion tops before pouring into the pan. Serve with cold thick
slices of tomato, or canned tomatoes icy cold, topped with a dash of
mustardy mayonnaise.*

STRAWBERRY OMELET WITH SOUR CREAM
For 1

3 eggs
1 tablespoon light cream [or half-and-half]
¼ teaspoon salt
2 tablespoons butter
¼ cup sour cream
½ cup frozen or fresh strawberries
Powdered sugar

[Preheat broiler.] Beat the eggs in a bowl, add the cream and salt. Beat with a fork for ½ minute. Heat the butter in a skillet until it sizzles. Pour in the beaten eggs. Stir once or twice with a fork. Lift the edges as the eggs begin to cook and let the liquid part run under. Shake the pan back and forth to keep the omelet free. When cooked but still soft on top, add half of the sour cream and half of the berries. Slide the omelet onto ovenproof platter. Pour remaining sour cream and berries on top, sprinkle lightly with powdered sugar, and run under a hot broiler for 10 seconds.

I like to eat [this] as a dessert with a cold Delicious apple. Try it.

BRIE QUICHE
For 6 or 8

8-inch torte pan lined with pie crust
4 eggs, separated
1½ cups half and half
1 pound Brie cheese (mashed)
⅛ teaspoon salt

[Bake the pie crust in a preheated 450° oven for 10 minutes. Reduce heat to 350°.] Beat the egg yolks with the cream, add the cheese and salt. Mix thoroughly. Beat the egg whites until stiff, stir one-third into the mixture, fold in the rest. Pour into torte pan and bake for 30 minutes or until custard is set. [Quiches are done when a knife inserted in the center comes out clean.] Cut in eighths or less and serve as is or with caviar. It may also be put into barque or tart shells for a cocktail party tidbit.

❧ Reader's Request

One of the lighter delectable dishes is known as

QUICHE LORRAINE
For 6

This is the recipe I use.

8-inch pie tin lined with pastry
4 slices crisp bacon, chopped
4 thin slices onion, sautéed until soft
8 paper-thin slices ham, shredded
8 paper-thin slices aged Swiss cheese
3 eggs
¼ teaspoon dry mustard
1 cup light cream, heated
Nutmeg

[Preheat oven to 450° and partially bake pie crust for 10 minutes. Reduce oven to 350°.] Sprinkle the bacon and onion over the bottom of pie crust. Add ½ the shredded ham, 4 slices of the cheese spread over the ham. Add the rest of ham and the cheese on top. Beat the eggs and mustard, [gradually] add the hot cream, and continue beating. Pour over the ham and cheese. Let stand 10 minutes. Sprinkle a tiny bit of nutmeg on top and bake until custard is set, [and a knife inserted in the center comes out clean].

To keep egg yolks from forming a hard crust in the refrigerator, slide them into a bowl and cover with cold water.

Piperade is a wonderful egg dish, but as someone once said, never before 10 AM unless you are addicted to garlic. It does disappear like magic on a brunch buffet.

PIPERADE
For 8 to 10

2 tablespoons butter
1 tablespoon olive oil (you may omit)
2 cloves garlic, crushed
½ cup thinly sliced onion
2 green peppers, slivered and blanched
4 ripe peeled tomatoes, chopped
1 tablespoon plus 1 teaspoon salt [divided use]
⅛ teaspoon white pepper
¼ cup chopped parsley
12 eggs
Cracked pepper
Chopped chives or parsley

Melt the butter, add the olive oil and sauté the garlic, onion and green peppers for 1 minute. Add tomatoes and cook slowly until all the liquid from the tomatoes has evaporated. Add 1 tablespoon salt, white pepper and parsley. Beat the eggs lightly with remaining teaspoon of salt and stir gently into the hot tomato mixture. Let them cook over low heat until set. They should never be hard-cooked. Slide onto a heated platter or serve in the skillet. Sprinkle with cracked pepper and chives.

For a large group as I usually have, I soft-scramble the eggs in a separate skillet and then pile them on top of the tomato mixture. Eat as soon as possible in either case. Anchovies are a nice addition for supper, but not for breakfast. I use smoked sausage with this frequently.

A quick Raclette: place Monterey Jack cheese on an ovenproof plate and bake in a preheated 450° oven until it begins to melt. Serve as a cocktail tidbit with small (hot) boiled potatoes and green onions.

Vegetables and Cooked Fruits

One could spend a lifetime expounding on the vegetable kingdom. Personally, I like to cook vegetables just underdone; the "dressing up" that follows finishes the cooking. I find vegetables take on a blissful state if they are made "interesting." These recipes are my most popular and flavorsome attention-getters, especially with the male half of the hungry horde.

Just a foreword: In selecting your fresh vegetables you should look for, first, clean vegetables, free from decay or bruised spots. Generally speaking, depend on your eyes rather than your fingers in judging vegetables. After you get them home, wash well, pare or shell, as the case may be, but never soak in water as vitamins and minerals will be lost.

Somewhere back in the days of the early Romans, recipe books advised cooks to add a dash of soda to green vegetables to keep them green, and unfortunately some people still think it necessary. It detracts from the flavor, changes the texture, and goodness knows what happens to the vitamins. Generally speaking, again, vegetables cooked in a small amount of water uncovered, turn out better, both in looks and taste—so don't make vegetable cooking complicated.

ARTICHOKE SOUFFLÉ

3 tablespoons butter
3 tablespoons flour
¾ cup milk
2 teaspoons grated onion
1 teaspoon salt
6 egg yolks
2½ cups mashed canned or freshly cooked artichoke bottoms
7 egg whites

[Preheat oven to 350°.] Melt the butter, add the flour, cook until
bubbly. Pour in milk [a little at a time] and cook until thick, [stirring
constantly]. Remove from heat. Add onion, salt, egg yolks and mashed
artichokes. Let mixture cool (until you can put your hand on bottom
of pan). Beat egg whites until stiff. Stir one third of them [into the
artichoke mixture]; fold in the rest. Pour into buttered 2-quart casserole. Bake for 35 to 40 minutes, or set in a pan of hot water and bake
1 hour, but test with a toothpick or cake tester. Serve as is or with
Hollandaise Sauce [page 224].

*Asparagus has been claimed the "aristocrat" of the vegetable world. It
comes from the royal family of the orchid and lily and has been held
in high esteem for at least 2000 years. It is believed to be a native of the
eastern Mediterranean and Asia Minor and grows wild over much of
that area today. The Greeks and Romans cultivated it; they cooked it
quickly. . . . Asparagus adds a touch of elegance to any dinner, so treat
it with the respect due it.*

*Fresh vegetable markets have all sizes of asparagus, from "grass" to
jumbo spears, flirting with the housewife. . . . Of course to really
appreciate the treasured taste of fresh asparagus you should cut it in
your own yard, then run, not walk, to a pot of boiling water and cook
it and eat it at once. But buy it as fresh as possible, take it home
quickly, and either cook it or refrigerate it. And do remember that thin
asparagus has more flavor than thick, or at least the vegetable market
buyers say so, and I agree with them, but the thicker stalks look more
elegant on a plate.*

In preparing asparagus, remove the "scales" with a paring knife or vegetable peeler and wash many times in cold water. Sand sticks like mad to these scales and in the tiny ridges of the stalk. The white part of the stalk should be broken off, too. Tie the stalks in a small bunch and stand in a deep pot, or lay flat in a shallow pan, cover and boil until tender, about 12 to 15 minutes.

Dress with melted sweet butter or any of the dressings suggested for broccoli, and of course Buca Lapi [see page 248]. Served cold with Vinaigrette Dressing, it is a surprise vegetable with a hot entrée; or my favorite way—mayonnaise whipped up with lemon juice and grated lemon peel on top. Or serve

ASPARAGUS SOUR CREAM

Asparagus
1 cup sour cream
¼ cup mayonnaise
2 tablespoons lemon juice
2 tablespoons bread crumbs
Butter

Combine sour cream, mayonnaise and lemon juice. Heat [but do not boil] and pour over asparagus that has been boiled and drained. Brown dry white bread crumbs in butter and sprinkle over the cream mixture. Run under the broiler until bubbly.

ASPARAGUS FROMAGE
For 4

4 mushroom caps
2 tablespoons butter
2 tablespoons flour
1 cup milk
½ teaspoon salt
⅛ teaspoon dry mustard
2 tablespoons sherry
10 ounces frozen or fresh jumbo asparagus spears
½ cup browned almond halves
¼ cup grated American cheese

Sauté mushroom caps in the butter. Remove and add flour to remaining butter, cook a minute, [gradually] add milk and cook until thick. Add salt, mustard and sherry. [Boil asparagus briefly and drain.] Place cooked asparagus on a serving platter, cover with the browned almonds, and top with mushrooms. Pour sauce over and sprinkle with cheese. Place under low broiler heat until cheese melts.

Green beans, more than any other vegetable, are served without one spark of imagination. Canned, fresh, or frozen, they can be delectable.

GREEN BEAN CASSEROLE
For 6

3 cups cut fresh or frozen green beans
1 cup slivered celery, cut slantwise
½ cup thinly sliced onion
1 cup sliced water chestnuts
½ cup sour cream
¼ cup mayonnaise
⅛ teaspoon curry powder
Salt and pepper

[Preheat oven to 300°.] Cook the beans, celery and onion al dente. Add water chestnuts. Mix with the sour cream, mayonnaise and curry powder. Season to your taste. Pour into a shallow casserole [lightly sprayed with cooking oil] and bake until hot. Run under broiler to brown.

Reader's Request

Spanish Green Beans are asked for time and time again by friends and customers. You can make them ahead of time and refrigerate to heat during the week.

SPANISH GREEN BEANS
For 4

[Preheat oven to 350°.]

    2 strips bacon, chopped
    ¼ cup onion, chopped
    2 tablespoons green pepper, chopped

Fry in heavy skillet until bacon is crisp and onion and pepper are brown. Add:

    1 tablespoon flour

Stir and add:

    2 cups canned tomatoes, drained
    1 cup canned green beans, drained
    Salt and pepper to taste

Place in a casserole [lightly sprayed with cooking oil] and bake for 30 minutes.

The magic of vegetables lies in their dressing. Read with your taste buds for a change.

If you insist on boiling your vegetables, use less water! One-half to one cup of water usually is enough to boil 6 servings of fresh, young, and tender vegetables. You must cook over low heat in a pan with a tight-fitting lid. Watch them—they cook fast.

❧ *Previously Unpublished*

GREEN BEANS WITH ONION AND COCONUT
For 6

4 tablespoons vegetable oil
½ cup thinly sliced onion
¼ teaspoon cayenne pepper, scant
4 cups cooked green beans, or canned green beans, drained
1 teaspoon salt
½ cup grated coconut

Heat the oil in a large skillet and sauté the onion slices until they are limp. Sprinkle with pepper and continue cooking for 1 minute. Add beans, salt and coconut. Use a spatula to flip the beans only until they are thoroughly heated. The ¼ teaspoon of cayenne pepper will make this quite hot so you may wish to decrease to a pinch.

I have to be a green bean fan. It is one vegetable that people are not afraid to taste. So I dress them up with lots of butter and things thrown in, like:

Almonds or Brazil nuts, sliced and browned in butter.

Keep a jar of dry bread crumbs on top of your range or in the refrigerator, made from all the leftover bread crusts or rolls. Toss and sauté a few in the butter you pour over the beans, with or without garlic.

Sauté fresh chopped mushroom stems with a dash of Beau Monde seasoning and swish the cooked beans around in them.

Sauté thin slices of sweet onions and serve on top of the cooked beans.

Finely diced bacon and onion sautéed together until the bacon is crisp and the onion soft, gives the Southern touch to green beans when tossed about liberally.

One teaspoon prepared mustard or horseradish added to ¼ cup butter.

Little pickled pearl onions, sliced water chestnuts, bamboo shoots, here and there in butter.

And, when I first started eating out in New York, I used to see on menus in Italian restaurants Asparagus Buca Lapi. The name always fascinated me so one day I tried it. I have never dared use the name, but I have Buca Lapied every vegetable known to man ever since. You merely pour hot melted butter over hot cooked vegetables, especially green beans, and sprinkle with grated Parmesan cheese. Try it sometime on any vegetable. Parmesan cheese surely has something to add flavor to vegetables; likewise Provolone.

Ⓑ *Reader's Request*

RED BEANS AND RICE
For 4 to 6

½ cup diced onion
¼ cup diced green pepper
2 tablespoons butter
3 cups canned or cooked red beans [or kidney beans]
1 cup diced cooked ham
Cooked rice

[Preheat oven to 350°.] Sauté onion and green pepper in butter until soft. Add beans and ham. Pour into casserole and bake for 30 minutes. Serve with a scoop of rice.

[Red beans, oval-shaped and about the size of navy beans, are a regional variant of kidney beans. Camellia brand is preferred by native Louisianans. Kidney beans, either light or dark, are often substituted. In New Orleans this dish is still widely served on Mondays, a tradition which evolved from the time when washer women came to homes to do the laundry, an all-day backbreaking chore. This dish is inexpensive, nutritious, and practically cooks itself. Many local restaurants still feature it on Mondays.— Editor]

How many beans? One cup of uncooked dried beans yields about 2½ cups of cooked beans.

Beets have such a divine color—too bad some dye man cannot catch the color for fabric.

BEETS IN ORANGE SAUCE
For 6

2 16-ounce cans baby beets
2 tablespoons grated orange peel
2 tablespoons cornstarch
2 tablespoons beet juice or water
1 cup orange juice
4 tablespoons lemon juice
2 tablespoons vinegar
2 tablespoons sugar
½ teaspoon salt
4 tablespoons butter

[Drain beets, reserving juice. Grate orange peel before squeezing.] Mix cornstarch with beet juice and add to orange juice, lemon juice, and vinegar. Cook until clear; add sugar, salt, and beets. Heat and add butter and grated orange peel. Serve hot.

PICKLED BEETS
For 6

Always add to a menu. Make them frequently and keep on hand.

1 16-ounce can whole baby beets
Vinegar to cover
6 cloves
1 tablespoon sugar
1 slice lemon
1 slice onion

Drain beets, cover with vinegar, add cloves, sugar, lemon, and onion. Bring to a boil, remove from heat and let stand for a few hours. Serve hot or cold.

Try fresh Brussels sprouts, sliced, cooked 6 minutes in a small amount of water. Drain, add butter and grapes. Season to your taste with salt and pepper and a tiny dash of cinnamon.

BRUSSELS SPROUTS
For 4 or 6

1 pound fresh or 20 ounces frozen Brussels sprouts
2 tablespoons chopped onion
2 tablespoons butter
1 cup sour cream

Find yourself a [steamer] . . . or put the sprouts in a strainer, water in the bottom of a pot and cover, but do not let the vegetables sit in the water. Anyhow, steam the Brussels sprouts about 10 minutes, or until tender. Sauté the onion in the butter, add the cream and heat [but do not boil!]. Add Brussels sprouts and mix well.

GREEN CABBAGE WITH BACON AND PARSLEY
For 8

1 large head green cabbage, cored
3 tablespoons sugar
3 tablespoons salt
2 cups boiling water
¼ cup butter [melted]
4 slices bacon, finely diced and cooked crisp
¼ cup chopped parsley
Salt and white pepper
[¼ cup pine nuts optional]

Cut the cabbage into 2-inch pieces. Cover with cold water; add the sugar and salt. Let stand several hours in the refrigerator. Drain. Put in a pot with boiling water; cover and cook for 8 minutes. Drain, add butter, crisp bacon and parsley. Correct seasonings. A variation is to add pine nuts, which are good added to any vegetable.

RED CABBAGE
For 8

3 pounds red cabbage
3 tablespoons butter
1 tablespoon sugar
½ cup vinegar
½ cup currant jelly
1 teaspoon salt

Remove tough outer leaves and core of cabbage. Wash and drain.
Slice very fine [with your food processor]. Melt the butter in a deep
skillet, add the cabbage, sugar and vinegar. Cover and cook 30 minutes or until tender. Stir frequently. Add jelly and salt; blend. Cook 10
minutes longer.

Slipping the least expensive vegetables into the menu is a feat worth trying.

MINT GLAZED CARROTS
For 6

12 young fresh carrots [or 1¾ pounds packaged baby carrots]
½ cup sugar
¼ cup butter [melted]
2 tablespoons chopped fresh mint or dried mint flakes

Wash, scrape and cook carrots in boiling salted water. Drain and
while hot, pour the sugar and butter over them. Cook slowly until the
carrots glaze, but do not brown. When almost ready to serve, sprinkle
with mint.

*Carrots always taste better when seasoned with lemon butter and
nutmeg.*

1½ teaspoons boiling water
2 tablespoons butter
1 tablespoon fresh lemon juice
⅛ teaspoon nutmeg
Chopped parsley for color

Mix and heat. Pour over boiled carrots and serve hot.

Cauliflower is a rugged individualist and there is nothing prettier than fresh cauliflower cooked whole and served in various ways. The simplest and most flavorful way is

CAULIFLOWER
For 6

1 whole fresh cauliflower
2 quarts boiling water
¼ teaspoon salt
½ cup milk
Butter
Paprika

Buy cauliflower that is white and firm and has fresh green leaves. Remove these leaves . . . cut off the stalk, and soak head-down in cold salted water. If there are any little bugs inside they will come out in a hurry.

[Preheat oven to 350°.] Drain and cook cauliflower in an open kettle in boiling salted water and milk—the milk is added to keep the cauliflower white. Cook until tender, about 20 minutes. Drain, place on an ovenproof tray, cover with cracker crumbs (made from the buttery kind), sprinkle with butter and paprika, and place in the oven to brown. Remove and serve at once.

You cannot reheat cauliflower very successfully; it takes on a strong, unpleasant taste and usually turns dark.

CELERY AMANDINE
For 4

4 [fresh or] canned celery hearts
2 tablespoons butter
1 cup canned consommé
1 teaspoon arrowroot or cornstarch
2 tablespoons cold water
Salt and freshly ground pepper
½ cup slivered almonds in their skins
2 tablespoons chopped parsley

[Preheat broiler.] Brown the celery in the butter. Add the consommé and simmer for 5 minutes. Add the arrowroot or cornstarch to the cold water and add to the casserole. Cook until thickened. Season to taste. Sprinkle nuts on the top (I like these browned in [additional] butter) and run under broiler for 1 minute. Sprinkle with parsley. Divine! And especially good with beef.

Other celery combinations I like:

Fresh celery cut slant-wise and thin, boiled 1 minute only in salted water, then combined with salted peanuts or pecans and whipping cream or a Thin Cream Sauce [page 223]; or combined with sliced sautéed mushrooms and browned almonds; or dressed with sweet butter and lots of chopped parsley.

In Italy, basil is called "Kiss-me-Nicholas" and any girl approaching a favorite young man with her basil sprig is hoping for a kiss.

How do you skin fresh peppers? Roast the peppers in an oven until the skins are well blistered (no harm will be done if they blacken a little). Then remove them from the oven, put them at once in a pot, and cover. Let the peppers stand (off the heat) for about five minutes. The steam will have loosened the skins and they can be easily removed.

❧ *Reader's Request*

Corn Pudding is the "Company" dish.

CORN PUDDING
For 8

¼ cup butter
¼ cup flour
2 teaspoons salt
1½ tablespoons sugar
1¾ cups milk
3 cups fresh or frozen corn
3 eggs

[Preheat oven to 350°.] Melt butter in saucepan, stir in flour, salt and sugar. Cook until bubbly; [gradually] add milk and cook until thick. Stir in the corn, either chopped or whole, but chopped makes a smoother pudding. Stir in the eggs that have been beaten until frothy. Pour into a well-buttered casserole and bake in a hot water bath for about 45 minutes.

❧ *Reader's Request*

FRESH CORN FRITTERS
For 6

1 pint grated fresh corn
½ cup milk from the corn and milk added to make the ½ cup
2 eggs, separated
½ cup flour
1 teaspoon salt
1 teaspoon baking powder
1 tablespoon melted butter

The uncooked corn is grated off the cob and mixed with the milk and slightly beaten egg yolks. The flour, salt and baking powder are mixed together and added and then the melted butter. The egg whites are beaten stiff and folded in last. Drop the batter on a greased hot griddle or frying pan and cook like pancakes. Serve with melted butter, syrup and scads and scads of crisp bacon.

[Use a sharp thin-bladed knife to cut the corn from the cobs. Then stand each cob in a tall-sided mixing bowl and rub the dull edge of the knife down the cobs to release the corn milk. — Editor]

⊱ *Previously Unpublished*

BRAISED CORN
For 12 to 14

12 ears of corn
½ cup butter
1 large onion, finely chopped
4 canned green chiles, chopped
4 cups peeled, seeded and coarsely chopped tomatoes
2 teaspoons salt
½ teaspoon chili powder
Grated Monterey Jack cheese

Preheat broiler. Cut the corn from the cob and set aside. Heat the butter in a large skillet with a lid and sauté the onion until it becomes yellow. Add the chiles and tomatoes and simmer uncovered for 15 minutes before you add the salt and chili powder. Add corn to the tomato mixture. Cover and cook for about 4 more minutes. Correct the seasonings. Turn into a lightly oiled ovenproof dish. Sprinkle with cheese and run under a hot broiler to brown.

Eggplant in the markets is a thing of beauty. I love to look at their satiny Victorian purples and reds, and after discovering they have an affinity for olive oil, I find them most succulent. And popular with all ages.

FRIED EGGPLANT

Cut one eggplant, medium size, in ¼-inch slices, soak in salted water (2 cups water, 2 tablespoons salt) for one hour. Drain and dry. Sprinkle with salt and pepper and roll in flour. Sauté slowly in butter or salad oil until brown on both sides, turning only once. Drain on paper. I like to use this as a base for stuffed mushrooms.

EGGPLANT AND MUSHROOM CASSEROLE
For 8

3 medium eggplants, peeled
1 cup finely chopped onion
½ cup butter [divided use]
4 eggs, beaten
1 cup mayonnaise
1 pound finely chopped fresh mushrooms
Salt and pepper
4½ ounces cream cheese, softened
¼ cup finely chopped parsley
Pinch of thyme
3 tablespoons grated Gruyère cheese
¼ cup fine white bread crumbs

Cover eggplants with water and 1 tablespoon salt, and let stand for 30 minutes. Drain and cook in fresh water until tender. Drain well. [Preheat oven to 350°.] Cut in cubes and place in large bowl. Sauté the onion in 2 tablespoons of butter until yellow. Add to eggplant. Stir in eggs and mayonnaise. Sauté mushrooms in 4 tablespoons butter. Add to the eggplant mixture. Mix thoroughly. Season to taste. Place in a buttered 2-quart casserole. Mix cream cheese with parsley, thyme, Gruyére and bread crumbs. Spread over top of casserole mixture. Sprinkle with 2 tablespoons melted butter. Bake until set and browned, about 40 minutes. You can make this ahead of time and refrigerate it until you're ready to bake and serve it.

This is the most versatile of all vegetable dishes. You may use it hot or cold, as an hors d'oeuvre, salad or main dish; keep it covered in your refrigerator for several days. I like to put Ratatouille in crêpes and use for a luncheon or brunch.

RATATOUILLE
For 8

3 medium-sized zucchini
1 medium-sized eggplant, peeled
4 tomatoes, peeled
2 green peppers
1 cup thin-sliced onion
1 clove garlic, minced
¼ cup vegetable oil or half olive oil
Salt and pepper
Parsley

Slice zucchini and peeled eggplant into ¼-inch slices. Cut tomatoes into medium dice. Seed the peppers, slice thin and blanch.* Sauté the onion and garlic in the oil until soft; do not brown. Add tomatoes, cook 1 minute. Mix in rest of ingredients, cover and bring to boiling point. Cook 5 minutes. Remove cover and cook at simmer heat until all liquid has evaporated. Correct seasonings; sprinkle with chopped parsley for added color.

[*To blanch green peppers, slice and put in a colander or strainer. Pour boiling water through it and drain thoroughly. This gets rid of the oily taste to which many object. —Editor]

RATATOUILLE IN CRÊPES

[Preheat oven to 350°.] Put ¼ cup of Ratatouille in each crêpe, roll loosely and place in a buttered shallow casserole. Sprinkle with grated Parmesan or with half Parmesan and half grated Swiss cheese. Place in oven until hot and run under broiler to brown. Allow 2 crêpes per person. I serve these as a vegetable with roast beef or lamb, but then I would serve Ratatouille with anything, because my guests think me smarter than I am. No doubt because I can pronounce Ratatouille.

There is no vegetable more exciting to the taste buds than fennel, either in a salad or as a vegetable.

FENNEL AU GRATIN
For 8 to 10

4 bulbs fennel
⅓ cup butter
⅔ cup heavy cream or Thin Cream Sauce [page 223]
Salt and white pepper
¼ cup grated Parmesan cheese
¼ cup grated Gruyère cheese

Wash fennel well, trim and discard the tops. Slice the bulbs and cook in boiling salted water until tender, not soft. Melt the butter and sauté until a light brown. Transfer to [lightly oiled] serving casserole, cover with the cream, sprinkle with salt and pepper. Cover with the cheese. Run under broiler to brown. You can prepare this vegetable ahead of time and refrigerate. To warm, bake at 350°.

❧ *Reader's Request*

This was served to a huge Sunday Morning Brunch . . . in Dallas, Texas. Husbands and wives alike were going back for seconds, so I thought it worthwhile to investigate. It was!

HOMINY AND MUSHROOM CASSEROLE
For 6

2 cups canned hominy, drained
1 cup canned mushroom soup
1 teaspoon Worcestershire sauce
½ teaspoon salt
Cornflakes rolled into crumbs
1 tablespoon butter

[Preheat oven to 300°.] Mix the hominy, mushroom soup, Worcestershire sauce and salt. Pour into a buttered casserole, sprinkle with the crushed cornflakes, and dot with butter. Bake until brown.

Mushrooms are considered a luxury unless you live near the source of supply. They should be handled with respect. Peel or scrub, depending on how you feel about it, and wash. Remove the stems and keep to chop for sauce or soup. Almost always you sauté them before using, so it is important to do this correctly:

For every pound of mushrooms, use 4 tablespoons of butter, ½ teaspoon salt and the juice of ½ lemon. Cook over low heat for 5 minutes, stirring occasionally. Then go on from there.

Served in a Thin Cream Sauce [page 223], they make a luscious vegetable. Serve them either sautéed or in cream, on toast or hot biscuits that are spread with deviled or Virginia ham for a delightful luncheon dish. Stuffed with seafood, chicken, or ham, they are an excellent entrée for a buffet supper or a tidbit for cocktails.

MUSHROOMS AU CRESSON IN CRÊPES
For 8

2 pounds fresh mushrooms
½ cup butter
½ cup finely chopped onion
½ teaspoon salt
2 tablespoons flour
½ cup dry white wine
2 cups sour cream
3 cups watercress leaves, not minced but leaves removed from
    stems, about 2 bunches
½ teaspoon Worcestershire sauce
16 thin crêpes [page 91 or purchased]

[Preheat oven to 350°.] Wash and slice the mushrooms. Sauté in the butter with the onion and salt. Add the flour, cook until bubbly. [Gradually] pour in the wine and cook until thickened, stirring. Add the sour cream, watercress and Worcestershire sauce and heat only. Correct seasonings. Put 2 tablespoonfuls in each crêpe, roll and place in a shallow 8 x 12-inch casserole or in a Crêpe Suzette pan. Bake until hot. Run under broiler to brown. This is a good first course for a seated dinner. Without the crêpes, this is a good hot cocktail dip for steak bits or meat balls. Sometimes I add a tablespoon of Dijon mustard to the mixture.

A popular Potluck luncheon is

MUSHROOMS AND ARTICHOKES IN MUSTARD CREAM
For 4

8 large mushrooms
¼ cup butter
1 tablespoon flour
½ cup milk
½ cup light cream
1½ teaspoons prepared mustard [Corbitt preferred Dijon]
1½ cups artichoke hearts (canned or frozen)
Pastry shells
1 tablespoon chopped chives

Sauté the mushrooms in the butter until tender. Remove. Add the flour, cook until bubbly, and [gradually] add the milk, cream and mustard. Cook until thick [stirring constantly]. Add the mushrooms and the artichokes, heated in their juices and then drained. Serve in thin pastry shells with the chives sprinkled on top. With this, fresh okra with lemon butter [page 251] and hot peeled cherry tomatoes and a Fruit Ring with Apricot Dressing [page 101].

MUSHROOM SOUFFLÉ
For 10 or 12

There will be more than enough to fill the Crown Roast of Lamb [page 197]. Put the rest in a buttered soufflé dish [or two 1½ quart dishes] and bake along with the lamb. This is a good way to use up mushroom stems also. And use this recipe any time, lamb or no.

> 1½ pounds fresh mushrooms
> ¼ cup finely diced onion
> 1 teaspoon salt
> Pinch of thyme
> 6 tablespoons butter
> 4 tablespoons flour
> 1½ cups hot milk
> 8 eggs, separated [beat whites until stiff]
> 2 tablespoons grated Parmesan cheese

[Preheat oven to 350°.] Wash, dry and chop the mushrooms fine. Sauté with the onion, salt, and thyme in the butter until the onions are soft. Add the flour and cook until foamy. Cook 1 minute more. Add hot milk slowly and cook until thickened, stirring constantly for about 5 minutes. Cool slightly and add the beaten egg yolks. Cool and stir in one third of the beaten egg whites. Fold in the rest and pour into the lamb roast cavity or soufflé dishes. Sprinkle with Parmesan cheese. Return to oven and bake for 40 minutes.

The onion might be classed as a lily of the field, and surely no cultivated plant has a history more ancient. . . .

A good cook will, no doubt, approach the pearly gates with an onion in one hand and a pound of butter in the other. So you had better learn your p's and q's about onions. The American variety of onion should be bought and used before it has begun to sprout, and in picking out your onions buy them with thin tight necks and crisp skin, regardless of color. Along with this, you should know too that onions contain vitamins B, G, and C, large amounts of minerals, protein, calcium and nitrogen especially, a volatile oil that gives a pungent smell and taste, and that one medium onion contains 125 calories. Our grandmothers had other knowledge—like onion syrup for colds, heated onion hearts for earaches and so forth. So, you cannot miss the pearly gates if you treat this glamour vegetable, fruit, or flower—named as you like—with respect.

Onions may be added to corn pudding, to fritters, to any green vegetable to give it a dash, to oyster stew, even to sauerkraut, to corn bread, to hot biscuits, to pie crust for meat pies—of course to any salad; in fact, to anything except perhaps vanilla ice cream.

A few things to remember about cooking onions may make them more acceptable:

Red Spanish onions are best for baking and sautéing.

White mild sweet onions for salads, or the purple ones.

Yellow ones for stuffing or French-frying.

Small white ones for boiling and creaming. Add a dash of vinegar or lemon juice to keep them white.

A taste teaser to be served with beef of any kind, or I like them with an all-vegetable dinner, or baked beans.

BROILED ONIONS ON TOAST

[Preheat broiler.] Slice large Bermuda or sweet white onions paper-thin. Place on a long shallow pan or ovenproof casserole. Pour a little olive or vegetable oil over and broil to a delicate brown on both sides, turning carefully with a spatula. Place on heavily buttered toast rounds [toasted in the same shallow pan]. Sprinkle with Parmesan cheese and run them under the broiler again for a few seconds before serving.

SCALLOPED ONIONS AND NUTS
For 6

12 small [white] boiling onions
1 cup diced cooked celery
4 tablespoons butter
3 tablespoons flour
1 teaspoon salt
⅛ teaspoon pepper
1 cup milk
½ cup light cream
½ cup blanched almonds or Spanish peanuts with skins
Paprika
Grated Parmesan cheese (optional)

[Preheat oven to 350°.] Wash and peel the onions and cook in boiling salted water until tender. Drain. Prepare the celery the same way. Make a cream sauce: melt butter in saucepan, add flour, salt and pepper; cook over low heat until bubbly; add milk and cream a little at a time and cook until thick, stirring constantly. Place the onions, celery and almonds or peanuts in layers in a buttered or lightly oiled casserole. Cover with the cream sauce, sprinkle with paprika and bake until bubbly and brown. Add Parmesan cheese, too, if you like.

[Helen Corbitt published this recipe using two different kinds of nuts. —Editor]

❧ *Previously Unpublished*

ONION AND APPLE CASSEROLE
For 4 to 6

4 large white onions
4 Rome Beauty apples
1 teaspoon cinnamon
2 tablespoons sugar
Salt and pepper
¼ cup butter

Preheat oven to 350°. Cut the onions into ¼-inch thick slices. Simmer for 10 minutes in just enough water to cover them; drain, saving the liquid. Peel, core and slice the apples. Lightly spray a casserole dish and fill with alternate layers of onions and apples. Mix the cinnamon and sugar together and add salt and pepper to your taste; sprinkle over the top. Dot with butter. Pour ½ cup of the water left from cooking the onions over the dish. Cover with a tight lid or foil and bake for about 1 hour.

Freshly cooked peas combined with sautéed mushrooms, and just enough heavy cream to "stick 'em," a dash of nutmeg and salt and pepper is a luscious party vegetable.

I find peas and rice combined make a pretty vegetable and one that is accepted by those who care for neither separately.

ૐ *Reader's Request*

I treat peas the same as beans to keep them from being just plain old peas! *And find that adding chopped chives or green onion tops, fresh mint, garlic salt, fresh or dried tarragon and Spice Islands Fines Herbes keeps everyone happy.*

HOSTESS PEAS
For 6

4 strips bacon
¼ cup minced onion
1 tablespoon water
2 tablespoons butter
3 cups cooked frozen peas
¼ cup shredded lettuce
½ teaspoon salt
1 teaspoon chopped pimento (you may add or omit)

Dice bacon and sauté until crisp; remove. Sauté onion in bacon fat until soft, remove and drain. Put the water and butter in a skillet, add the peas and lettuce, and cook until lettuce is wilted. Add bacon and onion and season. If you use the pimento, add just before serving.

A great company dish.

PEAS IN SOUR CREAM
For 8

20 ounces frozen or fresh young tender peas
1 cup sour cream
1 teaspoon horseradish
1 teaspoon chopped fresh mint
1 teaspoon Pernod (optional)
2 tablespoons thinly sliced scallions
1 apple with peeling, finely diced
Salt to taste

Thaw peas if frozen; cook until just tender, if fresh. In a large bowl, mix sour cream, horseradish, mint, Pernod and scallions. Add peas and apples. Season with salt. Chill. Serve as a salad or a cold vegetable.

SPINACH AND WHITE BEANS

2 pounds fresh spinach
4 tablespoons butter
½ cup finely diced cooked ham
2 cups cooked [or canned] white navy beans [drained]
2 tablespoons whipping cream
Salt and pepper
Whiff of nutmeg

Wash spinach and cut away heavy stems. Cook 1 minute in a covered container. Drain and put in your blender [or food processor] until finely chopped. Melt the butter in a large skillet. Add the spinach, ham, and beans. Stir in cream and cook until the consistency of mashed potatoes. Correct seasonings and add just a whiff of nutmeg. This is a good way to get your children to eat spinach.

CRESPOLINI

1 pound fresh or frozen [chopped] spinach
1 cup Ricotta cheese or dry cottage cheese
2 eggs
½ cup grated Parmesan cheese
16 thin crêpes
1 cup Thin Cream Sauce [page 223]
1 cup grated Muenster cheese
[Butter]

[Preheat oven to 375°]. Cook the spinach 1 minute if fresh, or defrost the frozen. Drain dry. Put in the blender and purée. Mix with the Ricotta cheese, lightly beaten eggs and the Parmesan cheese. Put 2 tablespoonfuls in each crêpe. Roll and place in a buttered shallow casserole. Cover lightly with the cream sauce and sprinkle with the grated Muenster cheese and a few dots of butter. Bake until bubbling. Run under broiler to lightly brown. Do ahead and bake later? Yes!

*The yellow crook-neck squash you find below the Mason-Dixon Line
are popular when stuffed. The white squash (cymlings—called patty
pan squash up No'th) are equally so. When they are over 3 inches in
diameter, forget about them. Both are pretty on a luncheon plate or
served on a silver tray garnished with parsley or watercress.*

STUFFED SQUASH
For 6

12 small squash

Cook unpeeled in boiling salted water until tender. Cool, cut hole in
the top and dig centers out with a teaspoon, being careful not to
break the squash as they are fragile.

    2 tablespoons onion, chopped fine
    1 teaspoon chopped parsley
    2 tablespoons butter
    1 cup squash pulp, seeds and skin, chopped fine
    3 tablespoons bread crumbs [divided use]
    1 hard-cooked egg, chopped fine
    1 teaspoon chopped pimento
    Salt and pepper

[Preheat oven to 350°.] Sauté onion and parsley in butter until onion is
yellow and soft. Add squash pulp, 2 tablespoons bread crumbs, egg
and pimento. Mix and season to your taste with salt and pepper. Fill
cavities of the squash; sprinkle with 1 tablespoon bread crumbs,
buttered*; place on a buttered tray and bake for 20 minutes or until
the crumbs are brown and sizzling.

[*To butter bread crumbs, melt butter, add bread crumbs and cook
until foamy.—Editor]

*Slivering vegetables instead of dicing them makes for better flavor,
if only psychologically.*

ᵌ❧ *Reader's Request*

When the squash is larger . . .

SQUASH PUDDING*
For 8

½ cup finely chopped onion
4 tablespoons butter
4 pounds yellow or white squash
1½ cups fine bread crumbs
4 tablespoons chopped pimento
1 tablespoon salt
¼ teaspoon pepper
2 eggs, beaten

[Preheat oven to 350°.] Sauté onion in butter until soft and light brown. Wash and slice squash. Cook in boiling salted water until it is soft. Drain and put through an electric blender [or food processor]. Add sautéed onion, bread crumbs, pimento and seasonings. Add eggs and beat thoroughly. Pour into a well buttered casserole and bake for 30 minutes.

[*Mea culpa! I have changed the name of this dish from Soufflé to Pudding because the ingredients and technique will not produce a true soufflé. They do make a delectable pudding.—Editor]

BAKED ACORN SQUASH
For 8

4 [medium] acorn squash
Salt and pepper
½ cup butter
½ cup chutney
½ cup grated coconut

[Preheat oven to 350°.] Wash squash and cut in half. Remove seeds and place the halves cut side down in a shallow pan [lightly sprayed with cooking oil], cover tightly with foil and bake until soft, [between 40 minutes and 1 hour]. Remove, sprinkle each half with salt and pepper; add 1 tablespoon butter or less depending on size of squash. Add the chutney and coconut. Return to oven and bake until bubbly.

ZUCCHINI FANS WITH MICHAEL SAUCE
For 4

Choose 8 small zucchini about 4 inches long, allowing two per person. I find one zucchini is never enough. Slice lengthwise almost to the stem end into as many thin slices as you can. The more slices, the prettier the fan. Cook in your steamer or in very little water until tender, about 6 minutes. Drain and arrange on a serving dish in fan shapes.

MICHAEL SAUCE (1 cup)
¾ cup sour cream
2 teaspoons tarragon vinegar
2 egg yolks, lightly beaten
½ teaspoon paprika

Cook all ingredients over hot water, not boiling, until thick and smooth. You must stir constantly. Spoon sauce over the fans, sprinkle lightly with salt and run under the broiler for 1 minute just before serving.

Peeled, cut in half lengthwise with the seeds left in, simmered just until tender in salted water and then served with Hollandaise Sauce [page 224], zucchini is a dish fit for a king.

❧ *Reader's Request*

Here is another special tomato treat to serve with chicken. The flavor is ecstatic.

TOMATOES SUPREME

[Preheat oven to 350°.] Wash medium-sized ripe tomatoes and cut in half crosswise. Cover with a mixture of ½ cup sour cream, ½ cup mayonnaise and ½ teaspoon of curry powder. Place on a lightly oiled or buttered pan and bake until soft.

Tomatoes have been included in low-calorie diets for years, and personally I feel they are overworked. They can be more palatable with the addition of herbs and seasonings. This dish is a favorite.

TARRAGON TOMATOES
For 6

3 ripe tomatoes
1 clove garlic, minced
⅛ teaspoon dried tarragon
⅛ teaspoon cracked pepper
A few sprinklings of Parmesan cheese

[Preheat oven to 350°.] Cut tomatoes in half [crosswise]. Combine garlic, tarragon, pepper and cheese. Sprinkle over the tomatoes and bake until tender, about 30 minutes. (Each tomato half has only 19 calories.)

Tomatoes are good, too, sliced and covered with heavy cream, salt and pepper and broiled until the cream bubbles. And sometime broil them plain with a thin slice of onion on top and Cheddar cheese. Heavens, put anything on them and broil—make them glamorous in your own inimitable fashion!

It has been said herbs are the wit of cooking, but even wit should be tempered. So herbs and spices should be used not with a heavy hand, but with a light and disciplined one, thus producing a subtle delight for the taste buds.

TURNIP PUDDING
For 6

8 medium white turnips, peeled and sliced
2 tablespoons onion, chopped
½ cup skim milk
Salt to taste
2 egg whites
Minced parsley or chopped chives

[Preheat oven to 350°.] Cook the turnips and onion in a steamer, or covered with boiling water, until just tender. Do not overcook. Drain. Mash or whip thoroughly in a blender or food processor. Heat the milk, add turnips, and cook until the milk is absorbed. Cool. Season and fold into the stiffly beaten egg whites. Pour into a lightly buttered casserole and bake until the pudding is puffy and lightly browned. Or skip the egg whites and serve sprinkled with chopped parsley or chives.

Variation: Substitute yellow turnips and bake in a scooped-out orange shell.

❧ *Reader's Request*

I have used this recipe for the cooking schools I have taught and the increase in the sale of turnips has been fantastic. The secret is to thin-slice the turnips and cook underdone. You may use rutabagas the same way, but these I like to cut in julienne strips.

TURNIPS AND PEAS IN CREAM

8 small white turnips, peeled and sliced paper-thin
2 tablespoons minced onion
3 tablespoons butter
½ teaspoon sugar
½ cup whipping cream
1 cup freshly cooked green peas
Salt and pepper
Chopped parsley

Cook the turnips in a steamer or in boiling water until tender. Drain. Sauté the onion with the butter and sugar for 1 minute. Add turnips and reheat. Add cream and peas and simmer until cream is reduced. Correct seasonings. Sprinkle with parsley.

VEGETARIAN SPAGHETTI SAUCE
4 cups

½ cup finely chopped onion
1 teaspoon finely chopped garlic
1 teaspoon finely chopped celery
1 teaspoon finely chopped parsley
½ cup olive oil
2 cups canned diced tomatoes
2 cups tomato purée
⅛ teaspoon paprika
Salt and pepper
¼ cup sherry

Sauté finely chopped onion, garlic, celery and parsley in olive oil until celery and onions are soft. Add tomatoes, purée and paprika. Cook until well blended and thick and season with salt and pepper. Add sherry and serve at once. Combined with fresh crab flakes or chicken it is a good buffet supper dish. Serve with a dish of grated Parmesan cheese nearby.

You may try anchovy butter on any green vegetable, but especially on fresh green beans.

ANCHOVY BUTTER
¼ cup

¼ cup butter
1 tablespoon lemon juice
1½ teaspoons anchovy paste

Cream butter, lemon juice and anchovy paste. Put on top of freshly cooked green beans and let it melt through them.

Dress vegetables with any flavor of butter you like: onion, chive, herbs, mint, garlic, Beau Monde seasoning, curry, watercress, parsley, all sorts of bread or cracker crumbs. Above all, experiment!

LEMON CHEESE BUTTER
½ cup

¼ cup butter
Grated rind of 2 lemons
1 teaspoon coarse salt (kosher salt)
1 teaspoon cracked pepper
¼ cup chopped parsley
¼ cup grated Gruyère cheese

Soften butter, add rest of the ingredients. Toss into hot cooked vegetables.

Previously Unpublished

PESTO
1 plus cup

1 cup olive oil
½ cup chopped parsley leaves
2 tablespoons fresh basil, stems removed
2 cloves garlic
Pine nuts or walnuts (optional)

Process this in a blender until smooth or chop the nuts by hand and use them as garnish. Pesto has a special affinity for sliced fresh tomatoes and it makes noodles and vegetables sing.

COOKED FRUITS

This dish is more similar to French apple sauce than American apple sauce and can be used as an accompaniment with meats or could be used in apple turnovers:

SAUTÉED APPLES

6 yellow or red Delicious apples
½ cup butter
½ cup sugar
1 tablespoon lemon juice

Peel and core apples; cut them into quarters and slice as thinly as possible. Melt butter in a large skillet over medium heat. Add apple slices, sugar and lemon juice; cook until soft. Lift and carefully turn with a spatula; do not let the apple slices brown. Taste and adjust the seasoning.

The Arabs knew about the lemon a long time before the medical researchers discovered Vitamin C. Its culture was preserved in the 12th and 13th centuries in Spain. The Spanish in turn brought lemons to America. In these days of salt-free diets, a squeeze of lemon juice gives the magic that salt normally provides. At any rate use lemons, Vitamin C and all. Flavor water for ice cubes with lemon juice for beverages, add a mint leaf or olive too. Combine with a little olive oil for vegetables and fish. Let celery stand in cold water and lemon juice for an hour. The celery will be more crisp, white and tender. Add lemon juice to water for pie crust. Use it in place of vinegar for dressings.

I have many choice hot fruits in my recipe file, but I find Curried Pears go with just about anything from lamb to lobster.

CURRIED PEARS

6 fresh pears or 12 canned halves
½ cup butter
½ cup brown sugar
1 tablespoon curry powder [or less]
½ teaspoon salt

[Preheat oven to 325°.] Peel, cut in half and remove core from pears. Mix and pile rest of ingredients in the cavities. Bake covered until soft. Remove cover and run under broiler until sizzling.

A fruit plate made of an assortment of canned fruits prepared the same way is a nice change for morning coffee or brunch.

I was brought up with a healthy respect for rhubarb. I like this recipe with meats of all kinds but chicken and pork in particular.

RHUBARB CRISP
For 6

1 package frozen defrosted rhubarb or 1 pound of fresh rhubarb
1 teaspoon grated orange rind
2 tablespoons orange juice
½ cup sugar [divided use]
¾ cup white bread crumbs, dried out in a 200° oven
Pinch of salt
4 tablespoons soft butter or margarine

[Preheat oven to 350°.] Place rhubarb in a lightly sprayed or buttered shallow casserole. [Grate the orange rind and then squeeze the juice.] Pour orange juice over. Mix half the sugar and all the rind together and sprinkle over. Mix crumbs with rest of sugar, salt and butter. Spread over rhubarb. Bake for about 35 minutes if frozen fruit is used, about 60 minutes if fresh. The crust should be a golden brown.

And Then Potatoes, Grains, and Pasta

There is nothing that smells better than potatoes baking. Idaho potatoes are the popularized ones, but California and Maine produce a fine type for baking or any other style of cooking. For me, Idaho takes the lead for baking because of its shape—long, flat, quicker cooking than the round kind. Just scrubbed and placed in a 350° oven and baked until done, about 1 hour, but timed to come out when you are ready to sit down; or rubbed in vegetable oil and salt; or wrapped in brown paper or aluminum foil to keep them from cooling off. Just bake them, and the whole family will succumb—even the curvaceous ones. Serve with sweet butter or sour cream, chopped chives, grated cheese, crisped salt pork—or all of them.

POTATOES ON THE HALF SHELL
For 6

6 Idaho potatoes
¼ cup milk or cream
1 egg
4 tablespoons butter
Salt and pepper
1 tablespoon chopped green onions [optional]

[Preheat oven to 350°.] Bake the potatoes, cut in half lengthwise and scoop out the potato. Mash, while hot, with the milk, beaten egg, and butter and beat until fluffy. Season with salt and pepper, and onion if you wish. Spread the shell with [additional] butter and pile lightly and high into it. Sprinkle with a smidgen of nutmeg or paprika or grated Parmesan cheese.* Bake until brown on top.

[*May be frozen at this point and rebaked as needed.—Editor]

⅔ *Reader's Request*

CHANTILLY POTATOES
For 6

6 large potatoes
2 tablespoons butter
¼ cup milk
Salt and pepper
½ cup whipping cream
4 tablespoons grated American [or Parmesan] cheese
Paprika

[Preheat oven to 350°.] Peel and wash potatoes and cook in boiling salted water until tender. Drain and mash with the butter and milk and beat until light and fluffy. Season with salt and pepper. Pour into buttered [or lightly oiled] casserole. Whip the cream until stiff and spread over the potatoes. Sprinkle with cheese and paprika. Bake until brown on top. These are especially good with spicy roast beef.

❧ Reader's Request

Hashed browned potatoes have always been a gastronomical delight for the man who eats away from home, because most housewives do not include them in their menu planning. . . . These potatoes were so popular at the Driskill Hotel in Austin, Texas, that I would be introduced as "The Hashed Browned Potatoes with Sour Cream Girl."

HASHED BROWNED POTATOES
For 6

6 baked potatoes (bake at least the day before and refrigerate)
2 tablespoons soft vegetable shortening
1 teaspoon salt
¼ teaspoon pepper
2 tablespoons melted butter
¼ cup sour cream

Peel and grate the cold baked potatoes on the coarse side of a 4-sided grater. . . . Heat the shortening in a heavy griddle or frying pan. Sprinkle potatoes lightly over the entire surface. Do not pack down. Sprinkle with salt and pepper and the melted butter. Cook over low heat until brown underneath and loose from the pan. You can lift up the edge to see if they are ready without stirring them. When browned, turn once and cook until the second side is brown. Stack in layers on a hot serving dish with warmed sour cream spread between them. ["Mr. Stanley" Marcus is a fan of these special spuds.—Editor]

AU GRATIN POTATOES
For 8

2 quarts diced cold baked potatoes
2 cups Mornay Sauce [page 226]
1 cup Medium Cream Sauce [page 223]
Dash of Angostura bitters
Grated Parmesan cheese
Paprika

[Preheat oven to 350°.] Mix the diced potatoes with Mornay and Cream Sauces; add a dash of Angostura bitters. Pour into a buttered 3-quart casserole and cover with grated Parmesan cheese. Sprinkle with paprika. Bake for 40 minutes.

My employees at Neiman Marcus called these Helen's Cottage Fried Potatoes. You may call them whatever you like. It is difficult to judge how many to fix; given the opportunity, some will eat them like potato chips. I usually allow one-half medium-sized Idaho potato per person.

BROILED POTATO SLICES

[Preheat broiler unit.] Scrub the potatoes and leave the skin on. Slice as thin as you possibly can and no thicker than ⅛-inch. While slicing, drop into cold water to keep from turning dark. When ready to prepare, drain and pour boiling water over for 5 minutes. Drain again and dry the potatoes. Place slices just overlapping, one layer thick in a buttered shallow casserole or skillet. (I use a Crêpe Suzette pan.) Season with salt, pepper and a dusting of paprika and grated Parmesan cheese. Dribble a little melted butter over. Broil on lowest oven rack, about 12 inches from the heating element, until brown. They will be crisp on top, soft on the bottom. You may also brown them in a 375° oven for 30 minutes.

LEMON STEAMED POTATOES

½ cup butter
16 small, peeled new potatoes
2 teaspoons grated lemon peel
1 tablespoon lemon juice
Coarse salt and cracked pepper

Melt the butter in a heavy skillet. Add potatoes, lemon peel and juice. Cover and cook until tender, shaking frequently. Sprinkle with salt and pepper. Toss again before serving.

Add chopped leftover bits of ham and Roquefort cheese to mashed potatoes and casserole them. Bake at 350° until hot. Add to your stuffed potato mixture, too.

❧ Reader's Request

Sweet potatoes are truly American. They were already here when Columbus arrived; the first settlers in the South made them one of their favorite foods and still think a real Southern dinner incomplete without sweet potatoes in some form or another. They have lots of vitamin A, and enough of vitamin C. There are two kinds, one dry and mealy and a light yellow in color; yams are darker and sugary.

SWEET POTATO CASSEROLE
For 6

6 medium-sized sweet potatoes
3 tablespoons butter
1 egg, beaten
2 tablespoons sherry
Salt and pepper
⅛ teaspoon nutmeg
1 tablespoon butter

[Preheat oven to 450°.] Bake scrubbed potatoes until they are done. [Reduce heat to 350°.] Remove, skin, and mash with butter. Add egg to potatoes with the sherry and beat until light and fluffy. Season with salt and pepper, pour into buttered casserole, sprinkle with nutmeg, and dot with butter. Bake for about 30 minutes.

[I've changed the name from "Sweet Potato Soufflé" to "Sweet Potato Casserole." Only Helen Corbitt could make a soufflé with just 1 egg! —Editor]

PECAN SWEET POTATOES
For 6

6 yams
Salted water
½ cup brown sugar
⅓ cup chopped pecans
1 cup orange juice
1 tablespoon grated orange rind
⅓ cup sherry
2 tablespoons butter

[Preheat oven to 350°.] Cook yams in boiling salted water until tender. Peel and cut in half lengthwise. Place in a casserole one layer thick, sprinkle with sugar, pecans, pour over orange rind and juice, and sherry; dot with butter, cover and bake for about 45 minutes or until all the juice has cooked into the potatoes.

Rice has been mentioned as far back as 3000 B.C. in India. Rice came by way of Madagascar to this country 275 years ago when a ship enroute from Madagascar to England was blown off course and put in at Charleston, South Carolina. The captain of the ship gave the governor a small amount of rice as a token of gratitude, and so began a great industry in America. Rice around the world has many ways of being prepared and many recipes are similar. For instance Pais Pidgeon in Jamaica is Hopping John [page 285] in the Southeast. Rice and Almond Pudding in Sweden has only one almond; the boy or girl who finds it in his serving will be the first to marry. In Finland, the finder will have a year of good luck. . . .

As far as I am concerned there is a genie in my kitchen—and it is rice. It will also fit if you are budget-minded. You may never find the end to the various things you can do with it. Uncle Ben's Converted Rice and I have had a love affair for years. I know others are good; I just like Uncle Ben's. You do not need a fancy gadget to cook rice; simply follow the directions on the package. The rice processors know what they are doing, but I always cook rice in a preheated 350° oven in a covered casserole for 45 minutes, regardless of how I may vary the preparation. I do not have to worry about it boiling dry. To me the taste and texture is better. For day-before preparation, I put everything in the casserole, refrigerate, and then put it in the oven at 350° 1½ hours before serving.

There is nothing better than Rice with Curried Fruit to serve with duck or any poultry, pork or ham. I do not recommend it for beef.

RICE WITH CURRIED FRUIT

½ cup chutney, finely chopped
2 cups melon balls (not watermelon)
1 cup diced fresh pineapple
1 banana, sliced
1 cup other soft fruit such as peaches, pears, grapes, etc.
2 cups chicken broth
2 teaspoons cornstarch
2 tablespoons curry powder (or less)
¼ cup [shelled] pistachios
½ cup slivered toasted almonds
¼ cup plumped raisins (Cover with warm water and let stand a
    few hours, then drain)
4 cups cooked rice, hot
Parsley, minced

Mix chutney, melon balls, pineapple, and chill well. [Chill unpeeled banana and soft fruits separately; add bananas and soft fruits to other fruits just before serving.] Mix chicken broth with cornstarch and curry powder and simmer until thickened. Add the nuts and raisins to the chicken broth sauce. Place the hot rice on a heated platter and top with the chilled fruit, then cover the fruit and rice with the curry-flavored sauce. Sprinkle with parsley.

This dish is to be a contrast in flavors and textures. The rice and sauce should be at the boiling point, whereas the fruit should be chilled so that you get the contrast in the hot and cold ingredients. Unfortunately, this dish is not designed for buffet or leisurely serving—it should be eaten immediately upon preparation.

EMERALD RICE SOUFFLÉ
For 6

4 eggs, separated
4 cups cooked rice [cooled]
1 cup raw spinach, minced
½ cup green pepper, minced
¼ cup onion, minced
⅓ cup grated Parmesan cheese
½ teaspoon paprika
1 teaspoon salt
½ cup heavy cream, whipped
Sour cream
Chives

[Preheat oven to 350°.] Beat egg yolks, add rice, spinach, green pepper, onion, grated cheese, paprika, salt and whipped cream. Mix thoroughly, fold in stiffly beaten egg whites. Pour into 1½-quart mold. Place in a pan of hot water and bake for 45 minutes.

A variation is to scoop out unpeeled whole tomatoes, leaving a thick shell. [Place upside down on a wire rack to drain.] Fill with rice mixture and place on a lightly sprayed shallow pan; bake until puffed and lightly browned.

Serve either preparation with sour cream and chives on top.

SAFFRON RICE
For 4

1 cup long-grained rice
1 tablespoon butter
1 tablespoon olive oil
2½ cups boiling chicken bouillon
¼ teaspoon saffron
¼ cup white wine
Salt and pepper

Brown rice in the butter and olive oil. Add the chicken bouillon, saffron and wine. Cover and cook over low heat until the liquid is absorbed. Season with salt and pepper.

❧ *Reader's Request*

ORANGE RICE
For 6

¼ cup butter
1 cup rice
½ teaspoon salt
2 cups chicken broth
½ cup dry white wine
Grated rind and juice of 1 orange
Pepper
Minced parsley [or toasted slivered almonds]

[Preheat oven to 350°.] Place butter, rice, salt, broth, and wine in casserole [buttered or lightly oiled]. Cover and bake until light and feathery, about 45 minutes. Add juice and rind; return to oven for 10 minutes. Correct seasonings, toss with a fork and sprinkle with parsley or almonds.

❧ *Reader's Request*

RICE WITH PINE NUTS
For 6

¼ cup butter
2 tablespoons minced onion
1 cup rice
2½ cups consommé (beef or chicken)
4 ounces pine nuts, toasted
¼ cup minced parsley
Salt and pepper

[Preheat oven to 350°.] Melt butter, add onion and sauté 1 minute. Add rice and consommé. Cover, bake for 45 minutes. Stir in pine nuts and parsley. Correct seasonings.

I like to substitute cooked rice for spaghetti in Tetrazzini dishes, for potatoes to be baked au gratin, or for potatoes in salad.

HOPPING JOHN
For 6 to 8

4 strips bacon
¼ cup chopped onion
2 cups black-eyed peas, fresh or frozen
½ cup raw rice
2 cups boiling water
Salt and pepper

Dice the bacon and fry with the chopped onion. Add to the peas, rice, and water. Cover and cook over low heat until the rice and peas are tender. Add seasoning.

This is served on New Year's Day in many homes—for good luck, you know!

RICE, CHILES, AND CHEESE CASSEROLE
For 6 or 8

3 cups sour cream
1 4-ounce can green chile peppers, seeded and chopped
4 cups cooked rice, packed
Salt and pepper
¾ pound Cheddar cheese, grated

[Preheat oven to 350°.] Mix sour cream and peppers. Season rice with salt and pepper. Put a layer of rice in bottom of a [buttered] 1½ quart casserole, then a layer of sour cream and a layer of cheese. Repeat with cheese on top. Bake until bubbly [about 40 minutes]. Or make ahead of time, refrigerate and bake when ready to serve.

Easy things to remember about rice:

1 cup makes about 3 cups cooked.

Chopped parsley or a pinch of saffron cooked with rice gives a different flavor and nice color for seafood dishes.

Substitute tomato juice for half the water for pink rice.

Garlic salt never hurts rice when you are using it with chicken.

❧ *Previously Unpublished*

SPANISH RICE WITH PEAS AND ARTICHOKES
For 6

2 tablespoons olive oil
1 cup chopped onion
½ cup chopped green pepper
1 cup raw rice
2 cups canned diced tomatoes
2 tablespoons vinegar
Salt and pepper
1 can artichoke hearts, drained and quartered
1 10-ounce package frozen green peas

Preheat oven to 350°. Heat the olive oil in a large skillet and sauté, or fry over low heat, the onion, green pepper and rice until the rice browns. Stir in the tomatoes, vinegar and salt and pepper, seasoning to your taste. Turn into a lightly oiled casserole, cover and bake until the rice is light and feathery, about 45 minutes. Toss the peas and artichoke hearts through the rice. Return to the oven for 15 minutes to reheat.

WILD RICE

is expensive, so you should follow directions to make it palatable. The box it comes in has the best rules to follow, but in case you have thrown it away: Wash and wash and wash in a sieve under running water, until the water is clear. Use:

3 cups water
1 teaspoon salt
1 cup wild rice

Bring to a slow rolling boil, and boil until the rice is flaky and tender when tested. Drain in a sieve, pour water through again, and steam dry over low heat to make fluffy.

With lamb, one of the popular rice dishes that "throw them" is cold cooked rice marinated in red French dressing, drained dry and combined with orange sections.

SHRIMP AND WILD RICE CASSEROLE
For 6

[Prepare 2 cups Thin Cream Sauce using chicken broth in place of milk, according to recipe on page 223.]

½ cup thinly sliced onion
¼ cup thinly sliced green pepper (you may omit)
½ cup mushrooms, thinly sliced
¼ cup butter
1 tablespoon Worcestershire sauce
Few drops Tabasco
2 cups cooked wild rice
1 pound cooked shrimp [shelled]

[Preheat oven to 300°.] Sauté the onion, green pepper, and mushrooms in the butter until soft. Add the seasonings, rice, shrimp and cream sauce. Place in a buttered casserole and bake until thoroughly heated. Or cook in a chafing dish. At any rate, serve it hot!

This is my favorite pasta dish. I use it as an entrée, as a vegetable and as a carrier for various seafoods in cream. As a buffet casserole it has no equal. One gal's opinion!

TONNARELLI
For 4

1 8-ounce package very fine egg noodles
1 4-ounce can sliced mushrooms or 1 pound fresh
3 tablespoons butter [approximate]
½ cup slivered leftover ham—you may omit, too
1 cup cooked peas
½ cup Parmesan cheese

Cook noodles until tender. Drain but do not wash. Slice the mushrooms; if fresh, sauté in additional butter. Add to the hot noodles with butter, ham, peas and the cheese, and toss until everything is well coated with the cheese. I have had guests ask if there were leftovers to take home—so it must be good.

Soothing! I call it mama food.

FETTUCINE ALFREDO
For 8

1 pound fettucine
1 cup butter, softened
1 cup cream at room temperature
2 cups grated or shredded Parmesan cheese

Cook pasta in 8 quarts of boiling water to which 2 tablespoons of salt have been added, about 8 minutes or until al dente. Drain pasta, but do not rinse, and immediately pour it onto a heated platter or into a heated bowl. Toss with butter, cream, and cheese until the cheese and butter are completely melted. Serve at once.

ꝣ *Previously Unpublished*

VERMICELLI À LA CRÈME
For 8

1 pound vermicelli, cooked and drained
½ pound bacon
3 cups creamy cottage cheese
3 cups sour cream
2 cloves garlic, crushed
2 cups minced onion
1 tablespoon White Wine Worcestershire sauce
2 teaspoons salt
3 tablespoons horseradish
½ cup grated Parmesan cheese

Preheat oven to 350°. Cook noodles according to the package directions or as described in the preceding recipe. (If vermicelli is not available, you can use other thin pasta.) Dice the cold bacon and fry until crisp; drain. Mix crisp bacon, cottage cheese, sour cream, garlic, onion, Worcestershire, salt and horseradish together. Turn into a buttered 3-quart casserole. Cover with Parmesan cheese and bake until the dish is hot and bubbly, about 40 minutes.

MACARONI SHELLS STUFFED WITH SPINACH AND CHICKEN LIVERS
For 6

12 largest size macaroni shells
3 quarts boiling water
1 teaspoon salt
1 teaspoon vegetable oil
1 pound fresh spinach
2 cups dry cottage or ricotta cheese*
½ cup grated Parmesan cheese
1 pound chicken livers
2 tablespoons butter
2 eggs, lightly beaten
Pinch of nutmeg
2 cups Thin Cream Sauce [page 223]
Salt and pepper
1 cup grated Gruyère cheese

Cook macaroni in the boiling water with salt and oil al dente, about
15 minutes. Drain, wash, and drain again. Wash spinach, put in a
covered pot [with only the water that clings to it]; cook 1 minute only.
Drain and put in your blender [or food processor] until chopped, but
not liquid. Mix with the [cottage or ricotta cheese and] Parmesan
cheese. Sauté the chicken livers in butter; slice. Add to the cheese
mixture with the eggs and nutmeg. Mix thoroughly. Season to your
taste. Stuff the mixture into the cooked macaroni and place in a
buttered shallow casserole. Pour over the cream sauce (seasoned with
salt and pepper). Sprinkle with the Gruyére cheese and bake. This is
a rich delicious pasta, and one shell should be enough. I usually add
a few more so the men can have two.

[*Rinse cold water through cottage cheese and drain thoroughly. Use
the curds.—Editor]

SPÄETZLE
For 6 to 8

2¼ cups sifted flour
1 egg, beaten
⅔ cup water
½ teaspoon salt

Mix into a soft dough. Form into a log about 2 inches in diameter; let stand 30 minutes. Slice thin and drop into boiling salted water. [Drain and serve with Veal and Pork Meatballs, page 182.]

Also serve späetzle with a sauce made from mixing ¼ cup butter with ¼ cup sour cream. Heat in a skillet [but do not boil] and drop the cooked späetzle in it. Shake over low heat until blended. Nice with roast beef.

MIXED NOODLES
For 6 to 8

1 8-ounce package fine noodles plus 1 cup [divided use]
5 tablespoons butter, divided use
¼ cup half-and-half
¼ cup grated Swiss cheese
Salt and cracked pepper

Cook 8 ounces of the noodles in boiling salted water until tender. Drain, but do not wash. Heat 2 tablespoons butter, half-and-half and cheese together; season to your taste. Fry the other uncooked cup of noodles in 3 tablespoons butter until brown. Toss with the hot cooked noodles.

When you ask your guests to have some groats, they usually say an embarrassed "no thank you," but Kasha, yes.

KASHA

1 cup butter [divided use]
1 cup pine nuts
1 cup thinly sliced onion
2 cups thinly sliced mushrooms
2 cups groats
6 cups chicken or beef broth [heated]

[Preheat oven to 350°.] Melt half of the butter in the casserole you will cook in and sauté the pine nuts until a golden brown. Remove the nuts, add the onions and mushrooms. Sauté until onions are soft, about 1 minute. Stir in the groats and broth; cover and bake for about 1 hour. Add rest of butter and nuts; toss lightly. Kasha is so good with beef, lamb and chicken and my men adored it. You may prepare rice the same way as this Kasha recipe.

❧ *Reader's Request*

GRITS SOUFFLÉ
For 6

2 cups milk
½ cup grits
1 teaspoon salt
½ teaspoon baking powder
½ teaspoon sugar
2 tablespoons melted butter
3 eggs, separated

[Preheat oven to 375°.] Scald milk, add the grits, and cook until thick. Add the salt, baking powder, sugar, and butter. Cool. Beat the egg yolks and add to the grits mixture. Beat the egg whites to a soft peak [and stir about ½ cup into the grits. Fold remaining whites into the batter.] Pour into a well buttered 1½-quart casserole and bake uncovered for 25 to 30 minutes. Cornmeal may be substituted for the grits.

GARLIC CHEESE GRITS
For 10 to 12

1½ quarts water [boiling]
2 cups grits

Cook together until done. Add:

½ cup milk
2 rolls [Kraft] garlic cheese
½ cup butter
Salt and pepper to taste
4 eggs, beaten
Parmesan cheese
Paprika

[Preheat oven to 300°. Mix ingredients except cheese and paprika until smooth.] Pour into a buttered casserole. Sprinkle with Parmesan cheese and paprika. Bake for 30 minutes.

Desserts

The men of my life like desserts. Ask them, and they will deny it, but all these many years the "gooier," the prettier, the bigger the desserts, the more the men eat of them. Dan Moody, one of Texas' most colorful governors, would go to court any day to take exception to the fact that he never liked cake without thick icing and ice cream on top of it. William A. Smith, one of the master builders of Houston, "a simple man" by his own words, would say, "Honey, they kill me!" but lap them up. Herman Brown, silent strong boss of many projects—and of me at the Driskill Hotel—always looked a little sheepish as he guiltily put them away.

❧ *Reader's Request*

What is easier or more gracious than serving Pots de Crème for dessert in the living room with coffee after dinner. The crème pots are available all over the country in china shops—so invest! Good too for holding vitamin pills, cocktail picks or whatever.

POTS DE CRÈME
For 8 except someone always wants two

3 cups half-and-half
9 egg yolks
¾ cup white sugar
¼ teaspoon salt
1½ teaspoons vanilla
Light brown sugar

[Preheat oven to 325°.] Heat the half-and-half. Beat egg yolks with sugar and salt. Beat in the hot half-and-half gradually with a French whip. Add vanilla. Strain and pour into pots de crème cups. Cover the pots and put in a pan of hot water 1-inch deep. Bake for 30 minutes or until a knife when inserted comes out clean. Remove pots and chill. Place a teaspoon of brown sugar on top of each dessert and run under the broiler to melt; cover and serve.

Use the same recipe but change the flavoring: omit the brown sugar (brulée). Add 6 ounces semi-sweet chocolate to the hot milk for Pots de Crème au Chocolat.

Or omit the vanilla and brown sugar and add 4 tablespoons of crème de cacao for another wonderful treat. Or you could flavor the custard with dark rum—watch it!—before baking. Omit running these variations under the broiler; they should be served very cold.

An easy and good dessert is to fill a large tray with whole strawberries, toasted crackers and a brick of cream cheese that has been rolled in granulated sugar. Let everyone help themselves. They can combine it any way they wish—cheese on strawberries, strawberries on cheese, cheese with crackers or whatever you serve. I like Matzo crackers with it.

FLOWERPOTS

are the answer to a party dessert. Actually miniature Baked Alaskas, but you can do so much with them.

At a recent party I built the decorations for the entire meal around the dessert. For a centerpiece, each table had a red clay pot filled with every kind of garden flower available, one with blue bachelor buttons, one with red geraniums, one with daisies, another with pink roses. Then I made the dessert's flowers fit in with the decorations of each table—a pot with roses went to the table with a bouquet of roses, daisies to the table with a daisy arrangement and so on. It was most effective, conversationally and decoratively.

Each Flowerpot is made by choosing a small clay flowerpot, which is first sterilized. [Place clean clay pots upside down on a jelly roll pan and bake them at 350° for 1 hour.] Cool slowly. Place a piece of plain baked cake in the bottom (to cover the hole). Pile with whatever ice cream you like—or sherbet—to three quarters full. Force a large ice cream soda straw into the middle of each pot, and cut it off even with the top of the pot. Pile meringue around the inside of the pot, leaving space over the soda straw open. Bake at 400° until the meringue is brown. Insert fresh flowers in the soda straw—it looks just like what it is, a flowerpot with fresh flowers. It is especially nice for men. They are intrigued by them.

At holiday time, use holly and tiny red roses or carnations. Place the pots on a large silver tray and surround with sprigs of holiday greens—effective.

You can make ahead of time and store in the deep freeze [for up to 3 weeks without meringue or 3 days with it]—all but the flowers, of course.

[Make meringue according to your favorite recipe or by this formula:

   3 egg whites
   2½ tablespoons sugar
   ¾ teaspoon vanilla (optional)

Beat the egg whites until frothy, then gradually add 2½ tablespoons sugar; beat until stiff. Add vanilla.]

ANGEL SOUFFLÉ

6 egg whites
Pinch of salt
Pinch of cream of tartar
1½ cups sugar
1 teaspoon lemon juice
1 teaspoon vanilla

[Preheat oven to 325°.] Beat egg whites with the salt and cream of tartar until stiff. Gradually add sugar and continue to beat until stiff peaks are formed. Add lemon juice and vanilla. Pour into a buttered square 9-inch cake pan or into a buttered ring mold. Bake for 45 minutes. Cool, slice and serve with a soft custard, flavored as you wish, and/or with any fresh fruit. [The center of a ring mold can be filled with custard and fruit.]

Reader's Request

CHERRIES JUBILEE
For 6

1 cup black Bing cherry juice
1 tablespoon cornstarch
¼ cup sugar
½ cup black Bing cherries [pitted]
1 tablespoon butter
2 tablespoons kirsch
2 tablespoons brandy

Bring [all but 2 tablespoons of] juice to a boil. Mix cornstarch, sugar and [remaining] juice and add to the boiling mixture. Boil 1 minute. Add the cherries. Remove from heat; add the butter, kirsch and brandy. Serve hot over vanilla ice cream. If you wish to ignite it, warm good cognac, pour over and light.

Liederkranz cheese, strictly American, and fresh pears or apples make a good dessert. Smelly, but good!

❧ *Previously Unpublished*

PEACHES À LA ROYALE
For 8

8 ripe peaches
1½ cups sugar, divided use
½ cup water
1 quart fresh strawberries
1 pint heavy cream
2 tablespoons cognac

Peel the peaches; cut them in half and remove stones. Boil 1 cup sugar and water together over high heat to make a syrup. Poach the peach halves in the syrup for about 10 minutes. Cool in the syrup.

Purée and strain the strawberries. Beat the cream, gradually adding ½ cup sugar, until the cream stands in stiff peaks. Add cognac to cream, then fold the cream through the berries. Taste and add more sugar if needed. Drain and pat the peaches dry and arrange in your best serving dish; cover them completely with the strawberry cream and chill for about an hour before serving. Sprinkle with macaroon crumbs or shaved chocolate [page 336] if you like.

A really elegant dessert is

MACAROON STUFFED PEACHES

6 fresh, frozen or canned peaches
1 dozen macaroon cookies (store bought)
1 egg yolk
2 tablespoons sugar
¼ cup butter

[Preheat oven to 325°.] If the peaches are fresh, cut them in half, take out the stones and a little of the pulp to make a deep space for the stuffing. Crumble the macaroons and stir in the other ingredients. Stuff the peaches with this mixture, spreading it in a smooth mound over each half. Put them in a buttered ovenproof dish and bake for about 30 minutes.

ᴣ❧ Reader's Request

APPLE AND PRUNE STRUDEL
For 8

4 strudel leaves (you buy a package)
3 large Rome Beauty or Granny Smith apples, sliced thin
½ cup sugar
¼ cup slivered almonds
½ cup chopped stewed prunes
Grated rind of 1 lemon
1 teaspoon lemon juice
⅛ teaspoon cinnamon
½ cup melted butter
1 tablespoon additional sugar

[Preheat oven to 350°.] Unfold 4 leaves of strudel dough from package. Mix the apples, ½ cup sugar, almonds, prunes, grated rind, lemon juice and cinnamon. Place 1 leaf of the dough on a piece of foil or a damp towel. Brush with the melted butter. Sprinkle with 1 teaspoon of sugar. Place the second leaf on top and repeat the butter and sugar process two more times. Place apple mixture on top of the leaves and roll lengthwise like a jelly roll, with the aid of the foil or towel. Place on a buttered tin and brush again with butter. Use a sharp knife to score diagonally into 8 portions. Bake until golden brown, about 50 minutes. Cut while warm. Serve with Lemon Hard Sauce [page 314].

ᴣ❧ Reader's Request

GLAZED APPLES

6 Winesap or similar winter apples
3 cups sugar
1½ cups water
⅛ teaspoon cinnamon

Pare and core apples. Cut into quarters. Mix sugar and water and boil 10 minutes. Add cinnamon and drop apple pieces into the syrup. Cook slowly until transparent. Place in a buttered casserole and keep warm. Keep any syrup left for another time. There will be.

ᛤ Reader's Request

CHOCOLATE MOUSSE WITH MARRONS

3 squares (3 ounces) unsweetened chocolate
3 tablespoons water
½ cup sugar
Pinch of salt
2 eggs, separated, whites beaten stiff
1 tablespoon cognac
3 tablespoons chopped preserved marrons [preserved chestnuts]
1 cup whipping cream

Melt chocolate in the water over low heat. Add sugar and salt; simmer
three minutes, stirring constantly. Blend a little of the chocolate
mixture into the egg yolks, then blend in all of it. Cool. Add cognac
and marrons. Fold in whipped cream and egg whites. Pour into a 1½-
quart soufflé dish and refrigerate or freeze, if you wish. I use a [lightly
oiled] ring mold and unmold on a silver tray. Fill the center with
unsweetened whipped cream and cover the whole thing with shaved
semi-sweet chocolate (white chocolate I prefer). Leave out the
marrons and cognac and substitute 1 teaspoon vanilla.

ᛤ Reader's Request

PEARS STEWED IN WHITE WINE
Serves 8

1½ cups dry white wine
1½ cups sugar
1 short cinnamon stick
4 whole cloves
1 lemon, sliced thin
8 whole peeled fresh pears

Mix wine, sugar, cinnamon stick, cloves and lemon [in a large heavy
pan with cover]. Bring to a boil and cook 5 minutes. Add pears, cover
and simmer until tender, about 30 minutes, depending on pear variety
and ripeness. Cool in the syrup; remove the cinnamon stick and
cloves. Serve the pears in a crystal bowl and pass with sour cream.

❧ Reader's Request

The most inexperienced bride can do this, so there is no excuse to skip the dessert when she is called upon to entertain. . . .

SABAYON
For 8

1 cup powdered sugar
6 egg yolks
1 cup milk
1 cup sherry

Beat the sugar and egg yolks until smooth. Place over hot water; add milk and sherry and beat until four times its former size. Serve hot in tall glasses, and hot!

❧ Reader's Request

The first time I served this was at a Confrerie des Chevaliers du Tastevin. After submitting the menu to "the committee" I was notified that all was approved except the dessert, which was too feminine, and what was I going to do about it. I said: "Serve it." Every man present had two helpings. It is a divine dessert and can be used with any kind of entrée. I sometimes serve lightly broiled sugared strawberries with it. You may halve the recipe, but why? Regardless of how few guests you have, it will all be eaten. It is one dessert of which seconds are always accepted with glee.

CARAMEL SOUFFLÉ
For 8

4 cups granulated sugar [divided use]
Butter for coating pan
12 egg whites
1 to 5 tablespoons water

[Preheat gas oven to 300°; set the thermostat for 325° for electric ovens.] Heat 1½ cups of the sugar in a skillet over medium heat until it becomes a brown syrup. Do not let it burn. Pour it into a 3-quart casserole or bundt pan, coating the sides and bottom. Cool. Rub the inside of pan and coating with butter. Beat egg whites until stiff. Gradually add 2 cups of sugar to the egg whites, beating constantly. Melt the remaining sugar in a skillet until it becomes a syrup. Add 1 to

5 tablespoons water* and cook until the syrup forms a thread [230° to 234° on candy thermometer]. Pour the syrup in a thin stream into the egg whites, beating constantly at medium speed on your mixer. Increase to high speed and beat for 12 minutes. Pour into the prepared pan and place it in a larger shallow pan filled with hot water. Bake for 60 to 65 minutes until the soufflé is firm but not browned. Turn out at once onto a serving tray. [Hold the platter close to the soufflé and turn it quickly over the dish. Remove the bundt pan slowly. It's best to work over a table or counter to keep the hot syrup from spilling out and causing a burn.] If you wish to prepare the soufflé early in the day, leave it in the pan and at serving time return to a 350° oven for about 20 minutes. It must be hot or warm to come out of the pan. Some of the caramel syrup will stay in the pan. Serve with English Custard (below). Men adore this dessert.

[*Corbitt published two versions of this recipe with different measurements of water. The amount added will determine how quickly it steams away and the syrup spins a thread. Ann Latham tested these two recipes extensively and I hope her insights will make them simpler for you.—Editor]

ENGLISH CUSTARD
For 10 to 12

¾ cup sugar [divided use]
3 cups milk
12 egg yolks
2 tablespoons butter
1 cup heavy cream (you may omit)
1 teaspoon vanilla

[Heat ½ cup of sugar and all of the milk together in a double boiler. Gradually whisk the remaining sugar into the egg yolks, beating until they are thick and lemon yellow. When the sweetened milk is hot, reduce heat and dribble about half of it into the egg yolks, stirring slowly with a whisk. Do not beat vigorously. Add the butter to hot milk. Return the egg yolks to the milk, stirring slowly with a wooden spoon to reduce bubbles. Scrape the bottom and sides of the double boiler frequently. When the custard coats a spoon and temperature reaches 170°, remove from heat. Cool, cover, and refrigerate. Before serving, beat the cream until it stands in stiff peaks, flavoring with vanilla. Fold the cream through the custard and ladle over the Caramel Soufflé.]

My mother made this dessert with lady fingers, a layer of macaroon crumbs, currant jelly and fresh raspberries, or other fruit in season, but she was Irish.

TRIFLE

2 dozen lady fingers, split
1 cup black raspberry jam
2 cups sliced fresh or frozen peaches
2 or 3 bananas, sliced
1 pint fresh strawberries, cut in half
½ cup sherry (or more if you like)
2 cups hot milk
4 eggs
¼ cup sugar
1 teaspoon vanilla
1 cup raspberries, drained if frozen
1 cup whipping cream

Line the serving bowl with one layer of lady fingers. Cover with jam. Layer the remaining lady fingers, peaches, bananas and strawberries. Add sherry to each layer of lady fingers. Refrigerate.

Prepare a soft custard: [scald the milk and gradually add about half of it to the eggs beaten with the sugar. Stir the eggs into remaining hot milk, and cook over hot water until thickened.] Cool and add vanilla. Pour over the prepared fruit and lady fingers. Add raspberries. Whip the cream and cover the Trifle.

There is nothing better than a good shortcake, and strawberry or peach is best. I like to make individual ones and serve on 12-inch crystal plates.

OLD-FASHIONED STRAWBERRY SHORTCAKE

2 cups flour
4 teaspoons baking powder
¾ teaspoon salt
⅓ cup sugar
½ cup soft vegetable shortening
½ cup whipping cream or half-and-half
¼ cup water
Sugared strawberries [or sliced peaches, sometimes]

[Preheat oven to 450°.] Mix the flour, baking powder, salt and sugar. Cut the shortening in with a pastry blender or two knives. Mix cream and water and stir in quickly. Do not over mix. Dump out on a floured board and pat about 1 inch thick. Cut with a 3- or 3½-inch biscuit cutter and put on an ungreased cookie sheet about 2 inches apart or drop by heaping tablespoonfuls. Bake for 15 minutes or until golden brown. Split and butter them. Cover first layer with sugared strawberries, slightly mashed. Cover with the other half and repeat with strawberries. Either be generous with the berries or peaches or don't make it. Serve with whipped or pouring cream. I like this dessert with lemon ice cream spread between the halves with the berries.

For Round Robin dinners I am often asked to make Crêpes Suzette, which I like to do, and here is my recipe.

CRÊPES SUZETTE
For 8

¾ cup plus 1 tablespoon butter
½ cup orange juice
2 teaspoons lemon juice
½ cup Curaçao
½ cup Grand Marnier
½ cup sugar
2 teaspoons grated orange peel
24 thin Crêpes [page 91]
Additional sugar
Cognac

Bring the ¾ cup butter (no substitute), orange juice, lemon juice, Curaçao and Grand Marnier to a boil. Remove from heat, add the ½ cup sugar and orange peel. This much may be done ahead of time. In fact, I keep this mixture in a covered jar in my refrigerator. When ready to make the dessert, melt the 1 tablespoon of butter in a crêpe pan or skillet. Place the crêpes in the pan, a few at a time. Spoon some of the sauce over them and heat over sterno or on the stove. Fold or roll, sprinkle lightly with additional sugar, add warm cognac or brandy and ignite; serve with some of the sauce. I sometimes heat Elberta peach halves and add to the sauce and serve with the crêpes, but then I am apt to add most anything.

I show off with this dessert frequently, as my friends will testify.

STRAWBERRIES ROMANOFF
For 6

1 pint vanilla ice cream
1 cup heavy cream
½ cup plus 1 tablespoon Cointreau, divided use
1 quart fresh strawberries
½ cup confectioners' sugar

Whip ice cream until it is creamy and fold in whipped cream and 6
tablespoons of Cointreau. Fold in strawberries, sweetened with
confectioners' sugar and 3 tablespoons of Cointreau. Blend quickly
and lightly and serve in chilled, stemmed glasses. The hostess should
do this at the table.

OLD-FASHIONED RICE PUDDING
For 6

3 eggs
½ cup sugar
¼ teaspoon salt
½ teaspoon vanilla or lemon extract
3 cups scalded milk
¾ cup cooked rice
Raisins (may be omitted)
Grated nutmeg

[Preheat oven to 350°.] Beat eggs slightly, add the sugar, salt and
flavorings. Pour in the scalded milk. Strain and pour into a buttered
casserole dish. Add the rice, and raisins if you wish. Sprinkle with a
few grains of nutmeg, set in a shallow pan of water and bake [about
45 to 50 minutes, until a knife blade inserted in the center comes out
clean]. Leave out the rice for a plain baked custard. I like to à la mode
warm rice pudding.

I like to serve this when I serve an entrée that has a sharp flavor, like the Chicken Piquante, Oriental Roasted Chicken or when I do not want to spend too much time and money on a dessert. It can look elegant and expensive too!

CARAMELIZED BREAD PUDDING
For 8

Put in top of double boiler:

2 cups brown sugar
8 slices of white bread, buttered and cubed

Combine:

6 eggs, lightly beaten
4 cups milk
2 teaspoons vanilla
½ teaspoon salt

Pour liquid mixture over the bread and brown sugar. DO NOT STIR. Cook over boiling water for 1 hour or until custard is formed. Serve warm. The brown sugar in the bottom forms a sauce. I find men like this and always ask for more. You may put the ingredients in a see-through soufflé dish and proceed as directed.

Crème Brûlée is a favorite dessert for holidays. . . .

CRÈME BRÛLÉE
For 6

2 cups cream [or half-and-half]
4 egg yolks
2½ tablespoons granulated sugar
1 teaspoon vanilla
¼ cup light brown sugar

[Preheat oven to 325°.] Heat cream in a double boiler. Beat egg yolks, adding granulated sugar gradually. Remove cream from heat and pour over egg mixture very slowly. Add vanilla. Pour into a 1½ quart casserole. Place in a shallow pan of hot water and bake uncovered about 45 to 50 minutes, or until set. [A knife blade inserted in center should come out clean.] When custard is set, sprinkle with the sifted brown sugar. Place under broiler for a minute or so until sugar melts. Chill. This is a rich smooth custard and should be served very cold.

CHEESE CAKE WITH SOUR CREAM TOPPING

¼ pound butter
1 pound graham crackers
1 teaspoon cinnamon
½ cup sugar

Melt butter, add crumbs, cinnamon and sugar. Mix thoroughly and line sides and bottom of 9-inch spring mold or pie pan.

1½ pounds cream cheese
4 eggs
1 cup sugar
1 teaspoon vanilla

[Preheat oven to 375°.] Whip cheese until creamy in your electric mixer. Beat the eggs, add sugar and vanilla. Add to the cheese and beat together until light. Pour into prepared pan and bake for 25 minutes or until the cake is firm. Remove and cool 10 minutes. [Increase the oven temperature to 475°.]

Mix:

2 tablespoons sugar
1 cup sour cream
½ teaspoon vanilla

Spread on top of cheese cake and return to the oven for 5 minutes. Cool and refrigerate for 24 hours. Spread with additional sour cream before serving.

Here is a romantic dessert for your Valentine, rich and smooth.

COEUR À LA CRÈME

8 ounces cream cheese
⅓ cup confectioners' sugar
⅛ teaspoon salt
¼ cup slivered preserved ginger
2 cups whipping cream (or equivalent amount of cottage cheese)
1 quart large strawberries

Whip cheese with electric mixer until fluffy. Add sugar, salt and ginger. Beat the cream until it holds stiff peaks and fold into the cheese mixture. Pour into a 1½-quart heart-shaped mold, or 2 smaller ones, lined with wet cheesecloth. Refrigerate overnight. Unmold on a serving tray, peel off the cheesecloth and surround with whole berries. Put a few berries in a blender, slightly sweeten and pass the sauce with the coeur. For a less caloric coeur, substitute 2 cups of cottage cheese for the whipping cream and beat until it is the consistency of whipped cream.

Do not be afraid of

GRAND MARNIER SOUFFLÉ
For 6

2 tablespoons butter
1½ tablespoons flour
½ cup scalded milk
½ teaspoon vanilla
5 eggs, separated plus 1 additional white
4 tablespoons sugar [divided use]
Additional sugar
2 tablespoons Grand Marnier liqueur
2 tablespoons whipped cream

[Preheat oven to 400°.] Melt butter, add flour and cook until golden. Slowly add scalded milk and cook until thick. Cook 5 minutes, stirring constantly. Add vanilla. Beat egg yolks with 3 tablespoons sugar. [Pour some of the hot sauce into the egg yolks, beating constantly; then pour the egg back into the sauce.] Beat 6 egg whites stiff, add 1 tablespoon sugar. Fold in half the egg whites, then the other half. Pour into a buttered and slightly sugared casserole. Bake for 20 minutes. Serve with 2 tablespoons of Grand Marnier added to 2 tablespoons whipped cream or pour warmed lighted Grand Marnier over, or both.

Traditionally speaking, pancakes are served at breakfast, but one may use them just about any time of the day. The young-fry, the debutantes, adore them, and as far as I know everyone else does, too.

I use pancake stacks for brunches and for desserts and never have any leftovers. The blueberry stack for all occasions. It is an impressive dessert to pass after a seated dinner, and so good. You make your basic griddle or pancake mixture, thin it with milk, then pour pancakes the size you wish. I do a 12- or 14-inch one, and use 10 to 12 cakes for a stack. You can make ahead and pile them on top of each other with wax paper between, and cover with a towel to keep from drying. When ready to assemble, [preheat oven to 350°] spread your tray with Lemon Cream Butter, then top with one pancake. Spread it with Lemon Cream Butter and a little of the hot Blueberry Sauce. Repeat until you have as high a stack as you wish. Pour more Blueberry Sauce over all and a goodly dollop of the Lemon Cream Butter. Put in oven for 3 minutes. Cut in narrow pie-shaped portions and pass.

PANCAKE STACKS
For 10 or 12 thin pancakes

2½ cups milk (about)
4 tablespoons melted butter
2 eggs, separated
2 cups flour
4 teaspoons baking powder
¼ cup sugar
1 teaspoon salt

Mix milk, melted butter and egg yolks. Sift together the dry ingredients and stir into the milk mixture. Fold in the stiffly beaten egg whites. Add more milk if necessary to make the pancakes thin. Cook and stack.

During my days at Neiman Marcus, the Thursday night buffets became very popular and the pancake stacks were asked for time after time. We made them with various accompaniments; lingonberries and sour cream with beef, Orange Butter [page 94] with chicken, maple syrup and ham juices with chicken and ham, cinnamon butter, whatever came to mind, always cut like a pie. The blueberry pancake was used with everything.

LEMON CREAM BUTTER
For 1 stack

½ cup butter
2½ cups confectioners' sugar
3 tablespoons lemon juice
Grated rind of 1 lemon

Cream butter, add sugar and beat. Stir in the lemon juice and grated rind. Beat until the consistency of whipped cream.

BLUEBERRY SAUCE
For 1 stack

4 10-ounce packages frozen blueberries or 3 cups fresh
1 cup cold water and juice
3 tablespoons cornstarch
6 tablespoons sugar
2 tablespoons lemon juice

Defrost berries and strain, reserving the juice. Combine water and juice; add the cornstarch and sugar. Cook over low heat until clear and thickened, stirring constantly. Add berries and cook 5 minutes. Remove from heat and add lemon juice.

If using fresh blueberries, mix 3 cups of sugar with 3 tablespoons of cornstarch; add 1½ cups of boiling water. Bring to a boil and let cook for 5 minutes, stirring carefully. Add 3 cups of blueberries, 1 tablespoon lemon juice. Add more sugar if necessary.

Cantaloupe filled with raspberries makes a delightful dessert.
À la mode with lemon ice cream is still better.
A combination of melon balls served in chilled glasses covered with champagne or Sauterne.
Cantaloupe filled with all sorts of fruit, but papaya from the Hawaiian Islands, grapes and bananas, makes a beautiful dessert. Lemon juice is a perfect accompaniment.
Honey dew melon quartered and filled with raspberry or lime ice. A cool and refreshing dessert.

COLD CHOCOLATE ALMOND SOUFFLÉ
Serves 8

1 tablespoon [envelope] unflavored gelatin
¼ cup rum
6 ounces [6 squares] semi-sweet chocolate [divided use]
1 cup light cream [half-and-half]
½ cup confectioners' sugar
½ teaspoon salt
2½ cups whipping cream
¼ cup slivered almonds, toasted and salted
Candied violets for garnish

Combine gelatin and rum in a cup and let stand 5 minutes. Put the cup in a pan of boiling water to melt the gelatin. Melt 4 squares of chocolate in heated cream; beat until smooth. Add gelatin, sugar, and salt. Let it cool until it begins to congeal. Beat whipping cream until stiff and set aside 1 cupful. Fold the rest into the chocolate mixture until smooth. Fold in almonds. Pour into a buttered 1-quart soufflé dish. Refrigerate. Serve topped with remaining whipped cream and sprinkled with 2 squares of shaved chocolate and crushed candied violets.

COLD LEMON SOUFFLÉ
For 8 to 10

1 tablespoon plus 1 teaspoon unflavored gelatin
¼ cup cold water
4 eggs, separated
½ cup lemon juice
¼ teaspoon salt
1 cup sugar [divided use]
1 teaspoon grated lemon peel
¼ teaspoon lemon extract
1 cup whipping cream
1 cup canned apricot halves

Soften gelatin in cold water. Set aside. Mix egg yolks, lemon juice, salt and ½ cup of sugar. Cook in double boiler until thickened. Stir in gelatin, lemon peel and lemon extract. Cool. Beat egg whites until soft peaks form. Gradually beat in rest of sugar, and beat until stiff. Whip the cream. Fold egg whites into custard as it begins to congeal, then fold in the whipped cream. Pour into custard cups and refrigerate. Unmold and serve with sauce of apricots puréed in the blender and sweetened to taste. Or pour into a 1½-quart soufflé dish or mold. I like to put a collar of foil around a 1-quart soufflé dish, tie securely, then remove before bringing to the table. This is a delicious soufflé to serve cold with any fruit and flavored whipped cream, if you wish.

You may use the same base for Cold Orange Soufflé, substituting ½ cup orange juice and 1 tablespoon grated orange peel for the lemon, and omitting the lemon extract.

❧ Previously Unpublished

HELEN CORBITT'S BANANAS FOSTER
For 4

4 tablespoons light brown sugar
2 tablespoons butter
½ teaspoon ground cinnamon
2 large bananas
1 jigger (1½ ounces) crème de bananes
½ teaspoon rum
1 jigger (1½ ounces) brandy
1 quart vanilla ice cream

Melt the sugar and butter together in a skillet until bubbly. Add cinnamon and bananas, which have been peeled and quartered lengthwise. Add banana liqueur and rum and simmer until the bananas are heated through and tender. Pour the brandy over the bananas and light. When the flame burns out, serve immediately over scoops of ice cream or fold into prepared dessert crêpes [page 91].

Slices of melon, peaches, fresh figs, or any other fresh fruit, arranged on a silver tray, a pretty, large plate or platter, and served with a bowl of Cream Cheese Sauce and a bowl of Melba Sauce is a luscious-to-look-at and -to-eat dessert. The Cream Cheese Sauce is made by adding cream to cream cheese and beating with a fork until the consistency of cream and easy to pour.

The idea is to pass the fruit, let those who partake select whatever they wish from the tray, spoon the Cream Cheese Sauce on top and pour the Melba Sauce over all. I always get a thrill when I serve this because everyone oohs and aahs both before and *after* eating it. It needs a pretty service though, and chilled plates to eat it from.

Dessert Sauces

I like my grandmother's hard sauce recipe the best, and break the rule of never serving two sauces for the same dish at one time. Rum Sauce hot and Hard Sauce cold over plum pudding is a delectable experience.

❧ Reader's Request

LEMON HARD SAUCE
1 cup

½ cup butter
1 cup granulated or 1½ cups confectioners' sugar
1 teaspoon lemon juice
½ teaspoon grated lemon rind

Cream butter, beat in sugar and flavorings.

HARD SAUCE
1 cup

¼ cup butter
1 cup fine granulated sugar
2 tablespoons brandy
A few grains of nutmeg

Cream butter in electric mixer until soft and fluffy. Gradually add sugar, beating continually. Add brandy and continue beating until light. Remove to a glass bowl or jar, sprinkle with nutmeg, and keep in a cool place for several hours before serving. Serve on hot puddings and pies.

SAUCE LAWRENCE
1¼ cups

1 cup Fudge Sauce [next page]
¼ cup orange juice
2 tablespoons grated orange rind
2 teaspoons Curaçao
Pinch of salt

Heat Fudge Sauce and add orange juice. Reheat and add grated orange rind and Curaçao. Serve hot over vanilla ice cream or flambé with brandy before serving. This is a use-it-all-at-one-time sauce.

CHOCOLATE SAUCE
1½ cups

¼ cup butter
¼ cup shaved bitter chocolate (about ⅔ of a square)

Stir over low heat until smooth, then add:

¼ cup cocoa
¾ cup sugar
½ cup cream [or half-and-half]
⅛ teaspoon salt

Bring to the boiling point. Remove from heat and add:

1 teaspoon vanilla

This may be stored and reheated over hot water as needed.

The fudge sauce I have used for years has always brought forth extraordinary comments from the men who swear they never eat any desserts. Now the only food they haven't tried it over is mashed potatoes.

FUDGE SAUCE
3 cups

½ cup butter
2¼ cups confectioners' sugar
⅓ cup evaporated milk
6 squares [6 ounces] bitter chocolate

Mix butter and sugar in top of a double boiler; add evaporated milk and chocolate and cook over hot water for 30 minutes. Do not stir while cooking. Remove from heat and beat. You may store in refrigerator and reheat as needed. If you wish to have a thinner sauce add cream, but do not add water.

You might try equal parts of hot Fudge Sauce and rum, well blended and folded into whipped cream and served over angel food or rum cake and vanilla ice cream. Sauce Hélène, for no reason at all—or because of me, if you like.

The extravagant corner of your emergency shelf should contain a jar of Melba Sauce—to dress up canned fruits and vanilla or peach ice cream for the unexpected guests. Or make your own! It is such a pretty color.

MELBA SAUCE
1 cup

1 cup frozen raspberries and juice, defrosted
1 teaspoon sugar
1 teaspoon cornstarch
[½ cup currant jelly (optional)]

Mix raspberries, sugar and cornstarch; cook over low heat until clear. Strain through a fine sieve and cool. The addition of ½ cup currant jelly gives a sparkle to its color.

The famous Peach Melba is a good company dessert; it is merely vanilla or peach ice cream mounded in the center of half a canned or fresh stewed peach and covered with Melba Sauce. Named for the famous singer.

❧ Reader's Request

I am always amused at the sophisticates who ask for this recipe. When they find it has peanut butter in it, the reaction is always the same— "Oh, Helen, really!"

PEANUT BUTTER SAUCE
2 cups

1 cup sugar
1 tablespoon white corn syrup
¼ teaspoon salt
¾ cup milk
6 tablespoons peanut butter
¼ teaspoon vanilla

Mix sugar, syrup, salt and milk and cook over low heat until thickened, stirring constantly. Add peanut butter and blend. Remove from the heat and add vanilla when cool.

❧ *Reader's Request*

A favorite dessert among those who like to use their taste buds to full advantage is Broiled Peaches with Rum Sauce. Peel and halve the peach, place flat side up in a pan covered with melted butter. Sprinkle generously with sugar and run under the broiler at low temperature until sugar is melted. Place in a glass serving dish and cover with:

RUM SAUCE
1 cup

½ teaspoon grated orange peel
2 tablespoons butter
¼ cup powdered sugar
½ cup whipping cream
2 tablespoons rum

Beat orange peel, butter and powdered sugar until smooth and fold in cream which has been whipped stiff. Add rum and blend carefully.

❧ *Reader's Request*

ROMANOFF SAUCE
1½ cups

1 cup sugar [divided use]
1 cup water
Grated rind of 1 lemon
2 tablespoons lemon juice
1 egg yolk
2 tablespoons butter
½ cup rum
Whipped cream

Cook ¾ cup of the sugar and water to a thick syrup (240° on your candy thermometer). Add grated lemon rind and juice. Beat egg yolk with remaining ¼ cup of sugar; add to the hot syrup and cook over low heat for 5 minutes. Add butter and rum and reheat but do not cook. Cool and add the rum sauce to whipped cream to suit your own taste and to make thickness desired. Serve on fresh strawberries, peaches or raspberries, or your favorite ice cream.

This recipe is excellent when you want a special sauce for fresh berries, especially wild ones.

CRÈME FRAÎCHE
2 cups

2 cups whipping cream
1 tablespoon buttermilk [with active culture]

Mix the cream and buttermilk together. Heat over low flame until just warm, 85° if you have a thermometer (and you should by now). Remove mixture and put in warm oven; stir every once in a while for 8 hours. It will be thick. Refrigerate before serving.

Custard Sauce has more friends than any other. . . .

CUSTARD SAUCE
2 cups

3 egg yolks
¼ cup sugar
⅛ teaspoon salt
1½ cups milk
1 teaspoon vanilla or lemon extract

Beat egg yolks slightly and add sugar and salt. Place in top of double boiler and stir in the milk. Cook over hot water, stirring constantly, until mixture coats the spoon. Remove and place in pan of cold water; beat in the flavoring and serve cold over gelatin desserts and fresh or canned fruits.

Grated orange or lemon peel added when using lemon extract and served over chilled, peeled fresh fruit or berries is delicious.

My mother always dipped her teaspoon in almond extract before measuring vanilla or lemon extract. I still do. If you like it, try it with other things, too.

BUTTERSCOTCH SAUCE
1½ cups

1 cup light cream
2 tablespoons butter
¾ cup brown sugar
1 tablespoon Karo syrup

Mix in a heavy pot and cook over low heat until the mixture is smooth and thick. Stir frequently while cooking. Serve warm or cold.

CARAMEL SYRUP
1 cup

1 cup sugar
1 cup hot water
½ teaspoon vanilla extract

Melt sugar in a heavy skillet over low heat. Stir constantly until melted and a light brown. Remove from heat and add hot water. It will be lumpy. Return to heat and cook and stir until lumps are dissolved. Cool; add vanilla.

ORIENTAL SAUCE
2 cups

2 cups sugar
1 cup water
2 tablespoons orange juice
1 tablespoon lemon juice
Slivered peelings of 1 lemon and 1 orange
    (be sure peeling is thin)
¼ cup slivered candied ginger
½ cup slivered blanched almonds, toasted

Mix sugar, water, fruit juices and peelings [zest] and cook until clear. Add ginger and cook to soft-ball stage [between 234° and 238° on a candy thermometer]. Remove from heat; add almonds and cool. Serve over chocolate or vanilla ice cream.

GRAND MARNIER SAUCE
2½ cups

1 cup whipping cream
½ cup sugar
3 teaspoons lemon juice
6 tablespoons Grand Marnier
1 teaspoon grated orange peel

Whip cream until soft peaks form. Fold in sugar and rest of ingredients. Spoon over any fresh fruit, but this is especially good on strawberries.

APRICOT SAUCE
1½ cups

1½ cups apricot jam
½ cup water
2 tablespoons sugar

Combine ingredients, bring to a boil, and cook for 5 to 10 minutes, stirring constantly. Rub the sauce through a sieve. You may add 1 or 2 tablespoons kirsch, brandy, or any liqueur.

Ices, Ice Cream, and Frozen Desserts

Unless you live where you can obtain really good commercial ice cream, hand packed and cared for, it would be smart to invest in an electric ice-cream freezer. You can whip up your favorite flavor with very little trouble and deep-freeze the leftovers.

This was part of my childhood.

THREE FRUIT SHERBET
2 quarts

1½ cups orange juice
¾ cup lemon juice
1½ cups mashed bananas (about 3)
3 cups water
2 cups skim milk
Sugar or artificial sweetener to taste

Mix all the ingredients and freeze in crank freezer or in refrigerator tray in your deep freeze. I like to take it out of the deep freeze when partially frozen and whip by hand or with an electric mixer. The sherbet can be frozen in a mold to be more decorative. Unmold on a silver tray and decorate with orange sections and green leaves.

BUTTERMILK SHERBET
2⅓ quarts

4 cups buttermilk
¾ cup lemon juice
1 cup sugar (or artificial sweetener to your taste)
1 cup light corn syrup
6 tablespoons grated lemon peel

Mix and freeze. Add:

2 cups puréed ripe avocado

Or, when fresh strawberries are ripe, omit avocado and add 1 cup of puréed strawberries, and cut the lemon juice to ¼ cup. The same with peaches, but they must be ripe. You can dress it up for company too. Pile the plain sherbet in half of a fresh or stewed peach, and pour puréed strawberries over. Slip a green leaf from the yard under the dessert crystal.

❧ *Reader's Request*

For the holidays

CRANBERRY SHERBET
1 quart

2 quarts fresh cranberries [a little more than 2 bags]
4 cups water
4 cups sugar
Juice of 4 lemons

Boil cranberries with the water for 8 minutes or until skins pop open. Put through a sieve, [add sugar and reheat, stirring constantly, until sugar dissolves. Cool and add lemon juice. Freeze. When ice crystals form, turn the sherbet into a large mixing bowl and beat until it is light. Return to freezer to harden.

This beautiful, tart ice is nice served in stemmed sherbet glasses to accompany a holiday bird. Children particularly enjoy this because they think they are being allowed to eat their dessert first. Serving sorbet between courses "cleanses the palate."—Editor]

This and the Lemon Velvet Ice Cream won hands down in the Ice Cream tasting.

AVOCADO SHERBET
1½ quarts

1½ cups mashed avocado
¼ teaspoon salt
2 cups sugar
1 teaspoon grated lemon peel
Juice of 12 lemons
1 quart milk

Mix avocado, salt, sugar, lemon peel and juice; add the milk and freeze. The curdled look will disappear in freezing.

FRESH PEAR ICE
1 gallon

2 cups sugar
4 cups water
4 cups puréed fresh ripe pears
½ cup lemon juice

Make a syrup of sugar and water over low heat. Peel and slice the pears, put in the blender and add to the syrup immediately to keep them from turning dark. Cool, add the lemon juice and freeze in your ice cream freezer.

This is a pretty dessert to bring to the table. It's good too in place of a more elaborate birthday cake: you can stick long Danish tapers into the ice, light them and present it. Spectacular!

PINEAPPLE ICE WITH PEACHES
For 8

3 pints pineapple ice or sherbet
2 pounds canned peaches (white ones are especially pretty)
26 ounces frozen raspberries
¼ cup kirsch
1 teaspoon vanilla
½ cup sliced blanched almonds, lightly toasted

Thaw ice enough to pack into a ring-shaped mold and return it to the freezer. Drain peaches, reserving syrup. Reduce the syrup by one half over high heat. Cool. Purée berries in blender. Strain. Combine reduced syrup, berry purée, kirsch, and vanilla. Pour over peaches and chill. Just before serving, unmold the ice and arrange the peaches in the center or around it. Pour the raspberry sauce over everything and sprinkle with nuts.

LEMON SHERBET MOUSSE
1 quart

1 6-ounce package lemon-flavored gelatin
1 cup boiling water
1½ tablespoons lemon juice
1½ pints lemon sherbet
1 cup slivered fresh pineapple or any fresh fruit
     or ¼ cup slivered preserved ginger

Dissolve gelatin in boiling water. Cool. Add lemon juice; blend in
lemon sherbet. Pour into a ring mold and chill until firm. Unmold and
decorate with fresh fruit or ginger.

A simple addition when not dieting: pass

1 cup whipped cream flavored with
4 tablespoons sugar
¼ cup lemon juice
Grated rind of 1 lemon

Quick Magic:

. . . chopped thin mints sprinkled over peppermint ice cream.

*. . . or crushed cinnamon stick candy crumbs on coffee ice cream
with a generous sprinkling of crème de cacao.*

*. . . or apricot purée mixed with Cointreau on orange ice or
vanilla ice cream—or both.*

. . . or crushed Almond Roca candy on strawberry ice cream.

*. . . or fresh or frozen blueberries mixed with crème de cassis on
lemon ice.*

These recipes I used a great deal in New York and at the University Tea House in Austin. In testing them . . . everyone who tasted was too enthusiastic for their waistlines.

FRENCH VANILLA ICE CREAM
Makes 1 quart

½ cup sugar
4 egg yolks
2 cups scalded milk
2 cups whipping cream
¼ teaspoon salt
2 teaspoons vanilla

Mix the sugar with the egg yolks and beat until thick. Pour in the scalded milk slowly, beating with a wire whisk. Boil until slightly thickened. Cool and strain; add cream, salt and vanilla. Freeze.

Variations can be added to 1 recipe of cooled French Vanilla Ice Cream before it is frozen:
GINGER ICE CREAM: Add ½ cup minced crystallized ginger.

PEANUT BRITTLE ICE CREAM: Omit sugar and add ½ pound of peanut brittle rolled out into crumbs.

CAROB ICE CREAM: Add ⅓ cup carob powder.

EGGNOG ICE CREAM: Heat and ignite 2 tablespoons brandy or bourbon before adding; sprinkle nutmeg over the surface.

GRAPENUT ICE CREAM: Add ¼ cup Grape-Nuts [cereal] and substitute almond extract for vanilla.

MINT ICE CREAM: Substitute 2 or 3 drops of peppermint oil or about ¼ teaspoon peppermint extract for vanilla and tint with green or pink vegetable coloring.

CHOCOLATE ICE CREAM: Shave 2 ounces [2 squares] of unsweetened chocolate into the milk as you scald it for making the base. You may want to increase the sweetener. Taste!

COFFEE BURNT-ALMOND ICE CREAM: Add 1 cup finely chopped toasted almonds and 2 tablespoons instant coffee.

COFFEE CARAMEL ICE CREAM: [Add 4 tablespoons instant coffee and increase the sugar to ¾ cup. In a heavy skillet, melt the sugar until it becomes a light brown syrup. Pour it into the scalded milk and coffee in a thin stream, stirring until it dissolves. Continue as directed under basic French Vanilla recipe.]

MOCHA ORANGE ICE CREAM: Add 4 tablespoons instant coffee and 1 tablespoon grated fresh orange peel; increase the sugar to ¾ cup. Heat and ignite 2 tablespoons Grand Marnier; let it cool before adding.

FRESH FRUIT ICE CREAM: [Purée 1 quart of ripe peeled and sliced fresh fruit in your blender, sweetened as if for table use. If you are using peaches, substitute ½ teaspoon almond extract for the vanilla. Strawberries often benefit from a squeeze of fresh lemon juice. Finish filling freezer can with whole milk.]

ICE CREAM BOMBE

    3 quarts vanilla ice cream
    2 cups cool Fudge Sauce [page 315]
    1 very cold 3-quart melon mold or 2 1½-quart size
    Whipped cream (optional)
    Crème de cacao (optional)

Coat the molds with vanilla ice cream about 1½ inches thick. Pack firmly and quickly. Do not let ice cream melt. Fill center with fudge sauce and cover with more ice cream. Cover with wax paper and press on the lid. Place in freezer overnight. When ready to serve, run a wet knife around the edge of the mold. Place a hot towel over for a minute, then turn upside down on to a chilled serving dish. Cut in slices at the table and serve with whipped cream and crème de cacao. Use same method for any flavored bombe.

❧ Reader's Request

It tastes just the way it sounds—like velvet.

LEMON VELVET ICE CREAM
1 gallon

1 quart plus 1⅓ cups whipping cream
1 quart plus 1⅓ cups milk
Juice of 8 lemons
4 cups sugar
2 teaspoons lemon extract
1 tablespoon grated lemon rind

Mix thoroughly and freeze.

A good frozen pudding to have on hand all year round, and especially at holiday time:

FROZEN HOLIDAY PUDDING

Pound cake
Kirsch
Crème de cacao
Cointreau
Brandy
1 pint pistachio ice cream
1 pint strawberry ice cream
1 pint vanilla ice cream
1 pint coffee ice cream

Cut the cake in ¼-inch slices to fit a loaf pan. Soak each slice in a different liqueur. Pack thin layer of pistachio ice cream in bottom of the pan, then place a slice of the soaked cake. Alternate the four ice creams and cake slices until the pan is full, the ice cream layer on top. Return to the deep freeze and leave for at least two days. Slice and serve on chilled plates. Neither the cake nor the ice cream should be more than ¼-inch thick, and the more layers of each you have the better the pudding. You can make it without the liqueur and have good results, too.

When I had Crêpes Brazil on my dessert menu in the Zodiac Room, everything else took second place. This is not the classic recipe but my version.

CRÊPES BRAZIL

16 thin dessert Crêpes [page 91]
1 quart Butter Pecan Ice Cream [see below]
2 cups Caramel Syrup [page 319]
1 cup whipping cream

Warm the crêpes, spoon the ice cream into each and fold once. Put a dollop of whipped cream on top and pour the Caramel Syrup over, letting your conscience be your guide.

You may buy the crêpes, ice cream and the caramel sauce, but why? Use my Caramel Sauce recipe and cook longer until the syrup is a thicker consistency.

BUTTER PECAN ICE CREAM

1 cup coarsely chopped pecans
6 tablespoons butter
3 tablespoons cornstarch
1 cup sugar
¼ cup dark brown sugar
2 cups milk
2 teaspoons vanilla
2 cups whipping cream

Toast the pecans in butter in a slow oven. Mix cornstarch and sugars in a heavy skillet, add milk and cook until thick, stirring constantly. Remove from heat, add vanilla and chill. Add cream and freeze in your freezer until partially done. Add pecans and resume freezing. Or whip the cream until stiff, fold in sugar mixture and pecans, pour into freezing trays and put in your deep freeze.

[Corbitt's inimitable ice cream flavor combinations are on pages 326 through 327.— Editor]

Cakes and Icings

Place baking pans in the center of the oven to permit free circulation
of air and heat evenly on all sides. When putting two or more pans in
the oven at the same time, stagger them on different shelves, so that one
is not directly above the other. There should be at least one inch between two pans on the same shelf; otherwise the trapped heat will cause
a "hot spot."

WHITE CHOCOLATE CAKE
2 layers

1 cup butter
2 cups sugar
4 eggs
¼ pound white chocolate melted in ½ cup boiling water
2½ cups cake flour
1 teaspoon soda
1 cup buttermilk
1 teaspoon vanilla

[Preheat oven to 350°.] Cream butter and sugar. Add eggs one at a time, beating well after each addition. Cool the chocolate melted in the water and add to the egg mixture. [Sift the flour and soda together. Beginning with the flour mixture] add the dry ingredients and buttermilk alternately to the chocolate mixture. Stir in the vanilla. Pour into well-buttered layer cake pans and bake 40 minutes or until done.

You may vary this recipe by the following: Add only egg yolks to butter and sugar. Use baking powder in place of soda. Then add beaten egg whites to mixture just before vanilla. Fold in 1 cup finely chopped pecans and 1 cup coconut. Bake in 2 layers. Frost either version with Colonnade Icing or Fudge Icing [pages 345 and 344].

❧ Reader's Request

This was my Aunt Laura's chocolate cake, black and moist. I love it with Colonnade Icing and bitter chocolate dribbled over. During the depression, while I was at the Presbyterian Hospital in Newark, New Jersey, I used to get up at three o'clock in the morning every Saturday and make these for anyone who could afford to buy them. And quite a few could.

CHOCOLATE CAKE
2 layers

[Preheat oven to 375°.]

　　2 squares [2 ounces] chocolate
　　½ cup boiling water

Melt together and cool. Then mix:

　　2 eggs, well beaten
　　1½ cups sugar
　　Pinch of salt
　　½ cup butter

Then add:

　　Cooled chocolate mixture
　　1 teaspoon vanilla
　　¾ cup buttermilk
　　1 teaspoon baking soda

Last, add:

　　1½ cups sifted flour

Bake for 35 to 45 minutes.

[Colonnade Icing recipe is on page 345. After the white icing has set, melt 1 ounce square of unsweetened baking chocolate with 1 teaspoon or more butter and dribble it from the tip of a teaspoon in an abstract pattern over the icing.—Editor]

When Neiman Marcus had its Irish Fortnight I had this cake served at the opening ball. It met with raves and still does every time it is served. . . . Being allergic to alcohol, I sometimes serve the cake with ice cream and hot Fudge Sauce [page 315] instead—and it is almost as welcome. Not quite!

IRISH COFFEE LIQUEUR CHOCOLATE CAKE

¾ cup butter, softened
2 cups sugar
¾ cup cocoa, sifted
4 eggs, separated
1 teaspoon baking soda
2 tablespoons cold water
½ cup cold coffee
½ cup Irish Coffee Liqueur [or Kahlua]
1¾ cups thrice sifted cake flour
2 teaspoons vanilla

[Preheat oven to 325°.] Cream butter and sugar. Add cocoa and beat in egg yolks, one at a time. Dissolve baking soda in water, and combine with coffee and liqueur. Add to the batter alternately beginning with the flour. Add vanilla. Fold in stiffly beaten egg whites. Turn into a greased and lightly floured 9-inch bundt pan. Bake for 45 minutes.

GLAZE
1 cup Irish Coffee Liqueur
1 cup powdered sugar

Turn cake out onto a plate while still warm and prick or pierce all over with a skewer. Combine liqueur and sugar and spoon this glaze mixture all over cake until it is completely soaked. Cover with foil and store in refrigerator.

I fill the center with Grand Marnier Sauce [page 320]. To serve the cake, I slice it, cover each slice with this sauce, and then add a good serving of Apricot Sauce [page 320].

ﷺ *Reader's Request*

The most talked about cake at Neiman Marcus is the

COFFEE ANGEL FOOD

1½ cups sifted sugar, divided use
1 cup sifted cake flour
½ teaspoon salt
1¼ cups egg whites (from 10 to 12 eggs)
1¼ teaspoons cream of tartar
½ teaspoon vanilla
1 tablespoon powdered instant coffee

[Preheat oven to 350°.] Add ½ cup of the sugar to flour. Sift together 4 times. Add salt to egg whites and beat with flat wire whisk or rotary egg beater until foamy. Sprinkle cream of tartar over egg whites and continue beating to soft-peak stage. Add the remaining cup of sugar by sprinkling ¼ cup at a time over egg whites and blending carefully into them with about 20 strokes each time. Fold in [vanilla and coffee]. Sift flour-sugar mixture over egg whites about ¼ at a time and fold in lightly with about 10 strokes each time. Pour into ungreased round 10-inch tube pan. Bake for 35 to 45 minutes. Remove from oven and invert pan on cooling rack.

Ice with Butter Cream Icing [page 343], adding 2 tablespoons of powdered coffee to the recipe. Whip until light and fluffy. Spread and sprinkle generously with slivered or chopped toasted almonds.

ANGEL LOAF CAKE

Bake an angel food cake in a loaf pan. Cut it lengthwise into 4 equal slices. Cover each slice with the following sauce and stack.

¾ cup sugar
1 tablespoon cornstarch
2 eggs
Juice of 1 lemon
Juice of 1 orange
2 tablespoons flour
1 cup whipped cream [from about ½ cup whipping cream]

1 10-ounce package frozen raspberries
Sugar to taste

Mix sugar, cornstarch, eggs, lemon and orange juice and flour; cook in top of double boiler until thick. Cool and mix with the whipped cream. Chill in the refrigerator. Do not freeze. Put the raspberries in blender; strain and add sugar if necessary. Slice cake and pour the strained raspberry sauce over each serving.

❧ Reader's Request

Rum Cake is a favorite all-year-round cake. This recipe is the one I use. It freezes well, too.

RUM CAKE

1 cup butter
2 cups sugar
4 eggs
3½ cups sifted flour
3 teaspoons baking powder
¼ teaspoon salt
1 cup milk
1 teaspoon rum extract

[Preheat oven to 325°.] Mix butter, sugar and eggs thoroughly. Sift flour, baking powder, and salt and add alternately with the milk and mix well. Add rum flavoring and bake 1 hour.

ICING
1 cup brown sugar
1 cup white sugar
½ cup water
Pinch of salt
1 teaspoon rum extract or 2 tablespoons dark rum

Mix both sugars, water, and salt, and boil well. Remove from heat, and add flavoring; pour half of the icing over hot cake while it is still in pan. Let cake cool, then turn upside down on plate and pour remaining icing over the cake.

ORANGE CHIFFON CAKE

2¼ cups sifted cake flour
3 teaspoons baking powder
1½ cups sugar
1 teaspoon salt
½ cup vegetable oil
5 egg yolks
¾ cup water
2 teaspoons grated orange peel
1 cup egg whites (from 7 or 8 eggs)
½ teaspoon cream of tartar

[Preheat oven to 325°.] Sift the dry ingredients together. Pour in the oil, egg yolks, water and orange peel. Beat until smooth (2 minutes with an electric beater). Set aside. Beat egg whites and cream of tartar together until stiff. Pour the flour mixture over egg whites a little at a time, gently folding in with a spatula. Do not beat. Pour into a 10-inch unbuttered tube pan and bake for 50 minutes. Increase oven temperature to 350° and bake an additional 15 minutes, or until the top springs back when you dent it with your finger. Turn pan upside down onto platter. Let stand until cold before removing pan.

Cover with Butter Cream Icing [page 343] flavored with 1½ teaspoons powdered coffee and ½ teaspoon of vanilla.

Cover the iced cake with shaved semi-sweet chocolate.

SHAVED CHOCOLATE
You need a large piece of chocolate to obtain large rolls or shavings of chocolate. Otherwise, buy the packages of 1 ounce squares or morsels and melt them over hot water. Pour into a loaf pan until you have a piece at least 1-inch thick. Refrigerate until it hardens. Remove from the pan and leave at room temperature for at least an hour. Take a heavy sharp knife—I use a French knife—place on top of chocolate, press down lightly and pull the knife over the chocolate toward you. The larger the piece of chocolate, the larger the shaving.

[This torte was a hit at the 1959 South American Fortnight, second only to Llinda Lee, a live Peruvian llama, which graced every floor of the store and was "stabled" at the Statler-Hilton.—Editor]

CHANTILLY TORTE
2 layers

6 eggs, separated
1½ cups sugar
2½ tablespoons flour
1 teaspoon baking powder
3 cups ground pecans
3 cups heavy cream, whipped

[Preheat oven to 350°.] Beat egg yolks, add sugar and beat with electric mixer for 15 minutes. Sift flour and baking powder and add gradually to the sugar and yolks. Add ground pecans and fold in the stiffly beaten egg whites. Bake in buttered cake pans for 30 minutes. Fill and cover with whipped cream and layers of shaved semi-sweet chocolate.

Or bake in sheets, pile high with the whipped cream and shaved chocolate for Black Forest Cake.

❧ Reader's Request

APPLE CAKE

2 cups sugar
1½ cups vegetable oil
2 teaspoons vanilla
2 eggs, beaten
Juice of ½ lemon
1 teaspoon salt
3 cups flour
1½ teaspoons soda
3 cups chopped peeled apples
1½ cups broken pecans

[Preheat oven to 375°. Mix together sugar, oil, vanilla, eggs, lemon juice and salt. Sift the flour and soda and add to liquids. Stir in apples and nuts.] Pour into buttered bundt or angel food tin. Bake for 1 hour or until a cake tester comes out clean. Serve plain or with Lemon Glaze, a variation of Sugar Glaze [page 341].

꙰ *Reader's Request*

This spice cake has always been popular as a "groom's" cake at weddings, and for tea parties. I always ice with Colonnade Icing [page 345] flavored with lemon juice and grated lemon peel.

PRINCE OF WALES SPICE CAKE
2 layers

⅓ cup shortening
1½ cups sugar
3 eggs
1½ tablespoons molasses
3 cups sifted cake flour
1½ teaspoons baking soda
1½ teaspoons cinnamon
¾ teaspoon cloves
¾ teaspoon nutmeg
1½ teaspoons baking powder
1½ cups sour milk [buttermilk]

[Preheat oven to 350°.] Cream shortening and sugar; add well-beaten eggs, then molasses. Sift dry ingredients together three times. [Beginning with flour mixture] add to creamed mixture alternately with sour milk. Pour into well buttered and floured cake pans. Bake for 20 to 25 minutes.

This was a recipe sent to me many years ago. I have used it for entertaining, a neighborly gift, and for travelers to munch on. It freezes well and wrapped in clear plastic will keep for days in the refrigerator.

POPPY SEED CAKE

¾ cup poppy seeds
¾ cup milk
¾ cup butter, margarine or soft vegetable shortening
1¼ cups sugar
3 eggs
1 teaspoon vanilla
2 cups flour
2 teaspoons baking powder
½ teaspoon salt

Soak poppy seeds in the milk overnight. [Preheat oven to 375°.] Cream butter and sugar. Add eggs one at a time, beating well after each addition. Add vanilla, milk, and poppy seeds, then flour sifted with the baking powder and salt. Mix well. Pour into a well buttered 9-inch tube angel cake or bundt pan and bake for 30 to 40 minutes. For a lighter cake, separate the eggs and fold in the stiffly beaten egg whites at the end.

This cake may be served plain, with confectioners' sugar sifted over or with a lemon juice Sugar Glaze [page 341].

The Houston Post *started me on the road to writing about food. The Food Editor, Ann Valentine, sent me the following cake recipe. . . . Good for holiday snacking and gifts.*

[Corbitt wrote a column called "Kitchen Klatter" for a number of years, which also appeared in Little Rock's Arkansas Gazette.—Editor]

BOURBON NUT CAKE

1 cup margarine [or butter]
2 cups sugar
6 eggs
4 cups sifted flour
2 teaspoons baking powder
2 teaspoons nutmeg
1 cup bourbon
¼ teaspoon almond extract
1 teaspoon vanilla
1 pound [4 cups] finely chopped pecans
7¼ ounces pitted dates, chopped
3 tablespoons coconut

[Preheat oven to 250°.] Cream margarine [or butter] and sugar, drop in whole eggs one at a time and stir after each addition. [Sift flour, baking powder and nutmeg together, reserving ¼ cup to dredge nuts. Add remaining flour mixture and bourbon, almond extract and vanilla alternately.] Flour nuts, dates, and coconut; add to cake batter lightly. Pour into buttered and floured angel food tin. Place a pan of water in the oven to prevent cracking and bake the cake for 6 hours. Also cover cake with aluminum foil for the first few hours of the baking period.

I use [this cake] for many occasions: a sweet for a cocktail party, a neighborhood gift at Christmas and with tea or coffee. Everyone likes it—calories and all—and you cannot fail. You may use it with or without an icing. If frosting, I use a lemon-flavored Butter Cream Icing. Forget to count the added calories.

DREAMLAND CAKE
2 layers

First Mixture:

> ½ cup butter
> 1 cup flour
> ⅛ teaspoon salt

[Preheat oven to 325°. Cream the butter and add flour and salt, sifted together.] Spread in two 9-inch square cake tins about ⅛-inch to ¼-inch thick.

Second Mixture:

> 2 eggs
> 1 cup brown sugar
> 1 teaspoon baking powder
> 1 cup walnuts, chopped
> ½ cup coconut
> ½ cup dates, chopped
> ½ cup candied cherries
> 1 teaspoon vanilla

Mix and pour second mixture over the first. Bake slowly for about 40 minutes. Ice with Butter Cream Icing [page 343] if you wish. Cut in squares.

SOUR CREAM POUND CAKE

1 cup butter
1½ cups sugar
4 eggs
2 cups flour
¾ teaspoon soda
½ teaspoon salt
¾ cup currants
½ cup sour cream
1 tablespoon Cointreau

[Preheat oven to 350°.] Cream butter, add the sugar and mix thoroughly. Add eggs and beat mixture until light. Sift flour, soda and salt together; add currants. Stir into the egg mixture alternately with the sour cream. Add the Cointreau and pour into a buttered and lightly floured angel food or bundt pan. Bake for 1 hour or until cake tester comes out clean. Turn out and while the cake is warm pour a lemon juice Sugar Glaze over. [See following]

SUGAR GLAZE
⅓ cup

1 cup sifted confectioners' sugar [pushed through a sieve]
1 tablespoon hot milk (approximate)

Place sugar in small bowl. Add milk gradually, blending well until mixture is thin enough to spread over cake.

[Lemon juice can be used instead of milk.]

❧ Reader's Request

It seems to me that the reputation of Carrot Cake has deteriorated. It is such a good cake, it should stay popular. This is the one I use.

CARROT CAKE
1 large cake

3 cups sifted flour
1½ teaspoons soda
1 teaspoon cinnamon
½ teaspoon salt
1½ cups liquid corn oil
2 cups sugar
2 cups grated raw carrots
1 8½-ounce can crushed pineapple with juice
1½ cups chopped pecans
2 teaspoons vanilla
3 eggs

[Preheat oven to 350°.] Sift flour, soda, cinnamon and salt together. Mix oil and sugar. Add half of the dry ingredients. Mix well and beat in carrots, pineapple, nuts and vanilla. Add the remaining dry ingredients and beat until well blended. Drop in eggs one at a time, beating after each addition. Pour batter into a well buttered and floured 10-inch tube pan. Bake for 1½ hours. When done leave in pan for 10 minutes, then remove. Cool thoroughly before icing with the following:

CREAM CHEESE ICING

8 ounces cream cheese
½ cup butter
1 pound confectioners' sugar
1 teaspoon vanilla
1 cup chopped pecans
[Milk]

Cream the cheese and butter. Add sugar, vanilla and pecans. Add a little milk, if necessary, to aid in spreading.

When you start talking about cakes, you could talk a volume. Surely everyone has a Betty Crocker Picture Cookbook. *I use its cake recipes. It is the icing that makes a cake popular.*

Really, you need only to have a few good icings, and you can make your own changes.

BUTTER CREAM ICING

½ cup butter
¼ teaspoon salt
2½ cups sifted confectioners' sugar
3 to 4 tablespoons milk
1 teaspoon vanilla

Cream butter, add salt and sugar, a small amount at a time, beating all the while. Add milk as needed, and flavoring. Beat until light and fluffy. Vary your flavors with almond extract, orange juice in place of the milk, and 2 teaspoons of grated orange peel; lemon juice and peel, likewise. Or add powdered coffee, 2 tablespoons. Or add 2 squares [2 ounces] of melted bitter chocolate. Add whatever you like.

SEA FOAM ICING

½ cup brown sugar
1 cup white sugar
4 tablespoons hot water
2 tablespoons strong coffee
¼ teaspoon cream of tartar
2 egg whites, stiffly beaten
¼ teaspoon salt
½ teaspoon almond extract
¼ teaspoon baking powder

Boil sugars, water, coffee, and cream of tartar until the mixture spins a thread or 248° on your candy thermometer. Remove from heat and pour very slowly into the stiffly beaten egg whites, continuing to beat until thick. Add salt, almond extract and baking powder, and beat until spreading consistency. Pile on the cake thickly, but do not use a heavy hand.

FUDGE ICING

2 cups sugar
2 tablespoons white corn syrup
1 cup milk
¼ teaspoon salt
2 squares [2 ounces] unsweetened chocolate, grated
1 teaspoon vanilla
2 tablespoons butter
[Light cream (optional)]

Mix sugar, syrup, milk, salt and chocolate. Cook over low heat to soft-ball stage, or 238°. Remove from heat, add vanilla and butter, and beat until cool. If it becomes too stiff, add hot thin cream until it has the correct texture for spreading.

Everyone who is dessert-minded gets the urge to do Petit Fours. It is as simple as falling off a log.

FONDANT ICING

2 cups granulated sugar
⅛ teaspoon cream of tartar
1 cup hot water
1 pound sifted confectioners' sugar (approximate)

Cook granulated sugar, cream of tartar and water to 226°. Cool to lukewarm and add confectioners' sugar till of a consistency to pour. [Place small cakes on a rack over wax paper to catch the drips. Ladle the icing over the cakes.] Keep in refrigerator covered with wax paper. Color if you wish, but lightly. Decorate with ornamental icing. Also, use for dipping almonds, fresh strawberries.

ORNAMENTAL ICING

2 cups sugar
1 cup water
3 egg whites
¼ teaspoon cream of tartar

Boil sugar and water until it forms a thread, or reaches 240°. Pour the syrup gradually into beaten egg whites, beating constantly. Add cream of tartar and continue beating until stiff. You can use it also for frosting the cake, and as thickly as you wish. Use it in a pastry tube for making flowers—it never melts or spreads.

This is a soft-on-the-inside, crusty-on-the-outside icing that never fails.

COLONNADE ICING

4½ cups sugar
1 cup water
6 tablespoons white corn syrup
6 egg whites, beaten stiff
⅓ cup confectioners' sugar

Mix sugar, water and syrup, and cook to the soft ball stage, 238° on your candy thermometer. Add slowly to egg whites, which have been beaten stiff but not dry, beating thoroughly until the icing is like cream. Add ⅓ cup confectioners' sugar. . . . Leftovers may be refrigerated, then heated over warm water to lukewarm and used as needed.

This icing goes on all the cakes you have liked, with variations:
With fresh coconut or toasted coconut flakes on chocolate or yellow cake.

With bitter chocolate melted and dribbled over it for a chocolate or angel food cake [see page 332 for Chocolate Cake].

Split layers of yellow cake and fill with lemon pie filling; ice lightly but deeply with Colonnade Icing.

Flavored with fresh lime or lemon juice and the grated rind, for angel food cakes.

Dusted with slivered nuts of all kinds for chiffon, layer and angel food cakes.

Fresh or frozen strawberries added for angel food and chocolate cakes.

Flavor with anything you like—peppermint, crème de cacao, or powdered coffee (add with the confectioners' sugar).

Pies and Pastries

Next time you make a cream pie, any kind, put a layer of whipped cream on top, then the meringue and you have three textures to savor. Or you may substitute ice cream for the whipped cream.

BLACK BOTTOM PIE

Prepare and bake a 9-inch Gingersnap Crust [page 359].

1 tablespoon unflavored gelatin
4 tablespoons cold water
2 cups milk
½ cup sugar
1 tablespoon cornstarch
¼ teaspoon salt
4 eggs, separated
2 ounces (2 squares) unsweetened chocolate, melted
1 teaspoon vanilla

Soften gelatin in cold water. Scald milk in double boiler. Mix sugar, cornstarch and salt together, stir slowly into milk and cook until thick. Add gradually to beaten egg yolks. Return to double boiler and cook 3 minutes longer. Stir in gelatin to dissolve. Divide in half; add melted chocolate and vanilla to one half of the mixture to make chocolate layer. Pour carefully into Gingersnap Crust.

CREAM LAYER
4 egg whites [left over from above]
⅛ teaspoon cream of tartar
½ cup sugar
1 tablespoon rum
1 teaspoon sherry
¾ cup heavy cream
1 tablespoon shaved unsweetened chocolate

Let remaining half of custard cool. Beat egg whites until frothy, add cream of tartar. Continue beating to a soft peak, and gradually add sugar. Fold meringue into cooled custard; add flavorings. Pour carefully over chocolate layer. Chill in refrigerator until set. When ready to serve, whip cream, spread on top of pie, and sprinkle with chocolate [see page 336 for directions on making chocolate shavings].

❧ *Reader's Request*

Coconut Cream or Meringue Pie was the golfers' favorite at the Houston Country Club. During the war years while I was manager there, I saved sugar and butter to be able to serve this pie on Saturday, regardless of anything else.

CUSTARD CREAM PIES

Prepare a 9-inch baked pie shell [page 358].

    1 ¾ cups milk [divided use]
    ¾ cup sugar [divided use]
    ½ teaspoon salt
    3 ½ tablespoons flour
    2 tablespoons cornstarch
    3 eggs [divided use]
    2 tablespoons butter
    ½ teaspoon vanilla
    ¼ teaspoon almond or lemon extract
    1 cup heavy cream

Scald half the milk and add ½ cup of the sugar and the salt. Bring to a boil. Mix flour, cornstarch, and 1 beaten whole egg plus 2 yolks with the remaining cool milk and beat until smooth. Add a little of the hot milk and blend. Combine both mixtures and cook over hot water until thick [enough to coat a metal spoon], stirring frequently. Remove and add the butter and flavorings. Beat until smooth. Beat the egg whites until frothy, add remaining sugar and continue beating until stiff. Fold the custard into the egg whites. Pour into baked pie shell.

[This custard mixture is the base of all cream pies—coconut, banana, toasted almond. Using uncooked egg presents food safety concerns. Please turn to page xii for a discussion and suggestions.—Editor]

COCONUT CUSTARD MERINGUE PIE: [Sprinkle ¼ cup coconut through the custard mixture and pour into a baked shell. Whip cream and spread over the top. Cover with ½ cup additional coconut and chill.]

When I use the meringue as a top, I whip and fold ½ of the cup of cream called for in the recipe above into the custard after it has cooled. Beat the egg whites with the sugar and pile on top. Sprinkle with ½ cup additional coconut and place in a preheated 450° oven until the coconut begins to brown.

CARAMEL CREAM PIE: [Caramelize ½ cup of the sugar called for in the recipe in a heavy skillet. Cool slightly before stirring it into the hot custard. Add remaining sugar to egg whites while you beat them.]

CHOCOLATE CREAM PIE: [Add 2 ounces (2 squares) of bitter chocolate. Banana Chocolate Pie is good. So are Chocolate Pecan and Toasted Almond.]

COFFEE CREAM PIE: Add instant coffee until it tastes as you like it—I like 2 tablespoonfuls. Toasted slivered almonds with it.

A most requested recipe.

SOUR CREAM APPLE PIE

Prepare a 9-inch unbaked pie shell [page 358].

    1 cup sugar
    2 tablespoons flour
    1 egg
    1 cup sour cream
    1 teaspoon vanilla
    ¼ teaspoon salt
    5 cups peeled, cored, and diced cooking apples

[Preheat oven to 350°.] Mix the sugar and flour. Add the egg, sour cream, vanilla and salt. Beat until smooth. Add the apples and pour into pie shell. Bake for 30 minutes.

    TOPPING
    ½ cup sugar
    5 tablespoons flour
    ¼ cup butter

Mix the sugar, flour and butter to resemble crumbs. Cover the pie and bake for 15 minutes longer.

This is a divine pie—a great favorite with non-dieters.

BING CHERRY PIE

Prepare a 9-inch baked Graham Cracker Crust [page 357].

1½ cups pecans, coarsely chopped
5½ cups drained Bing cherries
30 ounces canned sweetened condensed milk
Juice of 6 lemons
Red food coloring
1½ cups whipping cream
[Additional whipped or sour cream, optional]

Mix the pecans, pitted cherries, milk and lemon juice, and a few drops of red food coloring. Whip and fold in the cream. Pour into a prebaked crust. Chill. (Keep about 1 cup of mixture out of crust to pile in center after other mixture is set, if you want a high pie.) Cover with a thin layer of sour or whipped cream before serving, if you wish.

The very best pie I ever ate. I made it for a crusty friend who said, "It was so good I'd fight my Daddy for it."

LEMON CUSTARD PIE

Prepare an unbaked 9-inch pie shell [page 358].

4 large eggs
1 cup sugar
2 teaspoons flour
1 cup white corn syrup
Grated rind and juice of 1 lemon
4 teaspoons butter, just softened

[Preheat oven to 350°.] Beat the eggs, add sugar mixed with the flour. Add rest of ingredients. Pour into shell and bake for 60 minutes or until knife test shows it is done. Do not refrigerate.

FRENCH CHOCOLATE PIE

Prepare an 8-inch Meringue Crust from the following:

2 egg whites
⅛ teaspoon salt
⅛ teaspoon cream of tartar
½ cup sugar
½ cup finely chopped walnuts or pecans
½ teaspoon vanilla extract

[Preheat oven to 300°.] Combine egg whites, salt and cream of tartar in a mixing bowl. Beat until foamy. Add sugar, two tablespoonfuls at a time, beating after each addition until sugar is blended. Continue beating until the mixture stands in very stiff peaks. Fold in nuts and blend in vanilla. Spoon into a lightly buttered 8-inch pie pan and build the sides up ½-inch above the sides of the pan, but not out over the rim. If desired, the meringue can be squeezed through a pastry tube to make a fancy edge. Bake for 50 to 55 minutes. Cool.

4 ounces German's sweet baking chocolate
3 tablespoons water
1 tablespoon brandy
1 cup whipping cream
Shaved chocolate

Place baking chocolate and water in a saucepan over low heat. Stir until the chocolate has melted. Cool; add brandy to the chocolate. Whip cream to soft consistency. Fold chocolate mixture into whipped cream. Pile into meringue shell. Chill about 2 hours before serving. Garnish with shaved chocolate [page 336].

ॐ *Reader's Request*

DIXIE PECAN PIE

Prepare an unbaked 9-inch pie shell [page 358].

3 eggs
2 tablespoons sugar
2 tablespoons flour
2 cups dark corn syrup
1 teaspoon vanilla extract
¼ teaspoon salt
1 cup pecans

[Preheat oven to 425°.] Beat the eggs until light. Mix the sugar and flour. Add to the eggs and beat well. Add syrup, vanilla, salt and pecans. Pour into pie shell and bake for 10 minutes; reduce the heat to 325° and finish baking—about 45 more minutes.

ॐ *Reader's Request*

FRESH STRAWBERRY PIE

Prepare a baked 9-inch pie shell [page 358].

1½ quarts fresh strawberries
3 tablespoons cornstarch
1 cup sugar
2 tablespoons lemon juice
Whipped Cream

Wash and hull the berries and reserve half of the prettiest ones. Mash the other half, add the cornstarch and sugar, and cook until thick and clear. Remove from heat and stir in the lemon juice. Cool; add the whole berries, or if they are too large, cut in half, but save a few for garnishing. Pour into the pie shell, cover with whipped cream and garnish. It has a tartness combined with the strawberry sweetness that is interesting.

FRESH PEACH DUMPLINGS

3 cups flour
1½ teaspoons salt
1¼ cups soft vegetable shortening
1 tablespoon lemon juice
10 to 12 tablespoons ice water
8 fresh whole peaches

[Preheat oven to 425°.] Mix flour and salt. Cut in shortening with a pastry blender or two knives until it looks like cornmeal. Add lemon juice and water; mix quickly until mixture is free from the bowl. Add more water if necessary. Roll out on a floured board until thin. Cut into 6-inch squares. Wrap each around a peach, leaving the skin on and stone in. Bake for about 30 minutes. Cool, make a hole in top large enough to remove stone. It will slip out easily with an iced-tea spoon. The skin disintegrates in the baking. Put back in oven to heat, as they are better hot. Fill cavity with Hard Sauce [page 314].

Or, peel and remove stone, keeping peach as whole as possible. For each peach push into cavity:

1 tablespoon sugar
1 tablespoon butter
Pinch of cinnamon

Wrap each peach with pastry as directed above. Bake at 425° for 15 minutes, then reduce the heat to 350° and continue baking about 45 minutes, basting frequently with:

BROWN SUGAR SYRUP
1 cup brown sugar
½ cup water

Bring to a boil and continue to cook until a thin syrup is formed.

Serve dumplings with whipped cream, flavored with half lemon-half almond extract or with Hard Sauce.

❧ *Reader's Request*

FRESH STRAWBERRY-CHEESE TARTS OR PIE

Prepare 8 baked tart shells or 1 9-inch baked pie crust [page 358].

8 ounces cream cheese
½ cup sugar
1 teaspoon grated lemon rind
2 tablespoons lemon juice
2 tablespoons half-and-half cream or milk
Fresh ripe strawberries, stemmed and hulled

Mix the cream cheese, sugar, lemon rind, juice, cream or milk; beat until of whipped-cream consistency. (Leave the cheese out of the refrigerator several hours—it works better.) Line the tart shells or pie shell with the cheese mixture; fill with fresh whole ripe berries and cover with:

STRAWBERRY GLAZE
3 cups strawberries
1 cup sugar
3 tablespoons cornstarch
Whipping cream (optional)

Mash berries with the sugar and let stand for 30 minutes. Mix with the cornstarch and cook until thick and clear. Strain and cool. Pour over the berries and refrigerate. They are divine! I make small ones for buffet parties, and they are gobbled up in a hurry! Whipped cream on top for garnish.

FRESH BLUEBERRY TARTLETS

[Bake a crust for a tart or 9-inch pie tin using the Egg Pastry recipe on page 358 or buy frozen tartlet shells and bake according to package directions.]

8 ounces cream cheese
3 tablespoons sugar
3 tablespoons lemon juice
Blueberries

Mix cheese, sugar and lemon juice until consistency of whipped cream and spread generously inside the tart shells. Fill with fresh whole stemmed blueberries. Cover with:

BLUEBERRY SAUCE
1 cup fresh blueberries
2 tablespoons sugar (approximate)
2 tablespoons crème de cassis (optional)
Sour or sweet heavy cream (optional)

Crush berries in blender. Add sugar and cassis. Pour over berries. Serve plain or with sour or whipped cream.

LEMON ANGEL PIE

Prepare a 9-inch Meringue Crust with

4 egg whites
¼ teaspoon cream of tartar
¾ cup sugar

[Preheat oven to 300°.] Beat egg whites until frothy. Add cream of tartar. Continue beating, gradually adding the sugar until the mixture is stiff. Spread in a lightly buttered 9-inch pie tin and bake for 1 hour. Cool. Cover with Lemon Filling.

Mix:

6 egg yolks
¾ cup sugar
½ teaspoon salt

Add:

1 teaspoon grated orange rind
1 teaspoon grated lemon rind
3 tablespoons orange juice
3 tablespoons lemon juice
Whipped cream
Slivered blanched almonds

[Stir in citrus rind and juices.] Cook over hot water until thick. Cool and spread over top of the baked meringue. Cover with whipped cream and toasted almonds, or fold them into the custard.

SOUR CREAM PUMPKIN PIE

Prepare a 9-inch unbaked Graham Cracker Crust [page 357].

    12 ounces cream cheese
    ¾ cup sugar
    1½ tablespoons flour
    1 teaspoon grated orange peel
    ½ teaspoon grated lemon peel
    2 eggs plus 2 egg yolks
    1 cup cooked or canned pumpkin
    ⅛ teaspoon ground cinnamon

[Preheat oven to 350°.] Blend in your electric mixer the cheese, sugar, flour and grated peels. Add eggs and egg yolks; beat at medium speed until smooth. Mix in pumpkin and cinnamon; continue beating until light and smooth. Pour into prepared crust. Bake for 40 minutes or until the custard is set. Remove and spread with the following mixture:

    2 cups sour cream
    3 tablespoons sugar
    1 teaspoon vanilla

Bake 10 minutes longer. Remove from oven, cool and spread with a thin layer of additional cold sour cream.

This was the most popular pie for parties at the Driskill Hotel. Even the men ordered it.

ORANGE CHIFFON PIE WITH PRUNE WHIP TOP

Prepare a baked 9-inch Graham Cracker Crust [page 357].

    1 tablespoon gelatin
    ¼ cup cold water
    4 eggs, separated
    1 cup sugar, divided use
    ½ teaspoon salt
    1 tablespoon lemon juice
    ½ cup orange juice
    1 tablespoon grated orange peel

Soak the gelatin in the cold water for 15 minutes. Beat the egg yolks until light. Add ½ cup of sugar, salt, lemon juice and orange juice. Cook in a double boiler until thick. Add the grated orange peel. Remove from heat and add the gelatin. Stir until dissolved. Cool. Beat egg whites medium stiff, add the rest of the sugar gradually, and continue beating until stiff. Fold into the orange mixture and place in a graham cracker shell, piling high in the center.

    1 cup heavy cream
    1 tablespoon additional sugar
    ¾ cup chopped cooked prunes
    1 teaspoon grated lemon peel

Top with the whipped cream, into which the sugar, prunes, and lemon peel have been folded.

[Uncooked egg whites present safety concerns. Please turn to page xii for a discussion and suggestions.—Editor]

At the Houston Country Club I used to swirl crème de cacao in the whipped cream and sliver semi-sweet chocolate on top.

Use the same recipe for Lemon or Lime Chiffon, substituting lemon or lime juice and grated peel of each for the orange juice and peel. Sour cream is an interesting topping for the lemon pie, dusted with ground walnuts.

GRAHAM CRACKER CRUST

9-inch pie crust

    1½ cups graham cracker crumbs
    ½ cup confectioners' sugar
    ½ cup melted butter

[Preheat oven to 300°.] Mix and press firmly into a 9-inch pie tin. Sprinkle lightly with cold water and bake for 8 minutes.

Everyone has her own recipe for plain pastry. This is mine.

PLAIN PASTRY
Two 9-inch pie crusts or
12 individual tart shells

2 cups sifted all-purpose flour
1 teaspoon salt
⅔ cup shortening
6 to 8 tablespoons cold water

Sift the flour and salt together; cut in the shortening quickly and lightly with a pastry blender or your fingers. Stir in the cold water as lightly as possible to form a smooth ball. Roll out on a lightly floured board [or pastry cloth] to as thin a pastry as you like. . . . Roll out trimmings for cheese straws, or cut with a small round cutter for bases for cocktail spreads. Keep a container in your refrigerator for such things. Wrap unbaked dough in waxed paper and chill until you need it. [Bring to room temperature before rolling.] Remember to handle as little as possible, so the pastry will be light and flaky.

[Baked pie shells can be kept for several days in an airtight container.—Editor]

If you like a brown pie crust, sprinkle a little granulated sugar over the top or brush lightly with an egg beaten with a little water.

EGG PASTRY
1 tart pan or
2 9-inch pie crusts

2 cups [all-purpose] flour
1 teaspoon salt
⅔ cup soft vegetable shortening
1 egg
2 tablespoons cold water (approximate)
2 teaspoons lemon juice

[Preheat oven to 350°.] Sift flour with salt into mixing bowl. Cut in shortening with a pastry blender or two knives. Mix slightly beaten egg, water and lemon juice. Sprinkle over flour mixture, toss and stir until mixture is moist enough to hold together. You may need to add a little more cold water. Sprinkle flour on board to roll pastry on. Rub rolling pin with flour. Do not press down too hard on dough, but roll until dough is smooth and thin. Fit crust tightly into tart tin or pie pan, [lay a pie chain over the dough] to hold it firmly in place. Bake until golden brown.

An interesting crust:

COCONUT CRUMB CRUST
9-inch pie crust

1½ cups flaked coconut
2 tablespoons butter, melted
2 tablespoons sugar
¼ cup finely crushed graham crackers, ginger snaps, vanilla
    wafers or chocolate wafers
Pinch of cinnamon

[Preheat oven to 375°.] Combine coconut and butter and mix well. Add sugar and cookie crumbs, mixing thoroughly. Press firmly on bottom and sides of pie pan. Bake for 10 to 12 minutes or until lightly browned. Cool.

To serve, fill crust with ice cream. Serve immediately, or deep freeze to serve later. An all-time favorite, coffee ice cream in Coconut Crust with Butterscotch Sauce [page 319] and whipped cream.

GINGERSNAP CRUST
9-inch pie crust

35 gingersnaps
½ cup butter
1 tablespoon confectioners' sugar

[Preheat oven to 300°.] Roll gingersnaps with rolling pin to make fine crumbs; add melted butter and sugar and mix well. Press firmly into a 9-inch pie tin. Bake for 5 minutes.

It is good to have crumb crusts stored in your deep freeze. (Put wax paper or foil between them.)

TOASTED ALMOND CRUST
9-inch pie crust

1 cup [all-purpose] flour
½ teaspoon salt
¼ cup slivered almonds, lightly toasted
½ cup shortening
2 tablespoons cold water

[Preheat oven to 400°.] Mix flour, salt, and nuts. Cut in the shortening [until it is as fine as meal]; add the water. Mix to form a ball. Roll thin and fit into a pie tin. Bake until light brown.

Fill any crust with your favorite ice cream and freeze. When ready to serve, cut and serve with your preference of sauce or fruit poured over, and whipped cream, if you wish.

Strawberry Ice Cream Pie has always been the favorite.

1 9-inch Graham Cracker pie crust
1 quart strawberry ice cream

Press the ice cream into the shell and freeze. Serve with strawberries, fresh or frozen, and unsweetened whipped cream.

Other favorite combinations:

Lemon ice cream in Gingersnap Crust, served with fresh peaches or blueberries slightly mashed and sugared.

Coffee ice cream and raspberry sherbet in the Toasted Almond Crust with Fudge Sauce and whipped cream.

Vanilla ice cream, or a combination of flavors, packed in a baked pie shell and piled high with meringue made with 3 egg whites and 6 tablespoons sugar. Brown in a preheated 450° oven and place in the freezer. Serve with hot Fudge Sauce or Melba Sauce [pages 315 and 316].

Cookies

Cookies are a sign of hospitality and are as old as 1563. The American "cookie" comes to us from the Dutch who settled New Amsterdam (New York). The Dutch called a cookie a "koekje," a diminutive of "koek," meaning cake. As in many cases when adopting new food, the English took the sound and gave it their own spelling. The British today call our cookie and/or cracker a "biscuit" and sometimes a "tea cake."

The child who does not know the joy and comfort of reaching into a well-filled cookie jar has missed one of youth's greater compensations. And, too, cookie making can be child's play—and what a way to keep their idle hands busy.

There are so many kinds! From honest-to-goodness filler-uppers to the delicate fantasies everyone likes to serve at parties. And a box of homemade cookies makes your most difficult neighbor a slave forever. One piece of advice: Stir, but do not beat, cookie mixtures.

ಿ *Reader's Request*

CHOCOLATE CHIP MERINGUES
2 dozen medium or 3 dozen small

4 egg whites
¼ teaspoon salt
¼ teaspoon cream of tartar
1½ cups sugar
1 teaspoon vanilla
1 cup broken pecans
1 6-ounce package semi-sweet chocolate bits

[Preheat oven to 325°.] Beat egg whites until stiff, add salt and cream of tartar. Continue beating, adding the sugar a little at a time. Continue beating. Add vanilla, fold in pecans and chocolate bits. Drop by tablespoonfuls onto a cookie sheet or pan lined with foil, shiny side up. Bake until dry. Cool slightly and pull off the foil.

Omit the nuts and chocolate for Kiss Meringues.

ಿ *Reader's Request*

LACE COOKIES
5 dozen

3 eggs
¾ teaspoon salt
1½ cups sugar
1½ tablespoons melted butter
1½ teaspoons vanilla
¼ teaspoon grated nutmeg
4 teaspoons baking powder
3½ cups uncooked oatmeal

[Preheat oven to 350°.] Beat the eggs with the salt; add sugar gradually, then stir in remaining ingredients. Drop by teaspoonfuls onto a well buttered cookie sheet and bake for 10 minutes, or until a delicate brown. Remove from pan at once. [Cool on wire racks.]

SCOTCH SHORTBREAD
2 cakes

1 cup butter
½ cup confectioners' sugar
2 cups flour
¼ teaspoon salt
¼ teaspoon baking powder

[Preheat oven to 350°.] Cream butter, add confectioners' sugar and beat until light. Add the flour, salt and baking powder sifted together. Mix well and spoon into cake pans. Pat out to ¼-inch thickness. Prick with a fork. Bake until a delicate brown—about 20 minutes. Cut in pie shaped pieces. Or roll out and cut in 2 dozen squares before baking. Light brown sugar gives it a different flavor and good. Serve it hot. You may warm many times.

A favorite party cookie.

PECAN BALLS
About 5 dozen

½ cup vegetable shortening
½ cup butter
½ cup sugar
2 eggs, separated
2 tablespoons grated orange peel
2 teaspoons grated lemon peel
2 teaspoons lemon juice
2½ cups cake flour
½ teaspoon salt
1½ cups finely chopped pecans
½ pound glazed cherries (you may omit)

[Preheat oven to 325°.] You may substitute margarine for the shortening or butter, but the texture and flavor are better if you do not. Cream the shortening, butter and sugar. Add egg yolks, peels and juice; stir and add flour and salt, sifted together. Stir but do not beat. Chill for 30 minutes. Form into small balls. Roll in the slightly beaten egg whites, then in the nuts. Place on a greased cookie sheet. Make an impression in the center of each ball. Cut the cherries in half and press a piece into each cookie. Bake for 25 minutes. Nice for Christmas.

My favorite cookie:

LEMON CRUMB SQUARES
2 dozen

15 ounces sweetened condensed milk*
½ cup lemon juice
1 teaspoon grated lemon rind
1½ cups all-purpose flour
1 teaspoon baking powder
½ teaspoon salt
⅔ cup butter
1 cup dark brown sugar, firmly packed
1 cup uncooked oatmeal

[Preheat oven to 350°.] Blend together milk, juice and rind of lemon, and set aside. Sift together flour, baking powder, and salt. Cream butter, blend in sugar. Add oatmeal and flour mixture and mix until crumbly. Spread half the oatmeal mixture in an 8 x 12 x 2-inch buttered baking pan and pat down; spread condensed milk mixture over top and cover with remaining crumb mixture. Bake until brown around the edges (about 25 minutes). Cool in pan at room temperature for 15 minutes; cut into 1¾-inch squares and chill in pan until firm.

[*A condensed milk can no longer holds 15 ounces, so you will need to buy two. I decided to leave this in since Helen Corbitt was so fond of them.—Editor]

No Christmas cookie tray should be without a spice cookie, decorated with silver dragées, colored sugar, and all the things to add sparkle to your holiday table. This is a good one. You can also use them on your Christmas tree.

SPICE COOKIES
4 dozen

½ cup butter
½ cup sugar
⅔ cup molasses, New Orleans-type
1 egg [lightly beaten]
2¾ cups all-purpose flour
3 teaspoons baking powder
½ teaspoon salt
1½ teaspoons allspice

[Preheat oven to 375°.] Melt butter slowly in a large saucepan; cool. Add sugar, molasses and egg; beat well. Sift flour, baking powder, salt and allspice into first mixture. Mix well. Roll in wax paper; chill. Roll dough out evenly ⅛-inch thick on lightly floured baking sheet. (Cookies hold their shape better if you roll dough out on the baking sheet and remove the trimmings instead of rolling it on a pastry board and transferring the cookies to the baking sheet.) Cut in shape of Santas, stars or trees. Lift excess dough from around the cookies. Decorate with silver dragées, cinnamon drops and colored sugar. If cookies are to be used for Christmas tree decorations, make a hole in each with a skewer; enlarge holes so they won't close in baking. Bake for 8 to 10 minutes. Remove from baking sheet immediately and cool on cake racks.

❧ Reader's Request

Fudge Brownies, or Squares, are no doubt one of the most popular cookies for all ages. They are easy to make, can be served plain or iced, or rolled in powdered sugar. Cut in thin fingers and rolled in powdered sugar they are a good party cookie. Incidentally, when making your favorite Brownie recipe, coconut substituted for the nuts is a nice change, too.

FUDGE BROWNIE FINGERS
3 dozen

2 eggs
1 cup sugar
½ cup butter
2 squares [2 ounces] unsweetened chocolate
¾ cup sifted all-purpose flour
½ teaspoon salt
1 cup finely chopped nuts (walnuts or pecans usual;
     black walnuts divine)
1 teaspoon vanilla
[Confectioners' sugar]

[Preheat oven to 325°.] Beat eggs slightly; add sugar and stir. Add butter and chocolate melted together. Mix flour, salt and nutmeats and add to egg mixture. Add vanilla and stir until well blended, but do not beat. As I said before, never beat a cookie mix. Pour into a well-buttered 9-inch pan. Bake for 30 to 35 minutes. Cool and cut in 2-inch fingers. Roll in confectioners' sugar.

⅜ Reader's Request

One can usually eat a chocolate brownie and rest his conscience, but a butterscotch one—no—you always want one more.

BUTTERSCOTCH BROWNIES

4 tablespoons melted butter
1 cup dark brown sugar
1 egg
¾ cup [all-purpose] flour
½ teaspoon salt
1 teaspoon baking powder
½ teaspoon vanilla
¼ cup coconut
½ cup broken nuts

[Preheat oven to 350°. Cream the butter and sugar together until they are light. Mix in the slightly beaten egg. Sift the flour, salt and baking powder together and add them to the butter-sugar mixture. Stir in the vanilla, coconut and nuts. Spread in a buttered 8 x 8-inch pan and bake for 25 minutes.] Cool and spread with:

CARAMEL ICING
½ cup butter
½ cup brown sugar
¼ cup milk or half-and-half
1¾ to 2 cups confectioners' sugar
1 teaspoon maple or vanilla extract

Melt butter until brown, add brown sugar and cook, stirring constantly until sugar is completely melted. [Gradually] pour in milk and stir. Cool. Add confectioners' sugar and flavoring; beat until thick enough to spread.

This is a good picnic cookie—and a nice change from brownies.

CHOCOLATE COCONUT COOKIES
3 dozen

2 cups [all-purpose] flour
2 cups sugar
½ teaspoon salt
1 cup butter or margarine
3 tablespoons cocoa
1 cup water
2 eggs
½ cup buttermilk
1 teaspoon soda
1 teaspoon vanilla

[Preheat oven to 375°.] Sift together flour, sugar and salt. Set aside. Mix butter, cocoa and water. Bring to a boil, pour over flour mixture. Add well-beaten eggs, buttermilk, soda and vanilla. Pour into two buttered shallow cake pans approximately 9 x 9-inches. Bake for 30 minutes.

TOPPING
Mix and bring to a boil:

½ cup butter
6 tablespoons half-and-half
3 tablespoons cocoa

Add mixture to:

2 cups confectioners' sugar
½ teaspoon vanilla
1 cup shredded coconut
1 cup chopped nuts

Mix and spread over cookies as they come from the oven. Cut in squares.

PISTACHIO COOKIES
2 dozen

½ cup butter
⅓ cup sugar
1 egg, separated
½ teaspoon almond extract
¼ teaspoon salt
1 tablespoon grated lemon rind
1 tablespoon grated orange rind
1 cup [all-purpose] flour
Pistachio nuts, finely chopped

[Preheat oven to 350°.] Cream the butter, add sugar, egg yolk, extract, salt, lemon and orange rinds. Mix thoroughly until creamy. Add flour and mix. Shape into small balls. Roll each ball in unbeaten egg white, and then in chopped pistachio nuts. Make indentation in top of cookie with your thumb. Bake on greased cookie sheet for 12 to 15 minutes. [Cool on wire racks.]

ALMOND COOKIES
4 dozen

1 cup butter
1 cup sugar
1 egg, separated
¾ teaspoon vanilla
2 cups sifted cake flour
⅛ teaspoon salt
½ cup shredded almonds
3 tablespoons sugar
½ teaspoon cinnamon

[Preheat oven to 400°.] Butter a flat 10 x 16-inch pan and set in the refrigerator to chill. Cream butter; add the sugar and beat well. Stir in egg yolk and vanilla. Add sifted flour and salt. Spread mixture in pan. Beat egg white until stiff and spread over cookie mixture. Sprinkle with mixture of almonds, sugar, and cinnamon. Bake for 15 to 20 minutes. Cut in strips and remove from the pan while warm.

This cookie has many names and when I serve them they disappear like magic. Here is the oft-requested recipe.

CHINESE CHEWS
4 dozen cookies

1 cup butter
2 cups flour
1 cup [all purpose] light brown sugar, packed tightly

[Preheat oven to 350°.] Mix and spread evenly over an 8 x 12-inch pan. Bake for 15 minutes. Remove from oven and cool.

[Reduce the oven temperature to 325°.] Mix together:

4 eggs, lightly beaten
¼ cup flour
3 cups dark brown sugar
1 cup Angel Flake coconut
2 cups coarsely chopped pecans or walnuts
1 teaspoon salt
½ teaspoon vanilla

Spread on baked layer. Bake for 35 to 40 minutes or until cookie is firm. Dribble over top while cookie is warm:

1 cup confectioners' sugar mixed with
1 tablespoon orange juice
½ teaspoon grated orange rind

When cold, cut into fingers.

When cutting cookies, dip the cutters in flour before pressing into the dough. When rerolling the trimmings, lay them together. Wadding them together before rolling out toughens them. If you wish to mail homemade cookies to your children, pack them in popcorn to prevent breakage. They can eat the popcorn too.

FLORENTINES
3 dozen

½ cup whipping cream
3 tablespoons sugar
¼ cup [all-purpose] flour
⅓ cup slivered almonds, blanched
¼ pound diced preserved orange peel
4 ounces [4 squares] semi-sweet chocolate

[Preheat oven to 350°.] Mix cream, sugar, flour, nuts and orange peel together. Spread a cookie sheet with unsalted vegetable shortening and flour lightly. Drop the batter from a teaspoon onto the sheet, allowing ample space between each cookie. Bake until golden brown, from 8 to 10 minutes. Cool. Spread the cookie bottoms with the melted semi-sweet chocolate.

Don't you sometimes want just a plain sugar cookie?

PLAIN SUGAR COOKIES
5 dozen medium cookies

1 cup sugar
1 cup butter
3 cups sifted [all-purpose] flour
½ teaspoon salt
1½ teaspoons baking powder
1 egg
2 tablespoons plus 2 teaspoons cream
1 teaspoon vanilla
Additional sugar (optional)

[Preheat oven to 350°. Cream sugar and butter together. Add flour, salt, baking powder, sifted together. Beat egg, cream and vanilla together before adding.]

Mix well and turn onto well-floured board. Roll about ⅛-inch thick, cut and bake carefully on a buttered cookie sheet for about 12 to 15 minutes or until lightly browned. Sprinkle with granulated sugar before baking if you like.

ORANGE MARMALADE COOKIES
10 dozen medium cookies

½ cup butter
1 cup sugar
2 eggs
3 cups sifted [all-purpose] flour
½ teaspoon soda
½ teaspoon salt
1 cup thick orange marmalade

[Preheat oven to 350°.] Cream butter, add sugar and cream until light and fluffy. Mix in well-beaten eggs. Sift flour, soda and salt together and stir into egg mixture. Add marmalade and blend. Drop by tea-spoonfuls 1 inch apart on well-buttered cookie sheet. For small cookies, by half-teaspoonfuls. Bake for 12 to 13 minutes. Remove and cool. If you wish, cover with:

ORANGE ICING
2 teaspoons grated orange peel
1 teaspoon grated lemon peel
¼ cup orange juice
1 teaspoon lemon juice
3 tablespoons soft butter
3 cups confectioners' sugar
⅛ teaspoon salt

Mix grated peels and juices. Cream butter and sugar. Blend with juices. Add salt and mix until smooth.

These cookies keep well in a covered container, but disappear quickly.

Whether you buy or bake cookies, store them properly by keeping them at room temperature; crisp ones in a container with a loose cover, soft ones with a tight fitting cover. A wedge of fresh apple will keep them moist. If crisp ones become limp, place on an ungreased baking sheet and put in a 300° oven for 5 minutes.

PEANUT COOKIES
6 dozen small cookies

1 cup shortening
½ cup brown sugar
1 tablespoon corn syrup
1 tablespoon peanut butter
1 cup [all-purpose] flour
¼ teaspoon baking powder
1 cup chopped dry roasted peanuts

[Preheat oven to 350°. Cream the shortening and brown sugar together. Stir in the syrup and peanut butter. Sift the flour and baking powder together into the bowl and mix. Blend in the chopped nuts. Turn out onto a floured pastry board or cloth and knead briefly. Roll out into a sheet about ⅛-inch thick and cut into cookies. Place on a lightly greased cookie sheet and bake for 20 to 25 minutes or until they begin to color.]

⅛ Reader's Request

Everyone South of New York makes these sand tarts at Christmas time. They keep forever.

SAND TARTS
4 dozen

½ pound butter
½ cup sifted confectioners' sugar
2 cups sifted cake flour
1 cup chopped pecans
1 teaspoon vanilla
[powdered sugar]

[Preheat oven to 325°.] Cream butter; add sugar. Stir well and add flour, nuts, and vanilla. Shape into balls or crescents and bake on ungreased cookie sheet for 20 minutes or until a light brown. Roll in powdered sugar while warm.

This and That

There are always snippets of information left over at the end of every project of this size. Corbitt combined these and placed them at the backs of all but her last cookbook. It proved popular with earlier readers, so I am availing myself of the same opportunity. In an effort to make your hours in the kitchen more effective, here are hints my mother and friends, fine cooks all, have passed along to me. I've added a few of my own picked up during a gastronomically satisfying half-century spent in my own kitchens.—Editor

꙾ If you don't own a rolling pin, use a chilled cylindrical bottle of wine to roll pastry.

꙾ Something always needs to be grated: chilled citrus fruit is easier to grate. The extra flavor of freshly grated nutmeg and Parmesan cheese make it worth your effort. Either can be grated easily in a hand-held Zyliss or on a Japanese fresh ginger grater. Hard cheeses are easier to grate when they're at room temperature.

꙾ Cream cheese is always worked at room temperature.

꙾ You can judge the amount of butterfat in cheese by its firmness; hard cheese has less. Never heat no-fat cheese; the gum arabic used in it does just what its name implies.

꙾ To avoid a last-minute dither, make your sauces and gravies ahead of serving time and keep them hot in a preheated thermos bottle. Use

Lea & Perrins White Wine Worcestershire to flavor light colored sauces. Canned condensed soups are basically flavored cream/white sauces; for a quick sauce, thin one appropriately and dress it up with a little imagination!

❧ Egg whites give their greatest volume if you hold them at room temperature for 30 minutes before beating them. Be sure their bowl and beaters are scrupulously free of fat, which includes even a single drop of egg yolk. Use a wet teaspoon to fish out a speck of yolk or shell. On the other hand, heavy cream, along with the bowl and beaters, all need to be chilled to whip properly.

❧ When cake recipes begin "cream butter and sugar together" and continue by adding liquid and dry ingredients alternately, always add a little of the dry ingredients first to stabilize the batter.

❧ Prepare the bottoms of pans for chocolate cake by coating them with shortening and cocoa, rather than flour; it won't show white on the bottoms of baked chocolate layers.

❧ Use the back of a wooden spoon to force cocoa or confectioners' sugar through a coarse sieve. It is easier than sifting it.

❧ Lightly spray all sides of a freshly baked warm loaf of bread with butter-flavored cooking oil or rub them with butter to soften bread crusts.

❧ You can sour milk by stirring 1½ tablespoons of lemon juice or 1⅓ tablespoons of vinegar into a cup of "sweet" milk; allow it to sit for a few minutes. It's not as flavorful, but it works in a pinch.

❧ When the recipe directs you to "skim the surface," set one side of the kettle off the heat source. Convection currents cause the skim to gather toward the cooler side.

❧ Quick tip for removing fat from drippings: float one or more ice cubes on the surface of drippings; the ice quickly gathers the fat and can be discarded. When soups and stews are chilled overnight before serving, you can lift the solid cake of fat off easily the following day. If you are going to freeze or refrigerate the stew, leave the fat cake in place until you are ready to reheat. It seals the food under it. Keep bones overnight with soups and stews; food acids will leach calcium from them, enriching the dish.

❧ You make a *bouquet garni* by wrapping a stem of fresh parsley around several other herbs and vegetables. This makes it easy to remove them from the pot. The usual combination is a carrot, stem of celery and bay leaf tied together with parsley.

❧ A nylon mesh paint strainer from the hardware store makes a wonderful strainer for everything from fruit juice to chicken broth. It fits the old-fashioned conical colanders and is easy to wash out. (If you don't use your old conical colander any more, you can always make it into a lamp shade. I've seen them in pricey kitchen shops!)

❧ After you use the last pickle from a commercially prepared jar of sweet pickles, save the syrup. Drain a can of sliced beets, turn them into the pickle jar and refrigerate for several days in the reserved pickle juice. Voila! Pickled beets! Such an easy, inexpensive way to add color to a plate.

❧ Submerge fresh tomatoes, peaches, and even pears, in boiling water for 2 to 3 minutes, then dip them out and plunge into iced water. The skins will pull away.

❧ To keep fresh peaches from darkening during freezing, slice them into undiluted frozen orange juice concentrate. Dip them out and freeze as usual. There is only a slight orange flavor when they thaw.

❧ You can freeze bags of lemons when they are on sale; rinse and thaw in the microwave, about 45 seconds on half-power for each lemon, as you need them for cooking.

❧ Fresh artichokes will speak to you; hold each one up to your ear and squeeze lightly. If it squeaks, it still has moisture in the leaves. Also examine the stem ends to be sure they aren't hollow.

❧ To clean asparagus, use a thin knife blade to flip off each scale. Grasp both ends of each stalk and bend; the stem will break at the point at which it is tender enough to eat. Stand the spears upright in a jar containing about an inch of water, put a plastic bag over the tops and refrigerate for up to 3 or 4 days. If you don't own an upright asparagus pan, a metal percolator with the insides removed, will serve.

❧ How is the stem on an avocado like the little plastic thermometer on a turkey? They both pop up when they're "done." Look at the stem when your fingers can't decide if the fruit is ripe enough to eat.

❧ To clean fresh *dry* greens of every kind, first shake off the loose grit. Then add a drop or two of liquid dishwashing detergent to the first water in which you soak wet or dry greens. The super-wetting agent in the detergent causes dirt to slide off easily. Follow with a couple of good rinsings. Leeks need at least four wash waters to remove sand; use only the white parts.

❧ Use a sharp knife to slice rhubarb. A dull blade pulls strings along the ribs, allowing the lovely red color to leak out.

❧ Freeze nuts before shelling them; they slip out of their shells more easily. Fresh nuts have high oil content and should be stored in the refrigerator or freezer. Buy nuts at the height of their selling season, not when you first see them for sale in the early autumn; often those early ones have been stored from the previous year's crop.

❧ Potatoes can be baked and stuffed according to the recipe on page 277, then frozen on a cookie sheet. Package them in freezer bags for longer storage and rebake as needed.

❧ When cooking okra, add about 1 teaspoon of vinegar to the pan. It won't have that "slick" feeling.

❧ Spray cooking oil lightly inside molds before filling with gelatin mixtures; they will slip out easier.

❧ Look for dehydrated granules of fish stock at your market.

≥ Can you substitute ground turkey for beef to lower the fat content? Skinless ground white meat of turkey or chicken is lower in fat than beef. Dark meat of turkey, however, is not an effective substitute. Both require greater amounts of seasoning than does ground beef. Except for price, ground bison is a better substitute for beef.

≥ Land O' Lakes "Fat Free Half & Half" can substitute for light (coffee) cream in most of these recipes without altering the taste discernibly. When whipped cream is a "must," I like both the convenience and flavor of "Gossner Whipping Cream," an ultra high temperature (UHT) dairy product processed to stay fresh in its unopened aseptic box for six months without refrigeration. I dilute 1 cup of Gossner cream with 7 tablespoons of skim milk, plus 1 package of "Oetker Whip-it," a stabilizer. The addition of ½ cup of sugar gives a delicious reduced fat whipped cream.

≥ Decreasing the quantity you eat of certain foods may be more satisfying than decreasing the quality. It's more important to lower the fat in your daily lunch box sandwich than it is in your birthday cake.

Index

Page numbers in italics indicate photographs.